Pope Pius II, John Weever

The Hystorie of the Moste Noble Knight Plasidas, and Other Rare

Pieces

Pope Pius II, John Weever

The Hystorie of the Moste Noble Knight Plasidas, and Other Rare Pieces

ISBN/EAN: 9783337292027

Printed in Europe, USA, Canada, Australia, Japan

Cover: Foto ©ninafisch / pixelio.de

More available books at **www.hansebooks.com**

THE HYSTORIE

OF THE

MOSTE NOBLE KNIGHT PLASIDAS,

AND OTHER RARE PIECES;

COLLECTED INTO ONE BOOK BY SAMUEL PEPYS,

AND FORMING PART OF

THE PEPYSIAN LIBRARY

AT MAGDALENE COLLEGE, CAMBRIDGE.

PRINTED FOR THE

Roxburghe Club.

LONDON:
J. B. NICHOLS AND SONS, 25, PARLIAMENT STREET.

MDCCCLXXIII.

A lonneur de la saincte trinite
Louēge & bōne charte roy treschrestien
De latin en francois iay translate
Lystoire du treffort amoureux rien
Dauidus et de lucresse de mantoū
Que ēamoureux ont en durant leur vie

The Roxburghe Club.

MDCCCLXXIII.

THE DUKE OF BUCCLEUCH AND QUEENSBERRY, K.G.
PRESIDENT.

HIS EXCELLENCY MONSIEUR VAN DE WEYER.
MARQUIS OF LOTHIAN.
EARL OF CARNARVON.
EARL OF POWIS, *V.P.*
EARL BEAUCHAMP.
EARL OF CAWDOR.
EARL OF DUFFERIN, K.C.B., K.P.
LORD HOUGHTON.
LORD ORMATHWAITE.
SIR STEPHEN RICHARD GLYNNE, BART.
SIR EDWARD HULSE, BART
SIR WILLIAM STIRLING MAXWELL, BART.
HENRY BRADSHAW, ESQ.
REV. WILLIAM EDWARD BUCKLEY.
PAUL BUTLER, ESQ.
REV. WILLIAM GEORGE CLARK.
REV. HENRY OCTAVIUS COXE.
FRANCIS HENRY DICKINSON, ESQ.
GEORGE BRISCOE EYRE, ESQ.
THOMAS GAISFORD, ESQ.
HENRY HUCKS GIBBS, ESQ.
GRANVILLE LEVESON GOWER, ESQ.
RALPH NEVILLE GRENVILLE, ESQ.   *Treasurer.*
JOHN BENJAMIN HEATH, ESQ.
KIRKMAN DANIEL HODGSON, ESQ.
ROBERT STAYNER HOLFORD, ESQ.
ALEX. JAMES BERESFORD HOPE, ESQ.
HENRY HUTH, ESQ.
JOHN COLE NICHOLL, ESQ.
EVELYN PHILIP SHIRLEY, ESQ.
EDWARD JAMES STANLEY, ESQ.
SIMON WATSON TAYLOR, ESQ.
GEORGE TOMLINE, ESQ.
CHARLES TOWNELEY, ESQ.
REV. EDWARD TINDAL TURNER.
CHARLES WYNNE FINCH, ESQ.

PREFACE.

THE volume which is here reprinted, by the kind permission of the Master and Fellows of Magdalene College, Cambridge, forms part of the Pepysian Library, and bears at the beginning and end the two bookplates of its donor, one being his own portrait, and the other his cypher.

These plates, as well as the title-pages of the five principal pieces contained in it, and also the cover of the book with his arms stamped on the side, it has been thought well to reproduce in fac-simile, thus adding to the interest of the reprint.

The volume is composed of the following pieces bound up together:

I. The worthie Hystorie of Plasidas (1566), by John Partridge.

II. The Historie of the Lady Pandavola (1566), by John Partridge.

III. The History of the Lady Lucres of Scene (Sienna), and of her lover Eurialus.

IV. The Northren Mother's Blessing.

V. The Way to Thrift.

VI. The Life and Death of Sir John Oldcastle, Knight (1601), by John Weever.

Of these, No. V. is in prose, the rest in verse; No. VI. in Roman, the others in English letter.

No. I. is the story of the life, acts, and martyrdom of Saint Eustace, a patron saint of hunters, who, under his pagan name of Placidus, was a captain of the Roman guard, and was converted to Christianity by a vision of our blessed Lord, who appeared to him while hunting "a huge and lofty Bucke," and commanded him to forsake his idols.

The story, which was very popular, may be found in Caxton's

ii   PREFACE.

Golden Legend (fo. 331 v°. 1st edition), and also in chap. cx. of the Gesta Romanorum. In the English version of the latter book, published by the Club, the Emperor Trajanus of the Latin tale becomes the Emperor Avorios, and the knight Placidus figures only as "a certain knight," unnamed, and unidentified with Saint Eustace.

Mr. Collier, who reprinted the present poem in 1866, has given in his Bibliographical Catalogue (fol. ii. p. 117) a pretty full account of it; and in his Extracts from the Register of the Stationers' Company we find the licence for its printing, as follows :

> R^d of Thomas hackett, for his lycense for prynting of " an history of
> the mooste noble kynge plasadas, &c. .   .   .   .   .   . iiij d.

Of No. II. Collier could give no account, never having seen it. It tells of Pandavola, the fair daughter of Sylewma the King of Turkey, whose "comly corps" the people thronged from all parts to see; of her love for Alfyne, a knight of low estate, and of their tragic deaths.

The following is the licence for printing this book:

> R^d of Thomas Purfoote for his lycense for the pryntinge of the moost
> famose history of the worthy lady pandavolay, &c. .   .   .   . iiij d.

The story appears to be a translation from a foreign work, for Partridge, in some dedicatory verses addressed to Thomas Baynam, says he has

> this story brought
> Unto our vulgar speche.

but I can find no trace of the original.

These verses follow the poem, and are themselves followed by two other short pieces, one in praise of friendship, the other in dispraise of flattery. The poetry of these works of Partridge is but poor; they are, however, worth preserving, not for their own merits, but as a specimen of what was thought good enough to entertain our forefathers.

No. III. is told much better in prose than the two former are in verse, and is indeed written with some power; reading like a story from Boccaccio.

Its original author was Æneas Sylvius Piccolomini, afterwards Pope Pius II., himself a Siennese, who wrote in 1443 this "Opusculum de duobus amantibus Eurialo et Lucresia." *

The Spanish (12,491 d.), 4to, 1512, is entitled, "Historia muy verdadera de dos amantes Eurialo Franco y Lucrecia Senesa que acaescio en la cibdad de Sena en el año de Mil & cccc & xxxiiij, años en presencia del emperador Fadrique: fecha por Eneas siluio que despues fue elegido papa llamado Pio Segundo." The colophon is "Fin del presente tratado d'los dos amantes Eurialo franco y Lucrecia senesa. Fue impreso en la muy noble y muy leal cibdad de Seuilla por Jacobo cröberger. Año de mill q'nientos y doze, A. xxviij. de Julio."

The German version (12,403 c.) is contained in thirty-seven leaves 4to, and is illustrated with nineteen coloured woodcuts (of which one is employed twice over,) representing various points in the story. They are so quaint that it has been thought well to insert fac-similes of them in the present volume.

The first of them, with its border and initial letter (a C reversed doing duty for a D) heads the next page, and represents the translator, Nicholas von Wyle (or his messenger), presenting his book to his patroness, the opening words being

---

* This novel was very popular in its day, as may be supposed from the fact that no less than twenty-eight fifteenth-century editions are mentioned by Hain, in his Repertorium Bibliographicum (1826, vol. i. pt. 1, p. 25), as still extant, besides eight translations of the same century, three into Italian, two into German, and three into French; one of the latter being "Translate du latin en francoys par maistre Antithus chappellain de la saincte chappelle aux ducz de bourgogne a la priere et requeste des dames," and another, a poetical paraphrase, of which a copy is in the British Museum. It is supposed to be by Octavien de St. Gelais.

The same library possesses several early Latin editions, amongst which are A° 1476 Argentine (Granville 9,274); 1490 (?) Cologne (?) pressmark 3,835 $\frac{b}{1}$; 1497 Venice (12,450 d.); as well as one of the year 1648 in Vincent Obsopæus's book, De Arte Bibendi, &c. The Museum has also one of the German translations mentioned by Hain, and other Spanish and Italian versions.

Of the 1476 text (which is not mentioned by Hain) a reprint will be found in an appendix to the preface.

er durchleuchtigen hoch gebornen Fürstin und frawen fraw katherinen, Herzogin von österreich margrevin zu Baden, &c. und grevin zu Spanheim meiner gnedigsten frawen entbeut ich niclaus von wyle der zeit statschreiber zu Esslingen mein underthenig willig dienst zuvor.

He dates his dedication "Geben zu Esslingen auff Esto mihi,* Anno domini M.cccc.lxij." Then follows the author's dedication to Count Schlick: " Dem hochgeachten und volgeborn Ritter herren Caspern Schlicken herren des Nuwenburg keyserlichem Cantzler und houbtman zu Eger uñ zu dē Elenpogen seinem besundern herren entbeut[e]t Eneas Siluius poet und keiserliche Secretari vil und

* Probably *auf festo michi*, *i. e.* Michaelmas.

No. 1. To face page iv.

THE TRANSLATOR PRESENTS HIS WORK TO THE MARGRAVINE OF BADEN,
HIS PATRONESS.

enpfilcht heils sich im. Mariañus Sosinus mein lantzman von Senis burtig ein mann so guttig und so grosser kunst das ich zweifell ob ich seines geleichen ye gesehen habe, Hat mich dise tag her gebetten das ich im schreyb zwei lieb habende menschen." The colophon states the book to be "Geben zu Wyen 5 nones Julij, 1477."

Besides the early Italian translations mentioned by Hain there was one published in Venice by Matthias Pagan in 1554; and another in Daelli's Bibliotheca Rara, 1864. Both these are in the British Museum.

The French work of Octavien de St. Gelais consists of some 4,850 lines, beautifully printed by Antoine Verard, about 1493, on 92 leaves of vellum; the first of which has a large miniature, representing the author presenting his work to King Charles the Eighth. A fac-simile will be found as a frontispiece to the present volume.

There are also 129 smaller miniatures very well executed, but, as may be supposed from the number, compared with the length of the story, not all of them depicting incidents clearly distinguishable one from the other. Thus, one represents Eurialus writing a letter to Lucrece; another, Lucrece receiving it; another, Lucrece, with the forefinger of one hand on the forefinger of the other, considering what she shall say in answer. Another shews " Coñient Lucresse apperceut Eurial˙ et parla a lui" (fo. 38); and the next " Coñient Eurial˙ parla a Lucresse " (fo. 38v°); the two miniatures being almost exactly the same (much like No. 10 in the German set), only with a different action of the hands of the speakers. Two others (and these are two of the best in the book) show " Cōmēt Sozie mist Eurial˙ dedens une estable parmy du fein et comment il fut presq̄ trouve par dromo page neust este Sozias " (fo. 59), and "Cōmēt Lucresse amusa son mari en bas et le mena en la caue tant que Eurial˙ sen feust ale." (fo. 62 v°.)

Manuscript notes on the margin of the pages, such as these above quoted, accompany and explain the miniatures, one of which, as a specimen of the style, has been given in fac-simile at p. 112. It is from fo. 61 of the French book.

The first edition of the English translation is said to be that in the British Museum, a black-letter quarto (C. 21 c.) which Hazlitt dates c. 1549: but Lowndes mentions one by W. Copland, of 1547, which may be either the same or an earlier edition, or else perhaps a mistake for that of 1567 here reprinted, which is also from Copland's press.

There seems to be internal evidence that the Museum edition is *not* the first. It is too full of errors, and apparently errors of a copyist. See, amongst others, that pointed out in the note on p. 133, l. 16.

Mr. Henry Huth has a copy of an edition of 1560.

"The Excellent Historye of Euryalus and Lucretia" was licensed to T. Creede, October 19, 1596, but whether this was to be a reprint with a new title, or a new translation, is not known. Probably it was never printed, as Hazlitt mentions no copy, and there is none either in the British Museum or Bodleian.

There are two other translations in the British Museum; one (12 $\frac{\text{K.M.}}{287}$), by Charles Allen, printed in 1639, and another, in a volume (12,510 b.) containing also the Story of Hyppolitus, Earl of Douglas (1741), and the Secret History of Macbeth. It is entitled: "The Art of Love, or the History of the Amours of Count Schlick, Chancellor to the Emperor Sigismund, and a Young Lady of Quality of Sienna. By Æneas Sylvius, Poet Laureat, and Secretary to the same Emperor, afterwards Pope Pius the Second. London, 1741."

In the preface to the work the translator says

There is yet another advantage which our Author has above the Monsieurs in writing on a real not fictitious story. For though he gives his Lovers the names of Eurialus and Lucretia, it is plain from a passage* in his Epistle Dedicatory to the Count of Schlick that he drew his picture from the true Adventures of that Lord."

---

* The passage is as follows:

"The affair happened at *Sienna*, during the abode of the Emperor Sigismund in that City; you was there at the same time, and if I may believe my Ears, you bestowed some of your Time and Address in Love. It is the City of *Venus*. Your Friends, who know

PREFACE. vii

A very full account of the book and its story is given by Mr.
Furnivall in his preface to "Captain Cox, or Laneham's Letter,"
(p. xxxviii.) printed in 1871 for the Ballad Society.

It is the story of the beautiful Lucres of Sienna and her lover
Eurialus, a knight " of the contre of Francony" in the train of the
Emperor Sigismund; and tells how that her husband Menelaus
meets the fate of his Spartan namesake, and loses the love of his too
fair wife; how that Eurialus supplants him by the help of his trusty
friend Nisus, and of "Pandalus," cousin to Menelaus, and in spite
of the vigilance of Agamemnon, Menelaus's brother; and how that
Eurialus, called to Rome by his lord the Emperor, is forced to leave
his love, who shortly after dies of grief; and himself, though
married by the Emperor "to a ryghte noble and excellent ladye,
yet never enioyed after, but in conclusyon pitifully wasted his
painful life."

The French version, following the original, makes him a less
doleful end. The concluding lines are

> Jusqu a ce que cesar souverains
> Une femme lui donna chaste et tendre
> Du sang estoit dun noble duc venue
> La plaisante femme espousa
> Belle chaste et prudente tenue
> Sage homs estoit: moult lama et prisa
> Es oraisons quil faisoit tousiours a
> De la bonne Lucresse remembrãce
> C'il q' le corps a ame noublira
> Lame jamais sil a bonne prudence.

In the original there is a short Envoy or moral, of which the

you well, say that you were then much in Love, and that no Body was more gallant
than yourself; and believe that there was no Amour past at that Time that you had not
some Knowledge of. I therefore desire you to read over this History, and see whether
I have wrote Truth or not; blush not if it call to your Mind any Transactions of yours
that were like these, since you were a Man, and therefore subject to the Frailty of Man.
He who was never in love, is either a Stone or a Beast"—" oder ein unvernunftiges
tier." (German version.)

following French lines are a translation, and to them the translator adds a moral of his own.

<small>* Le Pape pre
auant sa pa
paulte uom
me enee sil
uie, aucteur
de ce liure, po^r
la cōclusion
de son eoure
dit a Marian'
an q'l il le
dirige.</small>

Mon cher ami Marianus tu as
Icy la fin du liure des amans
Lamour nen est fait ne eureux se bien as
Par tout vise; ce te suis affermans
Qui ce liure liront silz sont savans
Se garderont de choir en telz perilz
Le breuage damours ne soiët benans
Ou dalors plus que miel est mis.

LE TRANSLATEUR.

Histoire q' ay cy deuant translatee
Se p' bon sens on la veult digerer
Et qu il ne soit quen bien interpreter
A p'sonne ne veult mal suggerer
Toute vertu et bien veult ingerer
Peche finir et faictz p'nicieux.

The Envoy of the English translation which I add from Mr. Huth's copy of the edition of 1560, appears not to have formed part of the present edition. It points the moral of the story, showing that the joys of love—unlawful love is meant—of which the future Pope gives a somewhat graphic description, are surpassed by its sorrows.

LE A TO THE REDER.

Bi thys lytle thou mayst perceyue my frēd
The end of loue not fayned nor fortunable,
By which right pláynly thou mayst entend
That loue is no pleasure, but a pain pardurable,
And the end is deth which is most lamentable.
Therfore, ere thou be chayued with such care,
By others' peryls take hede and beware.

---

* A MS. note by the side of the text, in the same hand as the others which are found in almost every page, explaining the miniatures.

No. 3.   *To face page* ix.

THE TRANSLATOR PRESENTS HIS BOOK TO POPE PIUS THE SECOND.

> Fyrst by Eurialus, by whome perceyue thou maist
> The best it is to eschue shortelye
> To drynke of the cup, or of it to taste
> That savoured more of gall than of hony.
> Also I coulde shewe the hystoryes of many
> That yf they by tyme had made resystance
> They myght have eschued all such inconvenience.
>
> There was also the noble Troylus
> Whych all hys lyfe abode in mortall payne
> Delayed by Cresyde whose hystory is pyteous,
> Tyll at the last Achilles had hym slayne.
> Yet other there be, whych in this careful chaine
> Of loue have contynued all theyr lyfe dayes,
> Death was their end, there was non other waies.
>
> We redde also Piramis and thysbe
> Whych slew them selfe by theyr feruent loue,
> Of Hercules, and of the fayre ioyle,
> Wyth many other, whiche I coulde not attaine.
> And of Dido, whiche wyth her selfe stroue
> For love of Eneas whā she coulde not attaine,
> Tyll at the laste she had her selfe slaine.
>
> Yet coulde I shewe you of many other mo
> Yf leyser not wanted, but now I let it pas,
> Whiche by theyr love were constrayned also
> To mortal death, more pitye, alas!
> Therfore thys boke in English drawe was
> For an example, therby to eschew
> The paynes of love ere after they it rewe.

In the woodcut annexed (No. 3 of the German series) we see the translator presenting his work to its author, Pope Pius himself, who was still on the throne, and did not die till two years after the date of the translation. The bystanders appear to be remonstrating with him on his temerity, but he persists, and His Holiness receives the homage graciously.

Æneas Sylvius did not, however, look back with satisfaction on this work of his, which, while it professes to be a dissuasive from unlawful love, is so, not at all on the score of its immorality, but of its dangers and its hapless end; and portrays only too well the unscrupulous morals of the age and country in which he lived; and as he, when Pope, condemned, in his Bulla Retractationis, the antipapal opinions which as Imperial Secretary he had professed, so, in like manner, in his more advanced years, he was ashamed of and condemned this and any other writings of his youth which had an immoral tendency.

Nicolaus Beets, in his work "De Æneae Sylvii . . . . . morum mentisque mutationis rationibus" (Haarlem, 1839, p. 11) writes as follows : " Etenim animadvertendum est.Pium quum (a. 1463) in Bulla Retractationum scriberet 'Aeneam rejicite, Pium suscipite' morum non minus quam sententiæ politicæ mutationem respexisse, ut et inde apparet, quod eadem formula in utraque causa utatur. Voluptatibus enim nimium indulserat juvenis ; nunc senex scribit Carolo Cypræo, (Koelhoff, Cologne, MCCCCL[xx]viii, p. 352.) " De amore igitur quæ scripsimus juvenes contemnite, non morales* atque respuite; sequimini quæ nunc dicimus et seni magis quam juveni credite. Nec privatum hominem pluris facite quam Pontificem ; Æneam rejicite, Pium suscipite ; illud gentile nomen parentes indidere nascenti, hoc Christianum in Apostolatu suscepimus ;" and in the note, " Spectat hæc, quam citavimus Epistola, Carolo Cypræo scripta, *Tractatum de duobus amantibus* sive *narrationem de Eurialo et Lucretia se amantibus,* quam, petenti Mariano Sozimo amico scripserat Aeneas anno 1444, quum jam per duos annos Imperatori ab actis fuerat. Est sine dubio narratio satis lubrica, nec tamen plane bonis moribus noxia, quippe et eo consilio composita ut juvenes ab illicito amori deterreat; 'in amore autem quot latent mala si quis aliunde nescit hinc poterit scire.' (Aeneae Prologus.) Nec non ei insunt argumentationes morales optimae frugis. Multa tamen lasciviore modo sunt proposita, quae sine dubio plus fecerunt ut celebratissima fieret haecce historiola, quæ jam saec. xv. plures vidit editiones (Cf. Naaml. van boeken in der Nederl. gedurende de

---

* O mortales, 1551.

15ᵈᵉ eeuw gedrukt; by P. van Dummel, Amst. 1767, p. 2, 8, 15, 27, 56) quam quod inerat morale dogma. Doluit hoc Pius Secundus. Hinc scripsit in Epistola laudata duo contineri in eo libello, apertam videlicet sed heu lascivam nimis prurientemque amoris historiam, et morale, quod eam sequitur, aedificans dogma. Quorum primum fatuos atque errantes videbat sectari quamplurimos, alterum, heu dolor, pene nullos. Ita impuratum esse atque offuscatum mortalium genus."

The correct text of so much of the Epistle as relates to this subject will be found in the Appendix.

Alessandro Bracci, in his translation of Lucres and Eurialus, Firenze, 1489, recast the plot, with the intention but certainly not the effect of improving its morality. In Daelli's Bibliotheca Rara, 1864, vol. 38, there is an edition of Piccolomini's novel, and in the preface the editor says, " Alessandro Bracci non tradusse, ma rifece, o meglio guastó. Guastó la testura dello stile framettendovi di suo frigidi versi e anche un sonetto bisticcio.

> Amor m'ha ratto retto e, spento, spinto
> Che senza sarte in sirte surto gemo
> Avanti a' vanti in pene tante tinto.

Guastó la favola facendo morir Menelao scambio di Lucrezia e sposarla in seconde nozze da Eurialo. Crede cosí legittimar l'adulterio, e per esser piu morale, o com' egli dice piu jocundo, finge che Lucrezia che non aveva mai conceputo di Menelao e neppur di Eurialo ne' suoi congiungimenti impudichi, avesse di costui, dopo i legittimi nodi, otto figliuoli, tutti maschi e formosi. Egli la fa sopravvivere tre anni ad Eurialo, che muore di settentacinqu' anni ! Questo egli chiama nella dedicatoria del suo Rifacimento a Lorenzo di Pier Francesco de Medici *continuare tutto il processo della storia con cose piacevoli e joconde!*"

I have corrected this 1567 edition by Mr. Huth's copy of that of 1560, and by the copy of the earlier edition in the British Museum (which last Mr. Furnivall kindly collated for me), and these corrections, with others founded on a comparison with the original Latin, will be found in the notes.

No. IV. is "The Northren Mother's Blessing;" on which so much has been said by Mr. Furnivall in his "Forewords to the Babees Book, &c." (printed for the Early English Text Society,) p. lxix. under its other title "How the Good Wijf Tauȝte hir Douȝtir," and so much by Mr. Hazlitt in his "Early English Popular Poetry," vol. i. p. 178, that little more remains to be told, unless it be thought useful to add a comparison of the various versions of this popular piece, and, in order to make the present poem complete, to append a few stanzas which exist in the others but not in this.

It contains, as its other title denotes, a mother's address to her daughter, advising her how she should walk in the paths of this life, especially as a wife, a mistress of a house, and a neighbour, if she would thrive and bear a good name.

Our ancestors were somewhat prodigal of their advice to women, and often gave them, as in the present tract, very good advice.

Thus, Fitzherbert, writing about 1530, gives in his Boke of Husbandry a world of good counsel. After the precepts of Husbandry proper he writes a "Prologue for the Wyues Occupation."

"Now thou husbande, that haste doone thy dylygence and labour that longeth to an husbande, to get thy lyuynge, thy wyues, thy chyldrens, and thy seruantes; yet there are other thynges, that muste nedes be done or elles thou shalte not thryue. For there is an olde common sayenge, that seldome dothe the husbande thryue withoute the leue of his wyfe. By this sayenge it shoulde seme, that there be other occupations and labours that be moste conuenient for the wyues to do. And howe be it that I haue not the experyence of al theyr occupations and warkes, as I haue of husbandry, yet a lyttell wyl I speke, what they ought to do, though I tel them not howe they shulde doo, and exercyse theyr labours and occupations."

Then he begins to give her a "Lesson for the Wyfe," quoting

PREFACE. xiii

Solomon and Saint Jerome; and, after exhorting her to the love of her husband, he tells "What Warkes a Wyfe shulde do in generall," beginning " First, in a mornyng whan thou arte waked, and purposest to ryse, lyfte vp thy hande, and blesse the, and make a sygne of the holy crosse, In nomine patris, et filii, et spiritus sancti, Amen. In the name of the father, the sonne, and the holy gooste. And if thou saye a Paternoster, an Aue, and a Crede, and remember thy Maker, thou shalte spede moche the better." And then he goes on to tell her how she is to look after her house, her dairy, her children, her servants, her bakery, her brewery, her poultry, and her field and garden produce; impressing upon both husband and huswife "Tene Mensuram," " Eate within thy Tedure," *i.e.* tether. It is an interesting and amusing book, and in some parts a good parallel to our poem.

The other poems under this or like names differ so much in expression from the present piece and from one another, that they read more like translations or adaptations from some common original (perhaps written in 1391, "nine years before the death of Chaucer," as our title-page says; perhaps much earlier) than mere variations under the hand of a copyist. See on p. xix the lines from the version in the Cambridge University MS., the author of which desires his readers to pray for him *and* for the maker of the book.

Of the fellow-piece, "How the Wise Man tauȝt his Son," we find the prototype, consisting of 189 Anglo-Saxon lines, in an Exeter MS. of the tenth century. See Thorpe's Codex Exoniensis, p. 300.

It begins
    Ðus frod fæder
    Freo-bearn lærde,

that is to say, " Thus a wise father his dear son taught ; " and ends
    Swa þu min bearn gemyne
    Frode fæder-lare
    & þec a wið firenum geheald.

"So thou my son remember wise fatherly lore and thyself aye against sins preserve."

The " Wise Man " appears also to have been widely popular; he is mentioned in the Chartulary of Godstowe, p. 13. (Rawl. MS. B. 408).

"The prologue of the englyssh register. The wyseman tawht hys chyld gladly to rede bokys and hem well undurstonde, for in defaute of vndyrstondyng is ofttymes causyd neclygence, hurte, harme and hynderaunce, as experyens prevyth in many a place;" and then the writer goes on to say, that, as Latin is too hard for women, but they ought to know what their documents are, he means to translate for them the history or charters of their nunnery.

The several versions of the " Good Wife " which are now known, are

1. The present version; from a MS. " Reserved long in the Studie of a Northfolke Gentleman," says J. S. who published it in 1597.
2. That in the Cambridge University, MS. KK. 1, 5.
3. That in St. John's College (Cambridge) MS. G. 23.
4. That in the Ashmole MS. 61, fo. 7.
5. That in the Porkington MS. No. 10, fo. 135 v°.
6. That in the Lambeth MS. 853, p. 102.
7. That in the Trinity College (Cambridge) MS. R. 3, 19.
8. That in the Loscombe MS.

They all show signs, more or less clear, of their Northern origin.

No. 2 is printed in the Early English Text Society's issue for 1870, called " Ratis Raving," p. 103; and is entitled " The Thewis of Gudwomen." It is written, says the editor, in the Lothian dialect, and begins

> The gud wyf schawis, fore best scho can,
> Quhilkis ar thewis of gud women;

PREFACE. xv

> Quhilk*is* gar women be haldin deir,
> And pouer women princ*is* peir;
> Wit*h* sum Ill man*er*is and thewis
> That folowis ful women & schrewis.

It describes, but not like most of the others in the form of an address to a daughter, what is a woman's duty to God and to her neighbour. It contains 316 lines.

It is, perhaps, the same Rate, whose "Raving" we have in this book, who appears again in No. 4 (see p. xx).

No. 3 is of the same type and contains 306 lines; Mr. W. W. Skeat has kindly lent me a transcript of it for comparison. It is, he tells me, in Lowland Scottish, and was written out by a scribe named John de Ramsay, in 1487.

It varies considerably from No. 2, both in spelling and phraseology, and also in omission and addition of lines. I have marked in italics the differences in the first six lines.

> The gud *wiff* schawis *the* best scho can
> Quhilk ar *the* thewis of *a* gud woman
> Quhilk garr*is* women be haldin deir,
> And *makis* pouer women princis peir
> With sum ill *techis* and *ill* thewis
> That fol*lowis foull* women & schrewis.

No. 4, "How þe Goode Wyfe tauȝt hyr Douȝter," consists of 208 lines, and is printed in the volume containing Sir H. Gilbert's "Queene Elizabeth's Achademy," issued in 1869 by the Early English Text Society (extra series viii. p. 44).

No. 5 consists of 14 stanzas (168 lines), printed on p. 39 of the same volume, and is entitled, "The good wyfe wold a pylgremage."

No. 6 has 31 stanzas (219 lines), and is printed, as before said, in "The Babees Book," beginning on the 36th page; and has, in the footnotes, the collation of No. 7, which contains 32 stanzas.

No. 8, entitled "How the Goode Wif thaught hir Doughter," has 35 stanzas (175 lines), and was printed by Sir F. Madden in

1838; and again by Mr. Hazlitt in 1864, (Early Popular Poetry, vol. i.) with the addition of the opening stanza and some few readings from the 1597 printed text.

It is in the opening stanza that the several versions mostly differ. Thus in No. 4 it runs

> Lyst *and* lythe A lytell space,
> Y shall you telle A *praty* case,
> How þᵉ gode wyfe tauȝht hyr' douȝter
> To mend hyr' lyfe, *and* make her' bett*er*.

No. 5 begins

> The goode wyf wold a pylgremage
>   unto þᵉ holly londe:
> Sche sayd "my dere doȝttu*r*,
>   þou most vndor'stonde
> For to gowerne well this hous,
>   and saue thy selfe frow schond.
> For to do as I þᵉ teche,
>   I charge the þou fonde.
> Witt an' O & a ny,
>   seyd hit ys full ȝore,
> That lothe childe lore behowytt,
>   and leue childe moche more."

The first stanza of No. 6 is

> The good wijf tauȝte hir douȝtir
> Ful many a tyme & ofte
> A ful good wom*m*an to be,
> And seide "douȝtir to me dere,
> Sum good þou must lere
> If eu*ere* þou wolt þee."

all the stanzas, but the first and last, ending "my leve childe."

No. 7 varies but little.

No. 8 omits the first stanza, and ends the others alternately "My dere childe" and "My leve childe."

Stanzas 15, 16, and 27 of our poem are, with verbal variations, in No. 7, but not in No. 6; stanza 22 is represented in the Lambeth MS. by

(St. 18.) And what so thy meyne do, about hem þou wende,
And as myche as þou maist,* be at þat oon ende,
And if þou fynde ony defaute, do it soone ameende
So þei haue tyme and space, and may hem defende.
To compelle a dede to be doone & þere be no space,
It is but tyrannye with-out temperaunce & grace,†
Mi leue child.

See also stanza 17 of the same MS. on p. xix.
Stanza 26 runs in the Lambeth MS.

(St. 29.) Now haue y þee tauȝt, douȝtir, As ‡ my modir dide mee;
þinke þeron § uyȝt and day, forȝete þat it not be; ||
Haue mesure and lownes,¶ as ** y haue þee tauȝt,
And †† what man ‡‡ þe wedde schal, him dare care nouȝt.§§
Betere were a child vnbore
þan vntauȝt of wijs lore,||||
Mi leue child.

Instead of stanzas 28 and 29 of the present poem, No. 6 has

(St. 23.) Whanne þou art a wijf, a neiȝbore for to be,
Loue þan weel þi neiȝboris, as god haþ comaundide þee;
It bihoueþ þee so for to do,
And to do to þem as þou woldest be doon to.

---

* No. 8, for "And .... mayst," reads *Wilke dede þᵗ schalle be done.*
† No. 8, for "So þei .... & grace," reads
 [So] þei haue swiche for hem þᵗ may hem defende
 Mykelle note hym be houethe to don þᵗ house schalle holden.
‡ No. 8, for "as," reads *so.*
§ No. 8, for "þinke þeron," reads *þenk þer on bothe.*
|| No. 8, for "þat it not be," reads *nought þise þre.*
¶ No. 8, for "and lownes," reads *lowenesse & forthought.*
** No 8, for "as," reads *þᵗ.*
†† No. 8 omits "And."
‡‡ No. 8, for "what man þe," reads *what man þᵗ þe.*
§§ No. 8, for "him dare care nouȝt," reads *þan is he nought bycaught.*
|||| No. 8 omits "of wijs lore."

d

PREFACE.

> If ony discorde happen nyght or daye,
> Make it no worse, meende it if þou maye,
> Mi leue child.

which is found in none of the other MSS.

Stanzas 28 and 29 correspond to 26 and 27 in No. 8; and that version adds another stanza in this place which is peculiar to it.

> (St. 28.) Take ensaumple by hem, and lette alle folie,
> þat þou haue none defaute, ne þey or ȝe dyen,
> ȝif God þe sende children, þou hast þe more to done,
> þey askyn grete dispens, here warisone þei wille haue some,
> Care he hathe þt childryn schalle kepe, my leue childe.

No. 7, in place of the same two stanzas 28 and 29, and of st. 30 (st. 24 in No. 6), has its st. 23 and 24, which correspond in sense to our st. 19 and 27; and the following (25) which is neither in ours nor in No. 6.

> (St. 25) * With ryche Roobys and garlondes, and with ryche † thyng,
> Counterfete ‡ no lady as thy hosbond § were a kyng.
> With suche as he may the ayde,∥ apayde shalt þow be,
> That no countenaunce be lost for cause ¶ of thee:
> Ouyrdone pryde maketh nakyd syde,
> My leef chylde.

Stanza 21 is represented by 16 and part of 17 of No. 6.

> (St. 16.) And if þin husbonde ** be from home, lete not þi meyne †† goon ydil,
> But loke weel who dooþ myche eiþer litil,‡‡

---

* Collier in his edition of No. 8 prefixes *go not* to this line; but the sense does not need it.
† No. 8, for "with ryche," reads *swiche*.
‡ No. 8 prefixes *ne* to this line.
§ No. 8, for "hosbond," reads *lorde*.
∥ No. 8, for "ayde," reads *fynde*.
¶ No. 8, for "That .... thee," reads *þat he lees noght his manhed for þe loue of þe*.
** No. 8 reads *lorde*.
†† No. 8, for "þi meyne," reads *hem*.
‡‡ No. 8, for "But .... litil," reads *Loke þt þou wete wele, ho do mekylle or lytelle*.

And he þat weel dooþ, þou qwite * him weel his whyle,
And he þat dooþ oþer, serue him as þe vile,
　　A forn doon dede
　　Wole anoþer spede,
　　　　　　　Mi leue child.†

(St. 17.)　And if þi nede be greet & þi tyme streite,
þan ‡ go þi silf þerto & worche § an houswijfes brayde,
þanne wille þei alle do þe bettir þat aboute þee stande[s] ‖
þe work is the sonner do þat haþ many handis,
　　For manye handis & wight
　　Make an heuy worke light;
　　After þi good seruise
　　þi name schal arise,
　　　　　　　Mi leue childe. ¶

Our final stanza does not appear in any of the others, and in lieu of it No. 2 has

　　　　　And here I pray ye redaris all
　　　　　And als ye heraris, gret and small,
　　　　　That ay, quhen at thai one it luke,
　　　　　They pray for hyme that maid the buk;
　　　　　And fore al crystynne man, and me;
　　　　　Amen, Amen, for cherytte.

which is lacking in No. 3.

No. 4 has

　　　　　Ther' for' all' myȝhty god Inne trouc
　　　　　Spede vs Alle, both euen and morne;

---

* No. 8 reads þ^t *hathe wele done, ȝelde*

† No, 8, for "And he þat dooþ .... child," reads *He dothe an oþer tyme þe bette but he be a vyle, A dede well done herte it whemyth, my dere childe.*

‡ Omitted in No. 8.

§ No. 8 has *make*.

‖ No. 8 has *All þei schalle do þe better, þ^t þou bi hem standes*.

¶ No. 8, for "þe work ..... schal arise," has *many handys make light werke, my leue childe.*

d 2

And bringe vs to thy hyʒhe blysse,
That neuer more fro vs schall mysse
                Amen, quod Rate.*

No. 5 ends

(St. 14.) Far-well douʒttur, far-well nowe!
I go vn-to my pylgremage;
Kepe þe wel on' my blessynge
   tyl þou be more of a[ge],
let no merth ner' Jollyte
   þis lesson frowe þe swage;
Then þou schalt have þᵉ blys of heyvyn
   to thy errytage.
      Witt a O and a I,
         doʒttur, pray for' me;
      A schort prayer' wynnythe heyvyn',
         the patter noster and an' ave,
                Amen.

The last two stanzas of No. 6 (Lambeth) stand in the place of the last stanza of the Northren Mother's Blessing, and are as follows:

(St. 30.) Now þrift and þeedom mote þou haue my swete barn,†
Of alle oure former fadris þat euere were or aren,
Of alle patriarkis and prophetis þat euere weren alyue,
Her blessinge mote þou haue, and weel mote þou þriue!
   For weel is the child
   þat wiþ synne wole not be filid,
                Mi leue child.‡

(which corresponds to the last stanza of Nos. 7 and 8.)

(St. 31.) The blessynge of God mote þou haue, and of his modir briʒt,
Of alle aungils & of alle archaungils, and of alle holy wight,

---

* The title also of No. 4 is followed by the words "quod Rate," and in both cases it is misprinted *Kate*.

† No. 8 reads *my leue swete barn*.

‡ No. 8, for "þat wiþ .... leue child," reads *þat þryue may my dere child*.

PREFACE. xxi

And þat þou mowe haue grace to wende þe wey ful riʒt
To þe blis of heuene þere sittiþ god almyʒt,
Amen.

A harmony of the stanzas of four of the versions of the Northren Mother's Blessing.

No. 1. 1597.	No. 6. Lambeth.	No. 7. Trin. Coll.	No. 8. Loscombe.	No. 1. 1597.	No. 6. Lambeth.	No. 7. Trin. Coll.	No. 8. Loscombe.
Stanza. 1	Stanza. —	Stanza. —	Stanza. —	Stanza. 19	Stanza. 25	Stanza. 23	Stanza. 19
—	1	1	—	20	15	15	20
2	2	2	1	21	16	16	21
3	3	3	2	21	17	17	22
4	4	4	3	22	18	18	23
5	5	5	4	23	19	26	24
6	6	6	5	24	26	27	32
7	7	7	6	25	20	28	33
8	8	8	7	26	29	31	34
9	9	9	8	27	—	24	25
10	10	10	9	28	—	—	26
11	11	11	10	29	—	—	27
12	12	12	11	—	23	—	—
13	13	13	12	—	—	—	28
14	14	14	13	30	24	—	29
15	—	19	14	31	28	30	30
16	—	20	15	32	27	29	31
17	21	21	16	33	—	—	—
18	22	22	17	—	30	32	35
—	—	25	18	—	31	—	—

No. V., The Way to Thrift, is a short piece of 71 lines. It teaches by contraries, and might rather be called A Lamentation over Unthrift.

The last piece in the volume is The Mirror of Martyrs, or The Life and Death of Sir John Oldcastle, knight, a poem which deserved a better fate than to have been reduced, as it is said, to two, or at most three, extant copies. The present reprint will do a tardy justice to its merits.

Mr. Collier points out that the author applauds Spenser—"O greefe, that Spenser's gone!"—and borrows from Shakspere; but this latter obligation seems to be very doubtful, as far at least as concerns the lines on the battle of Shrewsbury, which are given by Collier as an instance of his borrowing.

> And all the Armie, ventrous, val'rous, bold,
> Hote on the spur, now in the spur lie cold.

Here so obvious a play on the name Hotspur was surely apt to occur both to Weever and Shakspere, without any borrowing on either hand.

The "first true Oldcastle" in Weever's dedication may be, as Mr. Collier says, a reference to Shakspere's "Old Lad of the Castle," and may intimate that he for the *first* time was showing Oldcastle in his *true* colours, whereas Shakspere had shown him in false ones; and to these false colours he may refer where he says the world

> With cowardise beginneth to empeach me.
> Page 185.

In the fourth stanza, however, there seems to be certainly a reference to Shakspere, when our author says

> The many-headed multitude were drawne
> By Brutus speech that Cæsar was ambitious;

for it is more probable that he refers to the play of Julius Cæsar, written about that time, than to the facts of history, or to Plutarch's version of them.

It is Oldcastle himself who relates his own prowess, his master's favour, his sufferings and death, martyred for his Lollard opinions; and who modestly says

> Becket is set; now doth Oldcastle shine;
> Him for a Saint within your Kalends hold."

Capgrave in his Chronicle of England gives a full account of Lord Cobham, but, though he gives him credit for his valour and ability, he does not estimate him so highly as in Weever's poem he estimates himself. Probably the contemporary view of the Lollards was as much too bad, amongst their opponents, as the distant view of the days of Elizabeth was too good, amongst the reapers of the seed they had sown. In the days of Henry the Fifth and Sixth their enormities were more visible than their virtues to the eyes of churchmen. In the days of Elizabeth their enormities were forgotten, and they were credited, as being the first fathers of the Reformation, with more virtues than they had possessed. Capgrave says " Thei [the Lollardis] trvsted mech on the witte and on the power of a certeyn knyte thei cleped Ser Jon Oldcastelle. He was cleped Cobham, for he had weddid a woman ny of the lordis kyn. A strong man in bataile he was, but a grete heretik, and a gret enmye to the Cherch. For his cause the archbishop gadered a Councel at London; for he sent out prestis for to preche, whech were not admitted be non Ordinarie; and he was present at her sermones; and alle thei that seide ageyn his prestis was he redy to smite with his swerde."

The Chronicle comes to an abrupt end in the very year in which Oldcastle was recaptured and put to death; and shortly afterwards Edward de Cherlton, fourth Lord Cherlton of Powis (the " Lord Powis, gouernour in Wales," of the 233rd page) received the thanks of Parliament for his good service in capturing "that notorious rebel," and delivering him over to the authorities of the State.

HENRY H. GIBBS.

Aldenham,
November 30, 1872.

NOTES.

Page ix, line 1, ioyle, *i. e. iole.*

„ 113, „ 1, The Emperour Sigismund. The Spanish version says "The Emperor Frederick III." whose secretary, indeed, Piccolomini was, and whose chancellor was Count Schlick.

„ „ „ 4, strete; it should be *gate*; orig. "porta."

„ „ „ 19, euery, *i. e. ivory; iuery*, 1560.

„ „ „ 24, deceyued; the original adds "and made, as we say, as horned as a stag."

„ „ „ 29, bente facioned; *bente, facyoned*, B. M. and 1560.

„ 114, „ 6, pytes, *i. e.* pits; *pyttes*, B. M.

„ „ „ 14, in warder; *inwarde*, B. M.

„ „ „ 19, cared, *i. e. carried;* Latin, "Non timida, non audax, sed temperatum verecundiæ metum, *virilem animum* sub femineo corde gerebat." The words underlined have been omitted in all three editions of the English. The French has "Et courage plus que viril auoit."

„ „ „ 27, presounte, *i. e. presenl*; the other two editions have *prefounte*. In the Latin it is "cesarem in funeribus habuit."

„ 115, „ 4, yene; *eyne*, 1560.

„ „ „ 21, fame, read *flame;* all English editions have *fame*, but the Latin is "Non tamen hac ipsa die vel in se *flammam* Lucresia cognovit."

„ 116, „ 1, they, read *the; thee*, 1560.

„ „ „ 10, Latin, "Excute conceptas e casto pectore flammas si potes infelix."

„ „ „ 16, louethe the, read *louethe the not*; Latin, "si virum fastidis."

„ „ „ 27, abrode. So in all three editions; it should be *abode, i. e.* delay; see p. 135, l. 31. The Latin has "Et dabit ante fidem; cur tuta timeam? Accingar, et omnem *moram* pellam."

„ 117, „ 8, Media; *Medea*, B. M.

„ „ „ 22, he put, &c.; French, "Deurialus rabatit le chappeau deuant les yeux."

„ „ „ „ ayne; *eyne*, 1560.

„ „ „ 26, couler; so also in the 1560 edition; *courler*, B. M.; it should be, perhaps, *courser*; French, "Sur ung boiart;" Latin, "Erat Eurialo spadix equus ardue ceruicis."

NOTES. XXV

Page 117, line 27, here, *i. e.* haīr; *heare*, 1560.
„ „ „ 30, manie, read *maine*, *i. e.* mane.
„ 118, „ 1, beinge alone; the Latin has here "sola fuit, claudere viam destinasset amori," which last four words the translator, or more probably the editor of a later edition of his translation, has omitted.
„ „ „ 4, chastye; so also in 1560; *chastitie*, B. M.
„ „ „ 6, fyers, *i. e. fierce*; Latin, "dira."
„ „ „ 8, aften; *often*, 1560.
„ „ „ 12, Zosias; Latin, Socias.
„ „ „ 32, dooste to=*dostow*, sometimes written for "dost thou;" *doest thou*, B. M.
„ 119, „ 16, thee, read *hee*, B. M.
„ „ „ 25, deade, *i. e. deed*; Latin, "facinus."
„ 120, „ 23, Perria; so in all English editions; it shoud be *Porcia* (see p. 160, l. 20). The Latin has "Porcia cathonis."
„ 121, „ 20, with thys wisdome; Latin, "Hic ubi ardere se vidit, diu prudentiam suam miratus est, seque multotiens increpavit." The French is
 "Mais quant il vit par effait reaulment
 Que Lucresse de bonne amour laymoit
 Sa prudence loua tres grandement
 Ma^s plusieurs foi^s luy mesme^s se lcrepoit."
„ 122, „ 2, goodes; so in all three editions; it should be *goddes*; Latin, "Diis equa potestas est cesarum."
„ „ „ 4, disroyl; so in 1560; *disroyle*, B. M.; it should be *dispoyl*; Latin, "pharetris et leonis *spolio* positis."
„ „ „ 11, beleuynge, *i. e. bellowing*; Latin, "mugientes."
„ „ „ 28, my, *probably* thy; Latin, "sed omnis tum salutis tum vite spes mee ex *te* pendet."
„ „ „ „ selefe; *selfe*, 1560.
„ 123, „ 1, sightes, read *sighs*; Latin, "suspiria."
„ „ „ 3, godlyhede, read *goodlyhede*; Latin, "venustatis."
„ „ „ 5, thy, read *the*.
„ „ „ 13, lefe, read *lese* (lose); Latin, "perdere."
„ „ „ 19, happe, read *happie*; Latin, "felix."
„ 124, „ 5, entre out of my syghte; Latin, "I ocius venefica;" German, "Mach dich bald hinweg;" French,
 "Vaten dicy pars bien legierement
 Vielle infecte, benefique et mauldicte."
„ „ „ 23, omit "is."
„ „ „ 8, bere; so in all three editions; perhaps a misprint for *vexe*; Latin, "parce literis ac nunciis me *vexare*."

e

NOTES.

Page 126, line 2, bautye; *beautye*, B. M.
,, 127, ,, 4, a lesse thinge; the Latin is more definite and less delicate, "transformari in pulicem vellem;" the French has,
"Plus voulentiers *puce* ie deuiendroye
Lors fenestre ne pourries fermer."
,, ,, ,, 14, chaunce; *chaunge*, 1560.
,, ,, ,, 15, that, read *thee*; B. M., *the*; 1560, y^e.
N.B. The letter used for "th" in the 1560 and 1567 editions, though not a correctly made *thorn* (þ), is, as in many other sixteenth-century books, a different type from the *y*
,, ,, ,, 18, thou haste none excuse; Latin, "nihil est quod objicias."
,, 128, ,, 12, Adriana; so in the Latin; *i. e. Ariadne*. Cf. Chaucer's " Man of Lawes prologue."
,, ,, ,, 23, I than synce am, *i. e. I then, since I am;* the " I " is not unfrequently omitted in early writers; Latin, " michi ergo nuptæ nobili."
,, ,, ,, 24, louers, *loues*, 1560.
,, ,, ,, 25, continuallye laste, read *continual, least*, 1560.
,, ,, ,, 29, y^e, read y^t.
,, 129, ,, 31, Deiphus; Latin, " Deiphebum Helena perdidit."
,, 130, ,, 11, note, read *not*.
,, ,, ,, 16, at all, read *shall;* Latin, " reditus festinus erit."
,, ,, ,, 19, Strusia, meaning " Tuscia," or [E]" truria," Latin.
,, 132, ,, 1, one; *on*, 15C0.
,, 133, ,, 10, sythen the wyndowes of ye towne shewed them selfe. The translator, or more probably the printer, has made a strange jumble of the sense. The Latin has, " Sene ipsa vidue videbant'," *Sienna herself seemed widowed;* in the French, " Sene venfue lore dire on pouoit;" but the printer of the 1560 edition, which this follows, has mistaken probably the " Sene " (or Sien) of some earlier edition for Sythen, and " widow " for widow (window), and made hopeless nonsense of the passage.
,, ,, ,, 21, may se in the bright mornonge what . . . . . . &c.; it should be, *may se the bright morninge! What measure is in love? It cannot be cloked—no more than a cough can!*
,, ,, ,, 24, naything, *i. e. neighing*; Latin, " hinnitus equorum." The Latin adds, " et prolixæ barbæ strepitus tuæ."
,, ,, ,, 25, here; *her*, 1560.
,, ,, ,, 31, voyde, read *viewed;* Latin, " spectatoque loco."
,, 134, ,, 1, caneil = *channel;* canell, 1560; Latin, " cloaca." French,
" Entre lostel du tauernier et cil

NOTES. xxvii

                De Lucresse ung grant euier auoit
                Tout plain de eaue."

Page 134, line 12, inioyninge, read *inioying*, see note on p. 138. l. 10; Latin, "amoris nostri *gaudium* nimium distulimus."

  „ „ „ 24, of bothe these; elles, &c., read *of both these illes, &c.*

  „ 135, „ 27, thoughte, read *though*.

  „ 136, „ 2, the; so in all three editions; it means *thee* (it seemeth to thee).

  „ „ „ 15, companye boystous; *companye of boystous*, 1560.

  „ „ „ 20, fearethe, read *fareth*, B. M.

  „ „ „ 21, chaunced; *chaunged*, 1560.

  „ „ „ 25, wayfer, read *wayter*, B. M.; Latin, "expectantem recreat Eurialum."

  „ 137, „ 14, at; so also in 1560; but omitted in B. M., thus making sense of the passage.

  „ „ „ 20, ropes, *i. e.* the porter's knot; Latin, "hos funes missos face." The German has "Lass fallen diese seiler." The corresponding lines in the French version are

            " Mais or auant ma volupte ma ioye
            Ostes ce sac môstres vous claremēt
            Despouilles vous faict tât q' voˢ voie
            Hors cet habit de porteur vitemēt
            Deceignes vous de cordes prōptement
            Ottroies moy q' ie vous puisse voir."

  „ 138, „ 10, enioynyng, read *enioyyng*, 1560; the French book has
            "Telles ioyes prouffiter ne voye mie;"
            Latin, "quid hæc amoris gaudia."

  „ „ „ 24, all, read *as*.

  „ 140, „ 5, rested, read *resysted*, B. M.; Latin, "obstabat mulier."

  „ „ „ 24, tymee, read *tyme*, 1560.

  „ 141, „ 17, answered, read *a sweard*, 1560; French,
            "Mon espee qui au coste pendoit;"
            Latin, "fidus ensis herebat lateri."

  „ „ „ 18, and there many seuauntes, read *there was many seruauntes*, B. M.

  „ „ „ 27, cyuyll lawe; Latin, "Lex Julia"

  „ 142, „ 8, one, read *on*, 1560.

  „ „ „ 20, *louynge*, read louynge; Latin, "vultu blando."

  „ „ „ 22, cane, read *can*, 1560.

  „ 143, „ 8, *founde* the pleasant . . . . . and after the *Courte* . . . . .; the Latin words, "Solebat hoc hominum genus pergratum esse matronis nostris," had got transposed in the printed copy, and the translator

e 2

xxviii   NOTES.

has made nonsense of the passage. It should run, "*founde* the love-letter. This kind of folk was wont to be pleasaunt to our matrons; but since the Emperour's *Courte* . . ."

Page 143, line 26, falth; *falleth*, 1560.
,,   144, ,, 10, cloued=*closed*; *cloced*, 1560.
,,   145, ,,   3, maysters, read *mayster*.
,,   ,,   ,, 12, soketh, read *seketh*, 1560.
,,   ,,   ,, 13, leue, read *lyue*, 1560.
,,   147, ,, 30, erre; so in all three editions; it means *ere*.
,,   148, ,,   9, reygneth; *it reygneth*, 1560.
,,   ,,   ,, 14, I bourne, read *it bournes*; Latin, "ardeat."
,,   ,,   ,, 18, rag; *rage*, 1560.
,,   ,,   ,, 22, mee, read *my*; French, "Pour q' mon cas damour cogneu te soit;" Latin, "meum amorem."
,,   ,,   ,, 26, it, read *in*.
,,   149, ,,   8, that the loue of us both lyke pearish; so also in 1560. The Latin has "Illa incensa et ego ardeo; ambo perimus. A line has been omitted by the copyist. B. M. has, "that the loue of us both *was* lyke, *she is kyndeled, and I burne, and we both peryshe*." In German it is "Dye ist entzund et ich briynne; in French,

"Elle brusle et je ars nen doubte point
Nous perissons remede ne trouuon."

The Spanish has "Ella arde y yo me abraso: y ambos, sino nos vales perceceremos."

,,   ,,   ,, 26, geeue=*give*; *geue*, 1560.
,,   150, ,,   3, hem, read *him*, 1560.
,,   ,,   ,,   5, Earle; French, "Conte soys seur palatin tu seras."
,,   151, ,, 32, rewarde, read *rewarded*; Latin, "premiandus."
,,   152. ..   5, done it by unknowne; so all three editions; Latin, "si potuisset te nesciente fieri." *By* may imply "in an unknown fashion," or may it perhaps be "per tmesin," un-*be*-known?
,,   ,,   ,, 11, A gylted bull; this is not, as might be imagined, the coat-armour granted to Pandalus "and his posteriars;" but the "aurea bulla" of the original—the patent of nobility. The French book says,

"Pandalus eut de macreau le salaire
Bientost apres fut conte palatin
De noblesse p' mieulx le tout parfaire
Les ornemens receut a ung matin
Ce fut assez tire pour ung hutin

NOTES. xxix

Sa lignée en est magnifique
Portant habis de velour et satin
Aux plus nobles par tout parifiee."

Here the author has a long reflection on nobility and its origin; which his translator has omitted, fearing Scandalum Magnatum. It is as follows:—

"Of nobility there are many grades, my Marianus; and, indeed, if thou look into the origin of any of them, thou wilt find, in my opinion, none, or certainly very few, that have not had an evil origin. For when we see those called noble who abound in wealth—but wealth is rarely the companion of virtue—who doth not see that their nobility has a degenerate birth? Usury enriches one, spoil another, ruin a third; this man gets wealth by poison, that by adulation, the other owes his place to adultery, while some get their profit out of lies; some make gain of their wives, some of their children; many are helped on their way by murder. Rare is he who gets together his wealth honestly. *No one makes a big bundle who mows not all kinds of herbs.* Men get riches together, and ask not whence they come, but in what quantity they come. This verse suits every one, ' Whence comes your having no one cares, but have you must.' But when the chest is once full, straightway a patent of nobility must be asked for—nobility, which thus sought is nothing else but the reward of iniquity. My ancestors were considered noble, but flatter me not; I think my forefathers were no better than others, whose antiquity is their only excuse, and that because their crimes are not in the memory of man. In my opinion no one is noble unless he be a lover of virtue. Of cloth of gold, of horses and dogs, of a row of lacqueys, of dishes, of tables, of marble palaces, villas, farms, fishponds, magistracies, forests, I make no account. For these, and all of these, a fool can get; whom if any one call noble, he must be himself a fool. 'Twas by pimping that our Pandalus got his peerage."

Page 152, line 22, hadde very; *hadde a very*, 1560.
  „   „   „   30, harden, read *harde* (B. M.)=heard.
  „   153, „   8, one, read *an*, B. M.
  „   „   „   26, appere; it should be *open*; Latin, "adaperiat."
  „   154, „   10, faylige, read *fayling*, 1560.
  „   155, „   18, emly; the "Emilie" of Chaucer's Knight's Tale, and Boccaccio's Theseide.

NOTES.

Page 155, line 27, nowe where doth; so all three English editions; read *nowe were dethe*, &c.; Latin, " nunc mori satius est quando hoc gaudium est, ne qua interveniat calamitas ; " German, " jetz wer leicht zu sterben;" Spanish, "agora seria conveniente el morir."

„ „   „   29, embrachynges; so also 1560; *embracynges*, B. M.
„ 156, „   2, chayret; *chayre*, 1560.
„ „   „   10, Athens, read *Antæus*.
„ „   „   12, dewe here (all editions)=*dewy hair*.
„ „   „   16, mytyng; *meting*, 1560.
„ 157, „   5, wel; *wyl*, 1560.
„ „   „   21, leue; *live*, 1560.
„ „   „   25, merely (all editions)=*merrily*.
„ „   „   30, fayth full; *faythfull*, 1560.
„ 160, „   19, snowned (all editions), read *suowned*, *i. e.* swooned; Latin, " exanguis cecidit."
„ „   „   20, Percia, *i. e. Porcia*.
„ „   „   23, beade, *i. e. bed*; *bede*, 1560.
„ „   „   25, were; *ware*, 1560.
„ 161, „   2, speke; *spake*, 1560.
„ 234, „   3, dread; so in original; read *dead*.

APPENDIX.

APPENDIX.

[The marginal corrections and additions are from the 1490 edition, unless it is otherwise stated. When the additions are incorporated into the text they are inclosed within square brackets.]

Enee Siluii poete Senensis de duobus amantibus Eurialo et Lucrecia opus- [From the print of the culum ad Marianum Sosinum feliciter incipit Prefatio. Vienna MS. of 1446. Argentine,

Agnifico et generoso militi domino Iaspari Slich domino noui castri, 1476.] Cesario cancellario, ac terrarum Egee Cubitique Capitaneo, domino suo precipuo, Eneas Siluius poeta, imperialisque secretarius *salutem plurimam* dicit, et se reddit *commendatum*. Marianus Sosinus Senensis, *conterraneus meus*, vir cum mitis ingenii tum *litterarum* multarum (*cuius* adhuc similem visurus ne sim, hereo), duos amantes sibi ut describerem rogatu*m* me hiis diebus feci*t*; nec referre dixit rem veram agerem, an more poetico fingerem. Scis qui vir sit; mirabere si tibi expendam, nihil ei preter formam natura inuidit, homontio est: nasci ex mea familia debuit cui paruorum hominum est cognome*n*: vir est eloquens, iuris vtrius*que* consultus: Historias omnes nouit: poetrie p*ar*itus es*t* : carmen facit et latinum et tuscum; philosophie tam scius qu*am* Plato, geome*ter* quasi Boecius, in numeris fere Macrobio similis: nullum instrumentum ignorat musicum; agriculturam quasi Virgilius nouit; nihil ciuile ignotu*m* viro. dum iuuenili adhuc stabant in corpore vires, alter Entellus erat luctandi magisterio. Non cursu non saltu no*n* gestu poterat sup*er*ari. Preciosiora sunt interdum parui corporis vascula, vt *gemme* lapilli*que* testantur ! nec ab re fuerit quod de Tethideo refert Stacius i*n* hunc referri. "Maior in exiguo regnabat corpore virtus." Dij formam huic homini et immortalitatem si dedissent, is etiam erat deus. Sed nemo sortitus est omnia inter mortales. Nullum adhuc noui cui pauciora quam huic defuerint: Quid qu*od* minutissima etiam didicit quasi alter Appelles sic pingit: Nihil emendatius es*t*, nihil lucidius, qu*am* sua manu scripti codices: Sculpit vt Praxiteles, nec medicine ignarus est: Adde virtutes morales qu*e* alias regunt ducuntq*ue*. Noui meis diebus pleros*que* studiis literarum deditos, disciplinis qui admodum abundabant; sed hii nihil ciuilitatis habebant nec rempublicam nec domesticam regere norant. Stupuit Plagarensis et furti villicum accusauit, qui

f

suem fetam undecim porcellos, [asinam] unum dumtaxat enixam pullum, retulerat: samicius mediolanensis grauidum se putauit, diuque partum veritus est, quia se uxor ascendit: Hii tamen iuris maximum lumen habiti sunt: in aliis vero vel fastum vel auaritiam invenies, hic perliberalis est. Plena semper ei domus est honestis hospitibus; nulli aduersus est, pupillos tuetur, egros solatur, pauperibus subuenit, niduas iuuat, nulli indigenti deest vultus eius: quasi socraticus, semper est idem: In aduersis fortem animum prebet; nulla fortuna inflatur: versucias, non vt exerceat sed vt caueat, quaslibet nouit: Ciuibus dilectus est, peregrinis amatus; nulli odiosus, nulli grauis: At homo tantarum virtutum cur nunc rem leuiusculam exigat? Haud scio, id scio nihil illi mihi negare fas esse. Eum namque, dum Senis essem, vnice dilexi; nec diminutus est amor quamuis separatus sit. Is quoque, cum esset ceteris nature dotibus preditus, tamen hac maxime pollebat, vt nullius erga se sterilem esse amorem sineret: Huius ergo rogatus non censui respuendos, scripsique duorum amantium casus, nec finxi: res acta Senis est dum Sigismundus imperator illic degeret.

Tu etiam aderas, et si verum hiis auribus hausi, operam amori dedisti. Ciuitas veneris est, aiunt qui te norunt uehementerque asserunt, quod nemo te gallior fuerit, nihil ibi amatorie gestum te inscio putant.

Ideo historiam hanc vt legas precor, et an vera scripserim videas. ¶ Nec reminisci te pudeat si quid huiusmodi nonnumquam euenerit tibi; homo enim fueras. qui nunquam sensit amoris ignes aut lapis aut bestia est. Ille namque vel per deorum medullas non latet igneam fauillam. Vale.

[Prefatio.]

Neas Siluius, poeta, imperialisque secretarius, salutem plurimam dicit mariano Zosino vtriusque iuris interpreti, conciui suo. ¶ Rem petis haud conuenientem etati mee, tue vero et aduersam et repugnantem: quid enim est quod vel me iam pene quadragenarium scribere, vel te quinquagenarium de amore conueniat audire? ¶ Juuenes animos res ista delectat, et tenera corda deposcit.

¶ Senes enim tam ydonei sunt amoris auditores, quam prudentie iuuenes: ¶ Nec quicquam est senectute deformius que venerem affectat sine viribus.

¶ Inuenies tamen et aliquos senes amantes, amatos vero nullum.

¶ Nam et matronis et puellis est despectum senium. ¶ Nullius amore tenetur mulier nisi quem viderit etate florentem.

APPENDIX.

¶ Si qu*id* alit*er* audis, .deceptio subest. Ego ve*ro* cognosco amatorium script*um* mihi non conuenire, qui iam meridie*m* pret*er* gressus, in vesperu*m* feror. Sed non minu*s* me scribere qua*m* te poscore dedecet. Ego tibi debeo morigerus esse: tu vide qu*id* postules. Nam quanto es natu maturior, tanto equius e*st* parere amicitie legibu*s*, quas si tua iusticia no*n* veretur mandando infringere, nec stultitia mea timebit transgredi obediendo. Tua in me tot sunt beneficia, vt nihil negare petitionum tuarum queam, etiam si admixtum sit aliqu*id* turpitudinis. Parebo igitur petitioni tue ia*m* decies multiplicate, nec ampli*us* negabo quod tanto con[u]itio postulas. Non ta*men* (vt ipse flagitas) fictor ero; nec poete vtemur tuba dum licet vera referre.

Quis e*n*im tam nequam est vt mentiri velit cum se ve*ro* pot*est* tueri? Quia tu sepe amator fuisti, nec adhuc igne cares, vis tibi vt duoru*m* ama*n*tium hystoriam texu*m*, nequ*i*tia e*st* que te no*n* sinit esse senem. Ero morigerus cupiditati tue et hanc inguinis egri caniciem prurire faciam; nec finga*m* quando tanta e*st* copia veri quid e*n*im est toto terraru*m* orbe amore co*m*munius? que ciuitas, quod oppidulum, que familia vacat exemplis? Quis trigesimu*m* nactus annum amoris ca*us*a nullum peregit facinus? Ego *de* me facio coniecturam, quem amor in mille p*er*icula misit. Ago sup*er*is gratias quod structas insidias milies fugi felicior astro marte quem vulcan*us* cum venere iacentem ferreo illaqueauit reticulo, deridendumque diis ceteris ostentauit. Sed alienos *non* meos amores attinga*m*, ne dum vetusti cineres ignis euoluo, scintillam adhuc viuentem reperiam.

Referam autem mirum amorem peneque incredibilem quo duo amantes (ne dicam amentes), inuicem exarsere; nec vetustis nec obliteratis vtar exemplis, sed nostri temporis ardentes faces exponam, nec troyanos, nec babilonios, sed nostre vrbis amores audies; quamuis ex [a]mantibus alter sub artico natus fuerit celo, forsitan et hinc sugere aliquid vtilitatis licebit: nam cum puella que in argumentum venit, amatore perdito, inter plorandum mesta*m* et indignantem exaluerit animam, alter vero post hac nunquam vere letitie particeps fuerit, commonitio quedam iuuenibus erit, his vt abstineant iugis. ¶ Audiant igitur adolescentule et hoc edocte casu videant ne p*ost* amores iuuenum se eant perditum: Instruit hec historia iuuenes ne militie se accingant amoris que plus fellis habet qu*am* mellis. Sed omissa lasciuia que homines reddit insanos virtutis incumbant studiis que possessorem suum gloria beare potest. In amore autem quot lateant mala si quis aliunde nescit, hinc poterit scire. Tu vale, et historie quam me cogis scribere attentus auditor esto.

[¶ Incipit opusculum de duobus amantibus.]*

---

* The Venice Edition of 1497 omits the Dedication and Preface, and begins with the words, ¶ Siluii Enee Poete, qui postea summi Pontificatus gradu*m* adeptus Pius est appellatus, Hystoria de duobus amantibus cum multis epistolis amatoriis, ad marianum compatriotam suum. Feliciter Incipit.

APPENDIX.

VRbem Senas, unde tibi et mihi origo *est*, intra*n*ti Sigismu*n*do Cesari quot honores impensi fuerunt, iam ubique uulgatum est. Palatium illi apud sacellum sancte marthe super uicum que ad cophorum[a] ducit portam strictam paratum fuit. Huc post*qu*am cerimonie peracte sunt c*um* uenisse*t* Sigismundus, quattuor maritatas obuiam habuit, nobilitate, forma, etate, ornatuque pares: no*n* mortales sed deas quisque putauit: si tres dumtaxat fuissent, ille uideri poterant quas referunt paridem *per* quietem uidisse. Erat Sigismu*n*dus, licet grandeuus, in libidinem pronus; matronar*um* alloquiis admodum oblectabatur, et femineis blandimentis gaudebat; nec suauius illi quicqu*am* fuit illustrium aspectu mulierum. Vt ergo has uidit, desiliens equo, inter manus earum exceptus[b] est, et ad comites versus, ait. "Similes ne unqu*am* hiis feminas uidistis. Ego dubius sum an facies humane sint, angelici ue uultus; celestes sunt certe." Ille oculos humi deiicie*n*tes, ut uerecundiores fiunt, sic pulchriores redduntur. Sparso namque inter genas rubore, tales dabant ore colores quales indicum[c] ebur ostro uiolatum, aut quales reddunt alba immixta purpureis rosis lilia. Precipuo tamen inter eas nitore Lucrecia fulsit, adolescentula nondum viginti annos nacta, in familia camelorum[d] prediuiti uiro Menelao nupta. Indigno tamen cui tantum decus domi seruiret, *sed* dign*o*, quem uxor deciperet, et (sicut nos dicim*us*) cornutum quasi ceruum redderet. Statura mulier*i*s eminentior reliquis; come illi copiose, et aureis laminis similes, *quas* non more virginu*m* retrofusas miserat, sed auro gemmisq*ue* incluserat: Frons alta, spaciiq*ue* decentis, nulla interfecta ruga: Supercilia in arcum tensa, pilis paucis nigrisq*ue* debito interuallo disiuncta: Oculi tanto nitore splendentes ut in solis modum respicientium intuitus [h]ebctarent; Hiis illa et occidere quos uoluit poterat, et mortuos cum libuisset in uitam resumere: Nasus *in* filum direct*us*, roseas genas oquali mensura disiungebat:[e] Nihil hiis genis amabili*us*, nihil delectabili*us* visu; Que, cum mulier risit, *in* paruam utrinq*ue* dehiscebant fouea*m* : Nemo has uidit q*ui* n*on* cuperet osculari. Os paruum decensq*ue* : Labra corallini coloris ad morsum aptissima : Dentes paruuli et in ordinem positi ex cristallo videbantur; *per* quos tremula lingua discurre*ns*, n*on* sermonem *sed* armonia*m* suauissimam monebat.

Quid dicam me*n*ti speciem an gule candore*m*? Nihil illo *in* corpore non laudabile: interioris forme iudicium faciebat exterior. Nemo hanc aspexit qui uiro non inuiderit. Erant insuper *in* eius ore multe facetie. Sermo is fuit qualem rumor *est* graccoru*m* matrem habuisse corneliam, siue hortensii filiam. Nec snauiu*s* aliqu*id* eiu*s* oratione, nec modesti*us* fuit, non ut plereq*ue* tristi facie honestatem oste*n*debat, sed alacri uultu modestiam: non timida, non audax, *sed* temperatu*m* uerecundie metu,[f] virilem animum sub femineo corde gerebat: uestes illi multiplices erant: n*on* monilila,[g] n*on* fibule, n*on* balthei,

[a] tophorum, 1490, torphorum, al. ed. colophorum 1648. dei Tofi, Ital.

[b] acceptus

[c] inclitu*m*

[d] camillorum

[e] disterminabat

[f] metum

[g] monilia

THE EMPEROR SIGISMUND RECEIVED BY FOUR LADIES OF SIENNA.

APPENDIX. xxxvii

non armille deerant. Redimicula capitis mirifica: multi vniones adamantesque cum in digitis tum in serto fuere, non Helenam pulchriorem fuisse crediderim, quo die paridem in conuiuio menelaus excepit. Nec ornatiorem: andromachen, cum sacris Hectoris initiata[a] est nuptiis. Inter has et Kathorina Peruchia [a] inuitata fuit, que paulo post diem functa extremum, cesarem in funebribus habuit qui et natum eius militia ante sepulchrum donauit quamuis infantem: huius quoque mirabilis forme decus elucebat, inferior tamen Lucrecia erat. Omnis de Lucretia sermo audiebatur: hanc Cesar, hanc ceteri commendabant intuebantur que; quocumque illa uertebatur eo et oculi sequebantur astantium.[b] [Et sic [b] astantium omitted. orpheus sono cithare siluas ac saxa fert traxisse sic ista homines quocunque volebat intuitu ducebat.] Vnus tamen inter illos plus equo in illam ferebatur Eurialus franco, quem nec forma nec diuitie amori reddebant ineptum: Duorum et triginta annorum erat: non eminentis stature, sed lete grateque habitudinis. Illustris[c] oculis, malis ad gratiam rubescentibus, ceteris membris non sine [c] Illustribus quadam maiestate decoris, stature correspondentibus. Reliqui curiales propter longinquam militiam omnes auro excussi erant; hic quia et domi abundabat, et propter amiciciam cesaris magna munera recipiebat, in dies ornatior conspectibus hominum reddebatur: longum famulorum ordinem pone ducebat. [Nunc auro illitis nunc muricis tirij sanguine tinctis non filis que vultum legunt[d] textis [d] nunc filis que ultimi legunt Seres vestibus vtebatur.] Tum equi tales illi erant quales in fabulis est ad Troyam uenisse Memnonis. Nihil huic ad excitandum illum blandum animi calorem quem amorem uocant, preter otium, deerat. Sed vicit[e] iuuenta et luxus; tum [e] vincit leta fortune bona quibus ille nutritur. Nec potens Eurialus sui: vt Lucretiam uidit, ardere puellam cepit; herensque uultui nihil satis uidisse putauit.[f] Nec [f] putabat. impune dilexit: Mira res. Multi egregia forma iuuenes: sed vnum hunc Lucretia; plures honesti corporis mulieres; sed hanc vnam eurialus sibi delegit.[g] Non [g] elegit. tamen hac ipsa die uel in se flammam Lucresia cognouit Euriali, uel ille Lucresie; sed amare se frustra uterque putauit. Vt igitur cerimoniis sacro cesaris capiti per-actis modus fuit, illa domum reuersa in Eurialum tota, in Lucreciam totus Eurialus, ferebatur. Quis nunc Tisbes et Pirami fabulam demeretur,[h] inter quos noticiam primosque gradus vicinia fecit, quippe[i] domos habuere [h] demiretur [i] quippe omitted. contiguas? Tempore creuit amor. Hii nusquam se prius viderant nec fama cognouerant. Hic franco, illa tusca, fuit: nec lingue commercium intercessit; sed oculis tantum res acta est, cum alter alteri placuisset. Saucia ergo graui cura Lucresia, et igne capta ceco, iam se maritatam obliuiscitur. Virum odit; et alens uulnerum[k] uulnus, infixos pectore tenet Euriali uultus. Nec nullam [k] "venerium." membris suis quietem prebet; secum que, "nescio quid obstat," ait, "vt amplius herere viro nequeam, nil me iuuant eius amplexus; nil oblectant oscula: fasti-

APPENDIX.

dium verba ingerunt: peregrini semper ante oculos est ymago qui hodie propior erat Cesari: excute conceptas e casto pectore flammas, si potes infelix. Si possem, non essem egra vt sum; Noua me uis inuitam trahit. Aliud cupido suadet, aliud mens. Scio quid ᵃ est melius; quod deterius est sequor. O ciuis egreggia ac nobilis, quid tibi ᵇ cum peregrino est? quid in extraneo vreris? quid thalamos aliene concipis vrbis? Si uirum fastidis, hoc eciam potest dare terra quod ames: Sed, hey ᶜ mihi, que nam illius est facies! quam non moueat eius forma, etas, genus, uirtus? certe mea pectora mouit, et nisi ferat opem dispereo.ᵈ Dii meliora dent. Vah! prodam ego castos hymenos, meque aduene nescio cui credam, qui, vbi ᵉ abusus me fuerit, abeat, uirque sit alterius, et me pene relinquat? Sed non is est eius uultus, non ea nobilitas animi uidetur, nec gratia forme illa est, ut timeam fraudes et amoris obliuia nostri: dabit ante fidem: Cur tuta timeam? Accingar, et omnem morem ᶠ pellam. Ego quoque ita sum pulchra ut non me minus ille velit quam ego ipsum cupiam Semper se mihi dabit, si semel ad oscula fuerit receptus mea. Quot me ambiunt prochi ᵍ quocunque pergo! Quot riuales ante fores excubant meas! Dabo amori operam: aut hic manebit, aut me secum abiturus abducet. Ergo ego et matrem et uirum et patriam relinquam. Seua est mater et meis semper infesta gaudiis. Viro carere quam potiri malo. Patria illic est ubi delectat uiuere. At famam perdam! Quid mihi rumores hominum, quos ipsa non audiam? Nihil audet qui fame nimis studet. Multe hoc alie fecerunt. Rapi helena uoluit; non inuitam asportauit Paris. Quid Dyanam referam uel Medeam? Nemo errantem arguit qui cum multis errat." Sic Lucresia: nec intra pectus minora incendia nutriebat Eurialus. Medias inter Cesaris curiam et Euriali domum Lucresia edes habuit: nec palatium Eurialus petere poterat quin illam ex altis se ostentantem fenestris haberet in oculis. Sed erubuit semper Lucresia cum Eurialum vidit; que res Cesarem dedit amoris comscium.ʰ Nam cum ex sua consuetudine nunc huc nunc equitaret illuc et hac sepe transiret animaaduertit mutari feminam Euriali aduentu, qui sibi quasi Mechenathes Octaueano astabat, ad quem uersus "en" ait: " Euriale, siccine vris feminas? mulier illa te ardet:" semel [vero], tanquam inuideret amanti, vbi ad edes Lucresie uentum est, Euriali oculos pilleo ⁱ contexit: "nec videbis," inquit, "quod amas; ego hoc spectaculo fruar." Tum Eurialus: "quid hoc signi est Cesar. Nihil mihi cum illa: Sed hoc facere incautum est, ne circumstantes in suspitionem abducas." Erat Eurialo spadix equus ardue ceruicis angustique capitis, quem et breuis aluus et obesa tergora spectabilem reddebant; animoso pectore choris luxuriantem, qui sonante tuba stare loco nesciebat: nutabat auribus et collectum fremens voluit ᵏ sub naribus ignem. Densa iuba, et dextro iactata

ᵃ quod
ᵇ tibi *omitted*.
ᶜ Heu
ᵈ dispero
ᵉ dum
ᶠ morem
ᵍ proci
ʰ conscium.
ⁱ pileo
ᵏ "volnebat"

xxxviii

THE EMPEROR COVERS EURIALUS'S EYES WITH HIS CAP.

LUCRETIA CONFIDES IN SOSIAS.

APPENDIX. xxxix

recumbebat in armo. Et cauans tellurem solido cornu, grauiter sonabat vngula. Similis illi fiebat Eurialus, uisa Lucresia: Que licet ᵃ dum sola fuit, claudere uiam destinasset amori,ᵇ vt tamen ᶜ illum aspexit nec modum flamme nec sibi ponebat. Sed ut siccus ager qui admisso igne comburitur, si chori perflant, altius flammescit, sic infelix Lucrecia exardebat. Ita est sane ut sapientibus uidetur. Humiles tantum casas inhabitat castitas: solaque pauperies affectu sano tenetur; et que domo se coercet modico, diuites edes nescit pudicitia. Quisquis secundis rebus exultat semper insolita appetit. Delicatas eligit domos et penates magnos dira fortune comes libido. Intuens igitur Eurialum quam sepe transeuntem Lucresia, nec ardorem compescere potens, diu secum cogitabat cui patefaceret. Nam qui tacitus amat magis uritur. Erat inter uiri seruos Sosias theutonicus, senex, heroque fidus, cui iam seruierat diu liberaliter: hunc aggreditur amans, plus nationi quam homini credens. Ibat magna procerum stipatus caterua per urbem Cesar, iamque Lucresie domum preteribat. Que vbi adesse Eurialum cognouit, "adeste," inquit, "Sosia, paucis te volo. Respice deorsum ex fenestra. Vbinam gentium inuentus est huic similis? Viden vt omnes calamistrati sunt, erecti, eminentibus humeris: Aspice cesaries et madido cirro contortos crines: O quales facies! omnes lactea colla ferunt. Quo sese ore ferunt, quam forti pectore! Aliud est hoc hominum genus quam terra nostra producat:ᵈ semen hoc deorum est aut celo missa progenies. O si ex his in virum fortuna dedisset! Nisi testes oculi essent: nunquam tibi narranti hec credidissem. Et si fama fuerit prestare omnibus gentibus germanos, credo subiectam boree eorum plagam ex frigore magno albedinem mutuari. Sed nostin tu aliquos?" "Quam plurimos," inquit Sosias. Tum Lucresia: "Eurialum franconem nosti?" "tanquam me," ait Sosias. "Cur tamen hoc rogas?" "Dicam," inquit Lucresia. "Scio quod in apertum non ibit: Hanc spem mihi tua bonitas facit. Ex hiisᵉ qui Cesari astant nemo est mihi Eurialo gratior. In hunc animus meus commotus est; nescio quibus exuror flammis. Nec illum obliuisci nec mihi pacem possum dare nisi ei me facio notam. Perge oro, Sosia: conueni Eurialum dic me ipsum amare. Nil uolo ex te amplius, nec tu frustra hoc nuntium facies." "Quid audio?" refert Sosias. "Heccine me flagitia facere aut cogitare? O hera: Prodam ne ego dominum? iamque senex incipiam fallere quod iuuenis abhorui? Quin potius clara progenies huius vrbis exstirpa nefandas flammas e casto pectore. Ne obsequere dire spei: extingue ignem. Non egre amorem pellit qui primis obstat insultibus: qui dulce malum blandiendo nutrit, duri et insolentis domini seruituti se dat, nec cum uult excutere iugum potest. quod si hoc resciret maritus, heu quibus te ille laceraret modis! Nullus diu latere potest amor." "Tace," inquit Lucresia. "Nihil loci terrori est. Nihil timet qui non timet mori. Quemcunque dederit exitum casus feram."

ᵃ libet
ᶜ amoris
ᶜ tamen omitted.

ᵈ perducat

ᵉ his

"Quo misera pergis?" Sosias retulit; "Domum infamem reddes, solaque tui generis eris adultera. Tutum esse facinus reris: Mille circa te oculi sunt. Non sinet genitrix occultum scelus, non uir, non cognati, non ancille, serui ut taceant, iumenta loquentur, et canes, et postes,ᵃ et marmora te accusabunt. Atque ut celesᵇ omnia, qui uidet omnia celare non potes deum. Disce quid pena presens conscie mentis [pauor] et animus culpa plenus seque ipsum timens: negata est magnisᶜ sceleribus fides. Compesce, obsecro, impii amorisᵈ flammas; expelle facinus mente casta horridum; metue concubitus nouos miscere thalamis mariti."

"Scio tectumᵉ esse quod dicis," rettulit Lucresia. "Sed furor cogit sequi peiora. Scit animus quantum precipitium instat, et ruit [sciens]. Vincit et regnat furor; potensque mente tota dominatur amor. Stat sequi quod regnum iubet amoris. Nimis heu nimis reluctata sum frustra: perfer, si mei te miseret, nuncium." Ingemuit super his [Sosias] "per que has" [dixit] "canas senectute comas, fessumque curis pectus, et fida que prebui generiᶠ seruitia te precor supplex siste furorem, teque ipsam adiuua: Pars sanitatis est uelle sanari." Tum Lucresia: "non omnis," ait, "ingenium reliquit pudor: Parebo tibi, Sosia, et amorem qui tegi non uult vincam; unicum effugium est huius mali; morte ut preueniam nephas." Exterritus hac Sosias uoce "moderare," inquit, "hera, mentis effrene impetus; coerce animos; nunc uita es digna, quia te nec[e] dignam putas." "Decretum est," ait Lucresia, "mori. Admissum scelus colateinᵍ uxor gladio vindicauit: ego honestius preueniam: morte committendum. Genus leti quero: laqueo, ferro, precipitio, veneno, vindicare castitatem licet. Vnum horum aggrediar." "Non patiar," inquit Sosias. At Lucresia, "si quis mori constituit prohiberi non potest," ait. "Prociaʰ Cathonis, mortuo Bruto, cum ferrum sibi substractum esset, carbones ardentes imbibit." "Si tam proteruus," inquit Sosias, "incumbat menti furor, tue uite magis quam fame consulendum est. Fallax sepe fama est, que malo melior, bono peior, nonnunquam datur. Temptemus hunc Eurialum et amori operam demus. Meus erit iste labor; tibique ni falor rem confectam dabo." His dictis incensum animum inflammauit amore: spemque dedit dubie menti. Sed non illi animus erat ut quod dixerat esset facturus, differre animum femina querebat, furorem que imminuere;ⁱ ut sepe tempus exti[n]guit flammas, et adimunt egritudinem dies. Existimauit Sosias gaudiis puellam producere donec vel cesar abiret vel mens illius mutaretur; ne, si negasset, aliusᵏ nuntius quereretur, aut in seˡ manus mulier ini[i]ceret. Sepe igitur ire atque redire se finxit et illum gaudere amore suo, et tempus ydoneum querere quo inuicem affari possent. dixit interdum, non fuisse loquendi opportunitatem; non nunquam se mitti extra urbem studiit, ac in reditum gaudia distulit. Sic diebus multis egrotum pauit animum. Et ne perᵐ omnia mentiretur, semel tantum adorsus Eurialum, "O quam hic dilectus es," ait. Nec illi, querenti

No. 6. *To face page* xli.

EURIALUS SENDS A LETTER BY A PROCURESS.

quid hoc esset, respondit. At Eurialus secreto ᵃ cupidinis arcu percussus, nullam ᵃ *om.*
membris quietem dabat, igne furtiuo populante uenas qui totas penitus vorabat
medullas: non tamen Sosiam nouit, nec Lucresie missum putauit, vt omnes
minus spei habemus quam cupiditatis; hic vbi ardere se vidit, diu prudentiam
suam miratus est, seque multotiens increpauit: "En Euriale quid sit amoris
imperium nostri! longi luctus, breues risus, parua gaudia, magni metus; semper
moritur et nunquam mortuus est quiamat. Quid tu hiis nugis ᵇ immisceas iterum?" ᵇ *om.*
Ac ᶜ cum se frustra niti videret, "quid tandem," ait, "incassum miser amori repugno? ᶜ *om.*
Num me licebit quod Iulium licuit, quod Alexandrum, quod Hanibalem? Viros
armatos refero. Aspice poetas: Virgilius per funem tractus ad mediam turrim
pependit: dum se muliercule sperat vsurum amplexibus. Excuset quis poetam,
vt laxioris uite cultorem: quid de philosophis dicemus diciplinarum magistris, et
artis beneuiuendi preceptoribus? Aristotelem tanquam equum mulier ascendit,
freno coercuit, et calcaribus pupugit. Diis equa potestas est Cesaris.ᵈ Non est ᵈ Cesarum.
uerum quod vulgo dicitur. 'Non bene conueniunt nec in una sede morantur
maiestas & amor.' Quis maior est amator quam noster Cesar? Quotiens hic
amori operam dedit? Herculem dicunt (qui fuit fortissimus et certa deorum so-
boles) pharetris et leonis spolio positis, colum suscepisse, passumque aptari digitis
smaragdos, et dari legem rudibus capillis, et manu que clauam gestare solebat,
properante fuso duxisse fila. Naturalis est hec passio. Sentit ignes genus
aligerum; Nam niger a uiridi turtur amatur aue. Et uariis albe iunguntur
sepe columbe; si uerborum memini que ad Pharonem siculum scribit Sapho. Quid
quadrupedes referam? mouet pro ᵉ coniugio bella iumentum: timidi scerui ᶠ prelia ᵉ per
poscunt, et concepti furoris dant Signa mugientes: Vruntur hircane tigrides: ᶠ cervi (1497).
Vuluificus aper dentes acuit: Peni quatiunt terga leones: cum mouit amor ardent
insane ponti belue. Nihil immune est; nihil amori ᵍ negatum: olim ʰ perit cum ᵍ *om.*
iussit amor. Iuuenum feroces concitat flammas, sensibusque fessis rursus extinctos ʰ odium
reuocat calores: Virginum ignoto ferit igne pectus. Quid ergo ⁱ nature legibus ⁱ ego
renitar. Omnia vincit amor et nos cedamus amori." Hec vbi firmata sunt lenam
querit, cui seras ᵏ ad nuptam ferendas committat [Eurialus]: Nisus huic fidus ᵏ ceras
comes fuit, harum rerum callidus magister. Hic prouinciam suscipit, mulier-
culamque conducit cui littere committuntur in hanc sententiam scripte.

" Alutarem te, Lucresia, meis scriptis, si qua mihi salutis copia
foret; sed omnis cum salus tum uite spes mee ex te pendet: ego
te magis quam me amo, nec te puto latere meum ardorem, lesi
pectoris Index tibi esse potuit uultus meus sepe lacrimis madidus,
et que, uidente te, emisi suspiria. Fer benigne te precor quod me tibi aperio.

g

APPENDIX.

Cepit me decus tuum, vinctumque tenet [eximia], qua omnibus prestas, uenustatis gratia : Quid esset amor antea nesciui : Tu me cupidinis imperio subiecisti. Pugnaui diu, fateor, violentum ut effugerem dominum : sed vicit meos conatus splendor tuus : Vicerunt oculorum radii, quibus es sole potentior : captus sum tuus, nec mei amplius compos sum. Tu mihi et cibi et potus vsum abstulisti : Te dies uoctesque amo, te desidero, te voco, te expecto, te cogito, te spero, de te me oblecto : tuus est animus ; tecum sum totus : Tu me sola seruare potes, solaque perdere : Elige horum alterum, et quid mentis habeas rescribe : Nec durior erga me verbis esto quam fueras oculis quibus me colligasti. Non peto rem grandem : ut alloquendi copiam habeam postulo, hoc tantum volunt littere mee, ut que scribo dicere possim coram te : Hoc si das, viuo, et felix viuo. Si negas, extinguitur cor meum, quod te magis quam me amat. Ego me tibi, et tue commendo fidei· Vale anime mi et uite subsidium mee." Has vbi gemma signatas accepit lena, festino cursu Lucresiam poscit : eaque sola inuenta, " Hanc tibi epistolam," inquit, " tota cesarea nobilior et potentior curia mittit amator ; vtque sui te misereret, magnis precibus rogat." Erat lenocinio notata mulier ; nec id Lucresiam latebat : permolesteque tulit nefandam feminam ad se mitti : Atque in cam versa, " que tc," ait, " scelesta, in hanc domum audatia mittit ? Que te dementia adire meam presentiam suasit ? Tu nobilium edes ingredi, tu matronas tentare ᵃ potentes, et violare audes legittimas faces ? Vix me contineo quin in capillos inuolem tuos. Tu mihi des litteras ? tu me alloquaris ? tu me respitias ? nisi plus quod me decet attenderem quam quod tibi conuenit, efficerem hodie ne post hac tabellas amatorias ferres. I ocius venefica, tuasque litteras tecum defer ! ymmo da potius vt lacerem ignique dedam !" Arripiensque papirum in partes diuersas scidit,ᵇ et calcatam sepe pedibus atque consputam, in cinerem proiecit. " Ac sic de te" [ait] "sumi supplicium, lena, deberet, igne quam viuo ᶜ dignior ! Sed abi ocius, ne te vir inueniat meus, et quas tibi remisi de te poscat penas : Caueto que admodum ne ᵈ ante conspectum redeas meum !" Timuisset talia mulier : Sed hec matronarum nouerat mores, et intra se inquit, " nunc uis maxime quia te nolle ostendis." Moxque ad illam " Parce," inquit, "domina : Putaui me bene facere, tibique placitum iri. Si secus est, da ueniam imprudentie mee : Si non uis redeam, parebo. Tu quem despicias amatorem uideris." Atque hiis dictis e conspectu recessit. Eurialo autem inuento. "Respira," inquit, " felix amator ! plus amat mulier quam amatur, sed nunc non fuit rescribendi ocium. Inueni mestam Lucresiam ; At vbi te nomino tuasque litteras debo, hylarem uultum fecit, milliesque papirum basiauit. Nec dubita, mox responsum dabitur." Et abiens vetula, cauit ne amplius inueniretur, ne pro verbis referret verbera. Lucresia vero, postquam anus euasit, fragmenta perquirens epistole, particulas

ᵃ temptare

ᵇ incidit

ᶜ vita [Leyd. ed.]

ᵈ ne om.

LUCRETIA TEARS THE LETTER.

quasque suo loco reposuit, et lacera verba contexuit, iamque legibile cirographum fecerat: Quod postquam milies legit, miliesque deosculata est, tandem inuolutum sindone inter preciosa iocalia collocauit. Et nunc hoc repetens nunc illud verbum, maiorem horatim bibebat amorem; Eurialoque rescribere statuit, atque hunc in modum dictatam epistola misit.

"Desine sperare quod assequi non licet, Euriale: Parce litteris ac nunciis me vexare: nec me illarum ex grege credito qui se vendunt: Non sum quam putas, nec cui submittere lenam debeas: Quere aliam incestandam: me nullus amor nisi pudicus sequatur: Cum aliis ut libet agito: Ex me nil postules; teque me indignum scias. Vale." Hec epistola quamuis durior Eurialo visa est et contraria lene dictis, viam tamen ostendit vltro citroque litteras missitandi. Nec dubitauit Eurialus credere cui fidem Lucresia prebuisset: sed angebatur quia sermonis ytalici nescius erat: Ideoque feruenti studio curabat ediscere. Et quia sedulum faciebat amor, breui tempore doctus euasit, solusque sibi dictauit epistolas qui prius ab aliis: mutuabatur quidquid etrusco sermone scribi oportuit. Respondit ergo Lucresie nil succensendum esse sibi quod infamem miserat feminam; cum id se peregrinum lateret qui vti alio nuntio non poterat; missionis amorem fuisse causam, qui nihil quereret inhonesti. Credere se fore pudicam castissimamque, atque id circo maiori dignam amore. Insolentem feminam honorisque sui prodigam nedum se non diligere, sed maximo odio prosequi; Pudicitia namque amissa, nil esse quod in femina commendetur: Formam esse delectabile bonum sed fragile caducumque, et cui, nisi pudor assit, nihil precii [a] detur: que pudicitiam forme adiunxerit eam [a] *om.* diuinam esse mulierem, ipsam [que] vtraque dote pollentem scire; ac propter[e]a coli a se, qui nihil ab ea peteret libidinosum, aut offuturum fame: optare se tantum alloqui, vt animum suum, qui scriptis plene ostendi nequit, verbis aperiat. Cum hiis litteris munera misit non solum materia sed etiam opere preciosa. Ad hec Lucresia sic rescripsit: "Accepi litteras tuas, iamque nil amplius de lena queror: quot me ames non magnifacior; quia nec primus es nec solus quem mea forma deceperit. Multi et amauerunt, et amant me alii. Sed vt illorum sic et tuus erit labor vatuus: [b] Habere verba tecum, nec possum, nec volo. Inuenire [b] vacuus. me solam, nisi fias hyrundo, non potes: Alte sunt domus, et aditus custodia clausi. Munera tua suscepi, quia oblectauit me opus illorum: sed ne quid tuum gratis apud me sit; ne ue hoc pignus videatur amoris, remitto ad te annulum quem matri mee vir dedit, ut apud te quasi precium sit venditoris iocalium. Nec enim minoris est gemma eius quam munus tuum. Vale." Hiis Eurialus sic replicauit.

xliv   APPENDIX.

[a] om.

"Magno in gaudio fuit ep*istol*a tua, qu*e* finem querelis facet de lena, sed angit me quod amorem paruipendis meum. Nam et si te [a] plures, nullorum tamen ignis comparandus est meo. At tu hoc non credis, qu*ia* loqui nequeo tecum: id si daretur, non me contemneres. O vtinam fieri possem hyrundo; sed libentius transformari in pulicem vellem ne mihi fenestram clauderes. At ego non quod nequeas, sed quod nollis doleo. Nam quid ego nisi animum respicio. Ach mihi Lucresia, quid dixti te nolle? An fieri possit, me nolis alloqui qu*i* tuus sum totus, qui nil magis cupio quam tibi gerere morem, quod, si iubes in ignem ire, citius obediam quam precipias? Mitte obsecro verbum hoc: si non datur facultas, assit voluntas tamen: ne me verbis eneca, qu*e* vitam oculis mihi prebes. Si non placet me alloquium petere quia non sit impetrandum, obsequar. Sed muta sententiam illam, qua meum laborem vacuum dixisti futurum. Absit hec crudelitas. Mitior esto amanti tuo. Si pergis sic loqui, fies homicida; nec dubita. Facilius tu me verbis interimeres, quam alius quiuis gladio. Desino iam plura poscere: vt redames tantum postulo: Nihil [hic] est qu*i*d obiicias: nemo pot*est* hoc prohibere: Dic te me amare, et beat*us* sum. Munuscula mea quouis modo apud te sint. Gratum est quod illa te aliquando mei admonebunt amoris. Sed parua illa fuerunt, et minora sunt que nunc mitto: tu tamen noli spernere, quod amator donat. Maiora[b] in dies ex patria debent afferri: Cum aderunt, ex me recipies. Anulus tuus nunquam ex digito meo recedet, et illum vice tua crebris osculis reddam madidum. Vale delicium meum, et mihi quod potes solatium dato."

[b] Majoraque

[c] om.

Ic cum frequenter replicatum esset,[d] in hunc tandem modum Lucresia dedit epistolam. "Uellem tibi Euriale morem gerere, teque (vt petis) amoris mei participem facere; Nam id tua nobilitas meretur, et mores tui deposcunt, vt incassum non ames. Taceo quantum mihi placet forma tua, et plena benignitatis facies: sed mihi non est vsui te vt diligam: nosco meipsam: Si amare iucipiam, nec modum nec regulam seruabo: Tu hic diu esse non potes, nec ego te, postquam in ludum venerim, possem carere. Tu me nolles abducere, at ego nollem manere. Mouent me multarum exempla qu*e* per peregrinos amantes deserte sunt, ne tuum amorem sequar: Jason Medeam [d] (cuius auxilio uigilem interemit draconem, et vellus aureum asportauit) reliquit:[e] Tradendus erat Theseus minotauro in escam, sed Adriane[f] consilio fretus euasit; illam tamen desertam apud insulam deseruit: Quid Dido infelix, que profugum recepit Eneam. Num illi peregrinus amor interitum dedit. Scio quanti periculi est amorem extraneum admittere, nec me tantis obiiciam discriminibus. Vos viri solidioris estis animi: furoremque magis compescitis.

[d] Medeam decepit
[e] om.
[f] Ariadne

EURIALUS RECEIVES A LETTER FROM LUCRETIA.

APPENDIX.   xlv

Feminia^a vbi furere incipit sola potest morte assequi terminum: Non amant sed ^{a femina}
insaniunt mulieres, et nisi correspondeat amor, nihil est amante femina terri-
bilius: Postquam receptus est ignis, nec famam curamus nec vitam: unicum
remedium est, si copia sit amati.^b Nam quo magis caremus, magis cupimus; ^{b amanti.}
nec discrimen timemus vllum, dum nostre libidini satisfiat. Mihi ergo nupte
nobili, diuiti, consultum est amori viam precludere; et tuo presertim, qui non
potest esse diuturnus, ne uel Rodopeya Phillis, dicar, vel altera Sapho. Ideo
te oratum volo: ne vltra meum exposcas amorem, et tuum vt paulatim com-
primas extinguasque: Nam id est viris quam feminis multo facilius; nec tu
si me (vt dicis) amas, id ex me querere debes, quod mihi exitio sit. Pro
tuis donis remitto auream crucem margaritis ornatam, que, licet breuis sit,
non tamen precio caret. Vale." Non tacuit Eurialus his acceptis sed vt erat
nouis scriptis incensus calamum suscepit, atque sub hac forma dictauit epistolam.

"Alue anime mi Lucresia que me tuis litteris saluum facis, etsi non
nihil fellis immisceas, sed hoc spero me audito distrahes. Venit
meas in manus epistola tua, clausa, et tua gemma signata. Hanc et
legi sepe et deosculatus sum sepius; sed hec aliud suadet quam
tuus videtur animus fuisse. Rogas me vt amare ^c desinam quia non expedit tibi ^{c amore}
peregrini flammas amoris sequi; Et ponis exempla deceptarum, sed hoc tam
ornate culteque scribis, vt mirari magis et amare tuum ingenium debeam quam
obliuisci. Quis est ille qui tunc amare desinat quando prudentiorem et sapien-
tiorem animaduertat amicam. Si meum imminuere^d amorem uolebas non ^{d minuere}
oportuit doctrinam tuam ostendisse. Nam hoc non est incensum extinguere,
sed ignem maximum ex parua conflare fauilla. Ego dum legi magis exarsi
uidens forme tue preclare et honestati coniunctam esse doctrinam. Verba
sunt tamen quibus rogas vt amare desistam. Roga montes vt in planum
veniant, atque fontes sua repetant flumina! tam possem ego te non amare,
quam suum relinquere phebus cursum! Si possunt carere niuibus sitie^e ^{e sithie}
montes, aut maria piscibus, aut feris silue, poterit et obliuisci Eurialus tui.
Non est pronum viris vt reris, Lucresia, flammas extinguere. Nam quod
tu nostro sexui ascribis, plerique vestro assignant: sed nolo hoc certamen nunc
aggredi. Ad ea me respondere oportet, que in aduersum rettulisti. Id circo
enim nolle te mihi iam-[que cor]-respondere amanti significas, quoniam multas
peregrinus amor decepit, exempla que ponis; sed possem ego plures referre quos
femine reliquerunt. Troylum, sicut nosti, Priami filium Crisis decepit: Dei

xlvi APPENDIX.

[a] perditit
[b] circe

[c] om.
[d] que om.

[e] et que pauca fuerunt.
[f] sum

[g] cesari
[h] trusia
[i] nec
[k] suauis mi

[l] om.

[m] finem statute.

[n] plalidussum.

[o] mihi
[p] dedignantur [1497].

phebu*m* Helena prodidit:[a] amantes cirtes[b] suos medicamentis vertebat in sues, atqu*e* in aliar*um* terga ferar*um*: Iniquu*m* est paucarum consuetudine totu*m* uulg*us* censere. Na*m* si sic p*er*gimus, et tu propter duos tres ve malos aut etiam decem viros omnes accusabis[c] horrebisqu*e*,[d] et propter totidem feminas cetere omnes erunt odio mihi. Qui*n* potius alia sumamus exempla qualis amor Anthonii Cleopatreq*ue* fuit; et aliorum quos epistole breuitas referri non sinit. Sed tu Ouidium legisti, inuenistiqu*e* post troyam dirutam achiuorum plurimos dum remeant peregrinis retentos amoribus, nunqu*am* in patriam reuertisse. Heserunt namqu*e* amatricib*us* suis, carere potius necessariis, domo, regnis, et aliis que sunt in patria queq*ue* gratissima uoluerunt, qu*am* amicas relinquere. Hec te rogo my Lucretia cogites, non illa qu*e* nostro amori sunt aduersa, et qu*æ* pauci fecerunt.[e] Ego ea mente te sequor, vt perpetuo te amem, simqu*e*[f] perpetuo tuu*s*: nec tu me peregrinum dixeris; magis namq*ue* ciuis sum quam qui hic nascit*ur*. Nam illum casus fecit ciuem, me vero electio. Nulla mihi patria erit, nisi vbi tu sis, et quanuis aliquando contingat me hinc abire, reditus tame*n* festinus erit: Nec ego in teutoniam reuertar nisi res compositurus ordinaturusqu*e* vt tec*um* esse qu*am* diu possim valeam; facile manendi apud te reperietur occasio. Multa hiis in partib*us* cesaris[g] negocia sunt; hec mihi committi expedienda curabo; nunc legatione fungar, nunc munus exerceo. Vicarium in strucia[h] cesarem habere oportet: ha*n*c ego prouinciam impetrabo. Ne[i] dubita suauium meum[k] Lucretia, meu*m* cor, spes mea: Si viuere absqu*e* corde possum, te et relinquere possum. Age iam tandem, miserere amantis tui, qui tanqu*am* nix ad solem liquescit: Considera meos labores et modu*m*[l] iam denique meis martiriis statue.[m] Quid me tamdiu crucias. Miror ego mei, qui tot mala perpeti potuerim, que tot noctes insomnes duxi, qui tot ieiunia toleraui. Vide qu*am* macer sum, qu*am* palidus:[n] parua res est que spiritu*m* alligatu*m* corpori detinct. Si tibi aut parentes, aut filios occidissem non pot[e]ras de me maius qu*am* hoc supplicium sumere: Si sic me punis qui*a* te amo, quid igitur facies qui tibi damnu*m* dederit aut malu*m*? Ah mea Lucresia, mea hera, mea salus, meu*m* refugium, suscipe me in gratia*m*; demum rescribe me tibi caru*m* esse! Nihil aliud volo, liceat me[o] dicere seruus Lucresie sum! Et reges et cesares amant, seruos vbi fideles nouerint, nec-[du*m* dignantur[p]] readamare qui amant. Vale spes mea, meusqu*e* metus." Vt turris que, fracta interius, inexpugnabilis videtur exterius, si paries admot*us* fuerit mox confrigitur, sic Euriali v*er*bis Lucresia victa est: Postqu*am* enim sedulitatem amantis aperte cognouit, et ipsa dissimulatum patefecit amorem, atqu*e* hiis litteris Eurialo sic aperuit.

EURIALUS RECEIVES "HEAVY NEWS" FROM LUCRETIA.

APPENDIX. xlvii

"On possum tibi amplius aduersari, nec te amplius, Euriale, mei amoris expertem habere possum. Vicisti; iamque sum tua. Me miseram, que tuas suscepi litteras; nimium multis exponenda sum periculis, nisi tua me fides et prudentia iuuet. Vide vt serues que scripsisti: In amorem iam tuum venio: si me deseris, et crudelis, et proditor, et omnium pessimus es. Facile est femellam decipere; sed quanto facilius tanto turpius. Adhuc res integra est; si putas me deserendam: dicito antequam magis amor ardeat. Nec incipiamus quod post modum incepisse peniteat. Omnium rerum respiciendus est finis. Ego, vt feminarum est, parum video. Tu vir es; te mei et tui curam habere oportet. Do me iam tibi, tuamque sequor fidem: nec tua esse cupio, nisi vt sim perpetuo tua. Vale meum presidium meeque ductor vite." Post hanc plures epistole misse vtrique sunt, nec tam ardenter scripsit Eurialus, quam feruenter Lucresia respondit: unum iam utrique[a] desiderium erat simul conueniendi, sed arduum ac pene impossibile [a vtrius que] videbatur, omnium oculis Lucresiam obseruantibus, que nec sola vnquam egrediebatur, nec unquam custode carebat; nec tam diligenter bouem Junonis Argus custodiuit, quam Menelaus iusserat obseruari Lucresiam. Vicium hoc apud ytalos late patet; feminam suam quasi thesaurum quisquis[d] recludit, meo[b] [b quisque] iudicio minus vtiliter. Sunt enim fere eiusmodi mulieres omnes, vt id potissimum cupiant quod maxime denegatur: Que vbi velis nolunt, vbi nolis cupiunt vltro: Ee[c] si liberas habent habenas minus deliuquunt: Exinde tam facile est inuitam [c Hee] custodire mulierem, quam in feruente sole pulicum gregem obseruasse: Nisi suapte casta sit mulier, frustra maritus nititur apponere scruantes eam: sed quis custodiet ipsos custodes? Cauta est, et ab illis incipit vxor. Indomitum animal est mulier, nullisque frenis retinendum. Erat Lucresie spurius frater; huic sepe tabellas commiserat Eurialo deferendas, hunc enim amoris sui conscium fecerat. Cum hoc igitur [conuenitur] Eurialum vt clam domi recipiat: habitabatque hic apud nouercam suam Lucresie matrem quam Lucresia sepe visitabat, et ab ea sepius visitabatur, nec enim magno interuallo distabant. Ordo ergo is erat, vt, clauso in conclaui Eurialo, postquam mater ecclesiasticas auditura cerimonias exiuisset, Lucresia superueniret, tanquam matrem domi conuentura, qua non inuenta, reditum expectaret, interim vero apud Eurialum esset. Post biduum statutus erat terminus; at hii dies tanquam anni visi sunt amantibus longi; vt bene sperantibus hore producte[d] sunt, male sperantibus correpte. Sed non arrisit amantum desideriis fortuna; presentit namque insidias mater: atque vt dies[d] [d perducte] venit, egressa domum preuignum excludit. Qui mox Eurialo triste nuncium tulit; Cui non minus quam Lucresia fuit molestum. Que postquam detectos [e hoc [al. ed.] agnouit dolos; hac[e] [animus commotus est: "nescio quibus][f] non successit: [f animus to quibus 1497.]

xlviii   APPENDIX.

^a aggrediamur [al. ed.] Alia," inquit, "eggrediamur ^a via : nec potens erit mater meis obsistere voluptati-
bus." Pandalus vero affinis erat, quem iam Lucresia fecit archan*orum* scium,
nec enim poterat ignit*us* anim*us* qu*i*escere. Significat igitur Eurialo hunc vt
alloquatur, qu*ia* fid*us* sit et conueniendi viam possit monstrare. At Eurialo non
videbatur tutum illi se credere, quem Menelao semper herentem intuebatur et
subesse fallaciam verebatur. Inter deliberand*um* autem iussus est Eurial*us*
rom*am* petere, atque cum pontifice maximo de coronatione transigere. Que res
tum sibi tum amice molestissima fuit. Sed oportebat cesaris imperium ferre.
Iter ergo [mora] duorum mensium fit. Lucresia interim domi manere, fenestras

^b mirare.   claudere, mestas induere uestes, nusq*uam* exire cernitur : mirantur ^b omnes, nec
causam noscunt. Sene ipse vidue videbantur, et, tanquam sol defecisset, cuncti
se putabant in tenebris agere. Domestici, qui eam sepe incubantem lectulo, et
nunq*uam* letam videbant, egritudini imputabant, et quicquid remediorum afferri
poterat perquirebant, s*ed* nunq*uam* illa vel risit vel thalamum egredi voluit, nisi

^c isse [al. ed]   postq*uam* redire Eurialum, et illi cesarem obuiam esse ^c cognouit. Tunc e*nim*,
quasi e graui sumno excitata, lugubri veste posita, et ornamentis redimita
priorib*us*, fenestras aperuit letabundaq*ue* illum expectauit. Quam ut cesar
vidit, "ne nega amplius, Euriale," inquit, "detecta est res. Nemo vnq*uam*
absente te Lucresiam videre potuit ; nunc, qu*ia* redisti, auroram cernimus. Quis
enim modus assit amori ? Tegi non potest amor, nec absconcli tussis." "Jocaris
mecum vt soles, cesar, et me in risum ducis," Eurial*us* ait. Ego quid hoc sit non
scio. Hinnit*us* equ*orum* [tuorum] et prolixe barbe strepit*us* tue illam forsitan excitauit." Atque sic effat*us* Lucresiam furtim aspexit, et oculos coniecit *in* oculos ;

^d consalutatio   eaque post reditum prima salutatio ^d fuit. Paucis deinde interiectis dieb*us* Nisus
Euriali fid*us* comes, dum anxius amici cause fauet, tabernam speculat*us* est que
post Menelai domum sita, in Lucresie cameram retrorsum habebat intuitum :
Cauponem igitur sibi consiliat, Spectatoque loco Eurialum adducit, et, "hac,"
inquit, "ex fenestra alloqui Lucresiam poteris." Media *inter* vtramq*ue* domum

^e hominum   cloaca fuit, nec homini ^e nec soli accessa ; trinmque vlnarum distantia fenestram
^f consedit   Lucresie determinabat. Hic diu conscedit^f amator, expectans si quis casus
Lucretiam ostenderet. Nec deceptus est : affuit tandem Lucretia, cumque huc
atque illuc respiceret. Quid agis, "ait Euralius," vite rectrix mee ? quo tendis
lumina, meum cor ? Huc huc dirige oculos, pr*e*sidium meum ! Tuus hic
Eurial*us* est ! me, me, assum, me respice !" "Tu ne hic ades," inquit Lucresia,
"O my Euriale ? Jam te alloqui possum ? Vtinam et amplecti valerem ?"
"At istud Eurial*us*, non magno conatu faciam : Scalam huc admouebo : obsera
thalam*um*, amoris nostri gaudia nimium distulim*us*." "Caue, my Euriale, si
me vis salu*am* : fenestra hic ad dextram est, vicinusq*ue* pessimus, nec cauponi

LUCRETIA TALKS TO EURIALUS ACROSS THE ALLEY.

APPENDIX. xlix

credendum est, qui parua pecunia et te et me perderet: sed alia incedamus via. Sat est si hinc sermoni nostro patet accessus," respondit Lucresia. "At mihi," inquit Eurialus, "mors est hec visio, nisi de ᵃ semel amplector, meisque brachiis ᵃ te teneo mediam." Diu ex hoc loco tractus est sermo, missaque per harundinem sunt munera. Nec Eurialus in donis quam Lucresia liberalior fuit. Sensit dolos Sosias; secumque, "frustra," inquit, "amantum conatibus obsto: nisi astans prouideo, et hera peribit, et domus infamiam subibit. Ex hiis malis satius est vnum auertere. Amet hera: nihil nocebit si clam sit. Ipsa pre amore ceca est, nec quid agat satis prospicit.ᵇ Si non potest custodiri pudicicia, satis est rumorem ᵇ perspicit. tollere, ne domus infamis fiat, ne ue paricidium commitatur. Adibo, et operam prebebo meam: Restiti quoad potui ne committeretur nefas; id quia non licuit, meum est curare," ait, "vt quod agitur occultum sit, et sic agere vt nemo sciat. Commune malum libido est, nec homo est quem pestis hec non agitet. Et ille castior habetur qui cautius agit." Dumque sic fatur Lucresiam egressam thalamo videt; Aggressusque feminam "Quid iam est," inquit "quod nihil amoris mihi communicas? Eurialus tibi nihilominus dilectus est, et vt clam ames, Videas cui des fidem. Primus sapientie gradus est, non amare; secundus vt sic ames ne palam fiat. Sola hoc sine internuntio facere non potes. Quanta mihi apud te sit fides, longo iam tempore didicisti. Si mihi committere vis, iube: mihi maxima cura est ne amor iste detegatur, et tu penam luas, et vir omnium [obtutationes ferat]." Ad hec Lucresia, "sic est vt ais, Sosia," inquit, "et tibi magnam habeo fidem; sed tu visus es nescio quomodo negligens, et meis adversus desideriis: Nunc quia sponte te offers, vtar obsequiis tuis, nec abs te decipi timebo. Tu scis quantum ardeo: diu ferre non possum hanc flammam: Iuua me vt simul esse possumus. Eurialus amore languet, et ego morior.ᶜ Nil peius est quam obstare cupidini nostre. ᶜ om. Si semel inuicem conueniremus, temperantius amabimus, et noster tectus erit amor. Vade igitur, Eurialoque viam vnicam me accedendi dicito. Si ab hinc quatriduo dum rustici frumentum afferunt, vectoris personam induat, opertusque sacco triticum per scalas in horreum ferat, tute scis thalamum meum ad scalas habere ostium. Itaque omnia Eurialo dicito. Hic diem manebo, et dum erit tempus sola in cubili ero. Ipse ostium impellat dum solus sit, et ad me ingrediatur."

Osias quamuis arduum facinus esset; maiora veritus mala, prouinciam suscipit; Eurialoque inuento cuncta ex ordine nunciat, que ille iudicans leuia libenter amplectitur, seque imperatis accingit; nec aliud queritur quam nimiam moram.ᵈ O insensatum pectus amantis! O men- ᵈ nimia mora. tem cecam! O animam audacem, corque intrepidum! Quid est tam inuium, quod

h

APPENDIX.

tibi peruium non uideatur? Quid tam asperum, quod planum non estimes? Quid tam clausum, quod tibi non sit apertum? Tu omne discrimen parui facis: tu nihil difficile censes. Inanis est apud te omnis custodia maritorum: Nulle te leges tenent, nulli metus: Nulli pudori obnoxius es: Omnis labor tibi est ludus. O rerum amor domitor omnium! Tu virum primatem, cesari acceptissimum, diuiciis affluentem, etate maturum, imbutum litteris, prudentia clarum, eo producis, vt, posita purpura, saccum induat, uultum fuco tegat, seruus ex domino fiat; et qui nutritus in deliciis fuerat, iam humeros ingestandis oneribus aptat seque publicum baiulum mercede locat. O rem mirandam peneque incredibilem! Virum aliquando consilio grauissimum inter caterinas vectorum cernere, atque in coluuie illa, feceque hominum, contubernium habuisse! Quis transformationem querat maiorem? Hoc est quod Ouidius methamorphoseos uult, dum fieri ex hominibus aut bestias scribit, aut lapides, aut plantas: hoc et poetarum eximius Maro sentit, dum Circes amatores in terga ferrarum[a] verti cantauit. Nam ita est ex amoris flamma sic mens hominis alienetur, vt parum a bestiis difforat. Linquens croceum tithoni aurora cubile, iam diem referebat optatum;[b] moxque suum rebus collorem apollo reddens, expectantem recreat Eurialum; qui tunc se fortunatum beatumque censuit, cum admixtum vilibus seruis nulli noscendum se vidit. Pergit igitur, ingressusque Lucresie domum, frumento se onerauit, positoque in horreum tritico, vltimus descendentium fuit, atque, ut erat perdoctus ostium maritalis thalami, quod in medio scalarum clausum videbatur, impellit, seque intro recipit, et reclusis foribus, solam Lucresiam serico intentam videt. Et uccedens propius, "Salue my Anime," inquit, "Salue vnicum vite presidium spesque mee! Nunc te solam ostende.[c] Nunc quod semper optaui semotis arbitris te amplectar; nullus iam paries, nulla distantia meis obstat oculis." Lucresia quanuis ordinem ipsa dedisset, primo congressu stupuit, nec Eurialum sed spiritum se videre putauit, vt que virum tantum ad ea pericula iturum sibi non suadebat; At vbi inter amplexus et oscula suum cognouit Eurialum. "Tu ne hic es," ait, "pauperculle? Tu ne hic ades Euriale?" Et rubore per genas fuso complexa est artius hominem, et media fronte conspicatur:[d] moxque repetens sermonem, "Heu quanto te," ait, "discrimini subiecisti! Quid amplius dicam? Iam me tibi carissimam scio. Iam tui amoris feci periculum. Sed neque tu me aliam inuenies. dii tantum fata secundent et amori nostro prosperum ventum dent. Dum spiritus hos reget artus preter te nemo Lucresie potens erit; Nec maritus quidem, si rite maritum appello, qui michi inuite datus est, et in quem animus nunquam consensit meus. Sed age, mea voluptas, meum delicium, abiicito saccum hunc, teque mihi tu quis es ostende. Exue vectoris speciem; hos funes missos face; Eurialum me videre concedito." Iam ille, depositis sordibus ostro fulgebat et auro, et amoris in officium pronus ibat. Tum Sosias ante ostium pulsitans, cauete

[a] ferarum

[b] adoptatum

[c] offendi.

[d] dissuauiata [al. ed.]

EURIALUS DISGUISED AS A PORTER.

MENELAUS AND BERTUS PICK UP THE CASKET.

APPENDIX. li

inquit amantes! nescio quod rerum querens Menelaus huc festinat: tegite furta vestra, dolisque virum fallite. Nihil est quod egredi putetis. Tum Lucresia: "latibulum paruum inquit sub strato est: illic preciose res sunt. Scis quid tibi scripserim, Si te mecum existente vir aduentaret: ingredere huc: tutus his tenebris eris: Neque te moueris, neque screatum [a] dederis." Anceps quod agat [a] secreatum Eurialus, mulieris imperium subit. Illa foris patefactis ad sericum redit. Tum Menelaus et vna Bertus assunt c[h]irographa nonnulla ad rempublicam pertinentia quesituri. Que postquam nullis inuenta sunt scriniis, "in latibulo nostro," inquit Menelaus, "forsitan erunt. I, Lucresia lumenque affer: hic intus querendum est." His exterritus Eurialus vocibus, exanguis fit, iamque Lucreciam odisse incipit; Atque intra se [dixit], "Heu me fatuum," inquit, "quis me huc venire compulit, nisi leuitas mea? Nunc deprehensus sum, nunc infamis fio: nunc cesaris gratiam perdo: quid gratiam! Vtinam mihi vita supersit! Quis me hinc viuum eripiet? Emori certum est! O me vanum et stultorum omnium stultissimum! In hanc sentinam volens cecidi! Quid hec amoris gaudia, si tanti emuntur? Breuis est illa voluptas, dolores longissimi: O si nos hoc pro regno celorum subiremus! Mira est hominum stultitia. Labores breues nolumus [b] pro [b] nolimus longissimis tolerare gaudiis: Amoris causa, cuius letitia fumo comparari potest, infinitis nos obiectamus angustiis! Ecce me ipsum, iam ego exemplum, iam fabula omnium ero: nec quis exitus pateat scio. Hinc si me deorum quispiam traxerit nusquam me rursus labor illaqueabit. O deus eripe me hinc! parce iuuentuti mee! Noli meas metiri ignorantias. Reserua me, vt horum delictorum penitentiam agam! Non me amauit Lucresia; sed quasi ceruum in casses voluit deprehendere. Ecce uenit dies meus! nemo me adiuuare potest, nisi tu deus meus. Audiueram ego sepe mulierum fallacias, nec declinare sciui. At si nunc euasero, nulla me vnquam mulieris tegna deludent." Sed nec Lucresia minoribus vrgebatur molestiis, que non solum sue sed amantis quoque saluti timebat. At, vt est in periculis subitaneis mulierum quam virorum promptius ingenium, excogita[t]o remedio, "Age," inquit, "vir: Cistella illic super fenestram est, ubi te memini monimenta nonnulla recondisse. Videamus an illic [c] [c] illi cirographa [d] sint reclusa:" Subitoque incurrens, tanquam vellet aperire cistellam, [d] chyrographa latenter illam deorsum impulit; Et quasi casu cecidisset, "proh mihi, vir!" ait, (1497). "adesto ne quod damni sentiamus. Cistella ex fenestra decidit: perge occius [e] [e] otius. ne iocules vel scripture dispereant. Ite, ite ambo! quid statis? Ego hinc, ne quis furtum faciat, oculis obseruabo." Vide audaciam mulieris! I nunc et feminis credito! Nemo tam oculatus est, vt falli non possit. Is duntaxat non fuit illusus, quem coniunx fallere non temptauit. Plus fortuna quam ingenio sumus felices. Motus hoc facto Menelaus Bertusque vna repente in uiculum se precipitant.

h 2

APPENDIX.

Domus etrusco more altior fuit, multique gradus descendendi erant. Hinc datum est Eurialo spacium mutandi locum, qui ex monitu[a] Lucresie in nouas latebras se recepit. Illi collectis iocalibus atque scripturis, quia cirographa[b] que quesierant non reperierunt, ad scrinia iuxta que latuerat Eurialus transeunt; ibique voti compotes facti, consalutata Lucresia recesserunt. Illa, abducto foribus pessulo; "Exi my Euriale, exi my anime," inquit, "veni gaudiorum summa meorum; veni fons delectationum mearum, scaturigo letitie [mee][c] fauum mellis; veni dulcedo incomparabilis mea! iam tuta sunt omnia; iam nostris sermonibus liber campus patet. Iam locus est amplexibus tutus. Aduersari osculis nostris fortuna voluit, sed aspiciunt dii nostrum amorem, nec tam fidos amantes deserere voluerunt. Veni iam meas in vlnas: nihil est quod amplius vereare, meum lilium rosarumque cumulus. Quid stas? quid times? tua hic sum Lucresia: quid cunctaris Lucresiam amplexari?" Eurialus vix tandem formidine posita sese recipit: complexusque mulierem, "nunquam me inquit tantus inuasit timor, sed digna tu es cuius causa talia tolerentur. Nec istec oscula et tam dulces amplexus obuenire cuipiam gratis possunt nec debent nec ego, vt verum fatear, satis emi tantum bonum. Si post mortem rursus viuere possem, teque perfrui, emori milies vellem, si hoc precio tui possent amplexus coemi. O mea felicitas! O mea beatitudo! Visum video an ita est? Teneo te an somniis illudor vanis? Tu certe hic es; ego te habeo." Erat Lucresia leui vestita palla, que membris absque ruga herebat, nec vel pectus vel clunes me[n]tiebatur. Vt erant artus sic se ostendabat. Gule candor niualis; oculorum lumen tanquam solis iubar; Intuitus letus; facies alacris; gene veluti lilia purpureis inmixta rosis; Risus in ore suauis atque modestus; pectus amplum; papille quasi duo punica poma ex vtroque latere tumescebant; pruritum quoque palpitantes mouebant. Non potuit Eurialus vltra stimulum cohibere, sed oblitus timoris, modestiam quoque ab se repulit; aggressusque feminam, "Iam," inquit, "fructum sumamus amoris." Rem verbis ingerebat. Obstabat[d] mulier: curamque sibi honestatis et fame esse dicebat, nec aliud eius amorem quam verba et oscula deposcere. Ad que, subridens Eurialus, "Aut scitum est inquit me huc venisse, aut nescitum: Si scitum, nemo enim est qui non cetera suspicetur; Stultum enim est infamiam sine re subire: Sin vero nescitum, et hoc quoque sciet nullus. Hoc pignus amoris est; moriar prius quam hoc caream." "Ach,[e] scelus est," inquit Lucresia. "Scelus est, refert Eurialus," bonis non vti cum possis. "An ego occasionem mihi concessam, tum quesitam cum optatam, mitterem?" Acceptaque mulieris veste, pugnantem feminam que vincere nolebat ab negotio vicit. Nec veneris hoc satietatem, vt Amoni cognita Thamar, peperit; sed maiorem sitim excitauit amoris. Memor tamen discriminis Eurialus, postquam vini cibique paulisper

Marginal notes:
[a] motu
[b] chyrographa
[c] om.
[d] obstat
[e] Ha

.

EURIALUS, ON HIS WAY FROM LUCRETIA'S HOUSE, OVERTAKES ACHATES AND NISUS.

hausit, repugnante Lucresia recessit. Nec sinistre quispiam suspicatus est quod unus ex baiulis putaretur.

Dmirabatur seipsum Eurialus dum viam pergeret secumque ait. O si nunc se obuium mihi daret cesar, meque agnosceret! quam illi habitus hic suspitionem faceret! quam me rideret! Fabula omnibus essem, et illi iocus: nunquam me missum faceret, donec sciret omnia. Dicendum sibi esset quid hec rustica vestis vellet; sed fingerem: non hanc sed aliam me dicerem adiisse matronam. Nam et ipse hanc amat: nec ex vsu est meum sibi amorem patere: Lucresiam nunquam perderem: que me suscepit seruauitque." Dum sic loquitur, Nisum, Achatem, Pliniumque cernit eosque preit; nec prius ab hiis cognitus est quam domi fuit, Vbi, positis saccis, pretextaque sumpta, rerum pandit euentum; Dumque quis timor quod gaudium intercessit memoriter narrat, nunc timenti similis, nunc exultanti fit. Inter timendum autem, " heu me stultum," inquit, "femine meum commisi caput! Non sic me pater ammonuit, dum me nullius femine fidem sequi debere docebat. Ille feminam esse dicebat animal indomitum, infidum, mutabile, crudele, mille passionibus deditum. Ego paterne immemor discipline, vitam meam muliercule credidi. Quid si me oneratum frumento aliquis agnouisset? ᵃ quod dedecus! ₐ cognouisset. quenam infamia mihi et meis posteris euenisset! Alienum me Cesar fecisset; tamquam leuem et insanum potuisset me contemnere. Quid autem si me vir dum scrinia versat latentem inuenisset. Seua est lex Iulia mechis. Exigit tamen dolor mariti maiores penas quam lex vlla concesserit. Necat hec ferro; necat ille cruentis verberibus; sed putemus virum pepercisse vite mee; num me in vinculis coniecisset, aut infamem cesari tradidisset? Dicamus et illius me manus effugere potuisse, quia inermis erat; quia mihi fidus ensis herebat lateri: At viro comitatus erat; et arma ex pariete pendebant captu facilia; in domo longus famulorum ordo. Clamores mox invaluissent, et ostia fuissent clausa: tum de me supplicium sumptum fuisset. Heu me dementem nulla me prudentia liberauit ab hoc discrimine sed casus tantum. Quid casus? Immo et promptum ingenium Lucresia: O fidam feminam! O amatricem sapientem! O insignem et nobilissimum amorem! Cur me tibi non credam? Cur tuam non sequar fidem? Mille mihi si non ᵇ assint ceruices omnes tibi committam: ᵇ om. tu fidelis es, tu cauta, tu prudens: scis amare, et amantem tueri. Quis tam cito excogitare potuisset viam, qua me querentes aueteret, vt tu ipsa cogitasti? Tu mihi hanc vitam seruasti; eandem tibi deuoueo. Non meum est sed tuum quod spiro. Non erit mihi durum perdere propter te quod per te teneo. Tu vite mee ius habes, tu necis imperium. O candidum pectus! O dulcem linguam!

APPENDIX.

O suaues oculos! O ingenium velox! O membra marmorea succique plena! quando ego vos reuisam? qua[n]do iterum corallina labia mordebo? quando tremulam linguam ori meo immurmurantem denuo sentiam? Papillas ne vnquam illas retractabo?" "Parum est," ait Achates, "quod in hac femina vidisti, quo propior femina, eo formosior est." "Non candali regis Lidia formosa vxor formosior fuit quam ista est. Non minor [a] illum voluisse nudam socio [b] demonstrari, vt plenius sumeret gaudium. Ego quoque itidem facerem si facultas esset; Lucresiam tibi nudam ostenderem. Aliter autem nec tibi effari quanta sit oius pulchritudo possem nec tu, quam solidum, quam plenum, fuerit meum gaudium, potes considerare. Sed congaude mecum, quia maior fuit mea voluptas quam uerbis exponi queat." Sic Eurialus cum Achate; nec pauciora secum Lucresia dicebat. Eius tamen tanto minor letitia fuit quo taciturnior. Aliis fidem non habuit vt rem posset referre. Sosie pre verecundia totum non audebat narrare.

[a] miror
[b] coningem socio.

Acorus interea Pannonius eques, domo nobilis, qui cesarem sequebatur, ardere Lucresiam cepit. Et quia formosus erat, redamari putabat, solamque femine pudiciciam obstare sibi rebatur. Illa sicut mos est nostris dominabus omnes uultu blando intuebatur. Ars est, siue deceptio potius, ne verus amor palam fiat. Insanit Pacorus, nec consolari potest, nisi Lucresie mentem persentiat: Solent matrone senenses ad primum lapidem sacellum diuine Marie, quod in bethleem nuncupatur, sepius visitare. Huc Lucresie, duabus comitata virginibus et anu quadam, proficiscebatur; Sequitur Pacorus violam in manu gestans deauratis foliis, in cuius collo epistolam amatoriam subtilibus inscriptam membranis asconderat. Nec mirere. Tradit onim Cicero yliadem omnem ita subtiliter scriptam sibi ostensam fuisse, ut testa nucis clauderetur. Offert violam Lucresie, seque commendat Pacorus. Respuit donum Lucresia: Instat Pacorus magnis precibus: Tum anus, "Recipe,"[c] inquit, "hera,[d] donatum florem. Quid times vbi nullum est periculum? parua res est qua potes hunc militem placare." Secuta est Lucresia anilem suasionem, violamque recepit. Parumper vltra progressa, violam alteri ex virginibus dedit. Nec diu post obuiam facti sunt duo studentes qui virgunculam vt sibi florem traderet non magno negocio induxerunt, apertoque viole stipite, carmen amatorium inuenerunt. Solebat hoc hominum genus pergratum esse matronis nostris. Sed postquam Cesaris curia Senas venit, irrideri, despici, et odio haberi cepit, quia plus armorum strepitus quam litterarum lepor nostras feminas oblectabat. Hinc graudis liuor et simultas ingens erat: querobant que toge vias omnes quibus possent nocere sagis. Vt ergo viole dolus patuit, ad Menelaum mox itur, epistolam que vt legat rogatur: Ille mestus domum pergit, vxorem increpat, [e] domum que clamoribus implet.

[c] respice.
[d] om.
[e] domum to vxor om.

PACORUS GIVES A LOVE-LETTER TO LUCRETIA, CONCEALED IN THE STALK OF A VIOLET.

PACORUS THROWS A SNOWBALL CONTAINING A LOVE-LETTER INTO LUCRETIA'S WINDOW.

APPENDIX. lv

Negat se ream vxor,^f remque gestam exponit, et anus adducit testimonium. Itur ad cesarem : fit querela : vocatur Pacorus : Is crimen fatetur, petensque veniam numquam se posthac Lucresiam vexaturum iureiurando confirmat. Sciens tamen iouem non irasci sed arridere periuriis amantum, sterilem flammam quo magis prohibitus erat eo diligentius sequebatur. Venit hiems, exclusis que ventis notis solam boream admittebat. Cadunt ex celo niues. Soluitur in ludum ciuitas : iactant matrone in vicos, iuuenes in fenestras, niuem. Hinc nactus est occasionem Pacorus ; epistolam alteram cera includit, ceramque niue tegit et cingit, factaque pila, in fenestram Lucresie iacit. Quis non omnia regi fortuna dicat ? quis non fauorabilem eius cupit flatum ? Fati enim plus valet hora benigni, quam si te veneris commendet epistola marti. Dicunt quidam nil esse quod in sapiente queat fortuna. Hoc ego hic sapientibus concedo : qui sola virtute gaudent, qui et pauperes et egroti, et in equo phallaris clausi, vitam se credunt possidere beatam, qualem adhuc nullum vel vidi vel fuisse putarim. Communis hominum vita fauoris fortunæ indiget ; hec quos nult eleuat, et quos nult deprimit. Quis Pacorum perdidit nisi fortuna ? Nonne prudentis consilii fuit in nodis viole clausisse tabellas, et nunc beneficio niuis epistolam transmisisse ? Dicet aliquis fieri cautius potuisse ? quod si hoc consilium iuuisset fortuna, et cautus hic et prudentissimus iudicatus fuisset. Sed obstans fatum pilam ex Lucresie manibus lapsam apud ignem duxit, ubi solutis calore niuibus, liquefactaque cera tabellas manifestauit, quas tum vetule que se calefaciebant, Tum Menelaus qui aderat, perlegerunt, nouasque lites excitauerunt, quas Pacorus non excusatione sed fuga vitauit. Hic rumor [ex vsu] venit Eurialo ; nam vir dum gressus et actus Pacori speculatur, insidiis Euriali locum facit. Verumque est quod dici solet, non facile custodiri quod a pluribus impugnatur. Expectabant amantes, post primum concubitum, secundas nuptias. Viculus inter edes Lucresie atque vicini perartus^a erat per quem pedibus utrumque parietem porrectis in ^a perarctus fenestram Lucresie haud difficilis prebebatur ascensus. Sed huc ascendere solum (1497). noctu licebat. Menelao petendum rus erat, ibique pernoctandum, qui dies ab amantibus tanquam saturnaliorum, expectabatur. Fit recessus ; mutatis Eurialus vestibus, in viculum se recipit. Stabulum illic Menelaus habebat, quod Eurialus, ducente Sosia, ingressus est. Ibi, nocte manens, sub feno latebat. Tum ecce Dromo qui erat Menelai secundus famulus, equis prepositus, impleturus presepia : fenum ex Euriali latere suscipit, eratque amplius suscepturus, ac Eurialum furca percussurus, nisi Sosias obuiasset. Qui vt discrimen agnouit, "da mihi hanc operam," inquit, "frater bone, ego pabulum equis prebebo.^b Tu ^b prebeo. interea loci vide an nobis cena instructa sit. Gaudendum est dum herus abest: Melius est nobis cum domina quam cum illo : hec iocunda est et

lvi   APPENDIX.

^a modio
^b sustinet
^c mucida
^d siluros [al. ed.]
^e porri (1497).

perliberalis, ille iracundus, clamorosus, auarus, difficilis: Nunquam nobis bene est dum ille adest. Vides vt ventres nostros iniquo castigat medio,^a qui semper esurit vt nos fame cruciet; nec sinit ^b muscida ^c frusta cerulei panis consumi, sed hesterna minuta seruat in mensem, vniusque cene silueos ^d et anguillas salsas in alteram differt; numerata fila sectilis pori ^e ne quid tangamus signata recludit. Miser qui per hec tormenta querit diuitias! Nam stultius nil quam viuere pauperem vt locuplex moriaris. Quanto melius nobis cum hera, que non contenta vitulis nos pascere et teneris hedis, gallinas quoque turdosque ministrat, et uini copiam melioris! I Dromo: cura ut quam vncta coquina sit." "Istud," inquit Dromo, "cure habebo, mensam potius quam equos fricabo. Herum ego hodie in rus deduxi, quod sibi male succedat. Nunquam mihi verbum dixit nisi vesperi cum me remisit et equos, renuntiarique domine iussit, non se rediturum hac nocte. Ah, laudo te Sosia, qui tandem odire cepisti domini mores. Ego iam mutassem dominum nisi me domina matutinis retenuisset offellis. Nihil dormiendum est hac nocte. Bibamus, voremus, donec veniat dies. Non tantum per mensem lucrabitur herus, quantum nos vna cena consumemus." Audiebat hec Eurialus libens, tametsi mores seruorum notabat, et idem sibi fieri non dubitaret. Et cum Dromo abisset,^f assurgens Eurialus, "O quam," inquit, "beatam noctem, Sosia, tuo beneficio sum habiturus, qui me huc duxti, et ne patefierem probe curasti. Vir bonus es, meritoque te amo, nec tibi non gratus inueniar." Aderat hora prescripta. Letus Eurialus, quamuis duobus perfunctus discriminibus, murum ascendit, ad apertam fenestram subintrat: Lucretiam iuxta foculum sedentem, paratisque obsequiis, expectantem reperit. Illa vt amantem cognouit, assurgens medium complexa est. Fiunt blanditie: dantur oscula: itur in venerem teusis volis, fessam que nauigio citheream nunc ceres reficit nunc bacchus.

^f Et cum domo abiissot Menelaus, utque dromo recessit (1490).

Eu quam breues voluptates sunt, quam longe solicitudines! Vix horam Eurialus letam habuerat. Tum ecce Sosiam qui reditum Menelai nunciat gaudiumque perturbat. Timens Eurialus fugere studet: Lucresia, mensis absconditis, obuiam viro pergit, reuersumque salutat. Et, "o my vir," inquit, "quam bene redisti. Nam ego iam te villicum inviscatum rebar. Quid tu ^g tamen rure tam diu. Caue ne quid olfaciam cur non domi manes. Quid me tua contristare absentia studes. Semper dum abes timeo tibi. Tu ne quam ardeas formido, vt sunt infidi vxoribus suis viri. Quo metu si me vis soluere, nunquam foris dormias. Nec enim sine te nox est mihi vlla iocunda. Sed cena hic iam; post cubitum ibimus." Erant tamen in aula vbi prandere

^g tu cum

EURIALUS CLIMBS IN AT LUCRETIA'S WINDOW.

No. 17. *To face page* lvii.

EURIALUS AND LUCRETIA AT SUPPER.

familia solet; ibique virum detinere Lucresia nitebatur, Donec Eurialus abeundi spacium suscepisset, cui necessaria est morula quendam: Menelaus autem foris cenatus erat, seque in thalamum recipere festinabat. Tum Lucresia: " Parum me amas " inquit, " Cur non potius domi apud me cenasti? Ego quia tu aberas nec commedi hodie nec bibi quicquam. Venerunt tamen villici ex rosalia nescio quid vini portantes: optimum esse ferebant trebeanum. Ego pre mestitia nihil gustaui : Nunc, quando ades, eamus si placet in cellarium introrsum, gustemusque vinum, si vt illi dixerunt tam suauissimum sit." Hisque dictis, lanternam [a] [a] laternam dextra,[b] virum sinistra manu recepit, et in infimum penarii descendit: tanquam [o] dextera diu nunc hunc nunc illum cadum terebrauit, ac cum viro petis[s]auit, donec Eurialum putauit abiisse. Ac ita demum ad ingratos hymeneos cum viro transiuit· Eurialus intempesta nocte domum repetiit. Sequenti luce, siue quod sic expediebat cauere, siue suspitio mala fuit, muro fenestram Menelaus obstruxit. Credo, ut sunt conciues nostri in coniecturas acuti, suspicionumque pleni, timuisse Menelaum loci commoditatem, vtque parum videbat, vxori occasionem demere voluisse. Nam et si nihil conscius erat illi, vexatam tamen feminam, multis dietim tentatam precibus uon ignorabat; et animum cognoscebat mulieris instabilem, cuius tot sunt voluntates quot in arboribus folia. Sexus enim femineus nouitatis est auidus, raroque virum amat cuius copiam habet. Sequebatur ergo viam maritorum pervulgatam, quorum opinio est infortunium bonis excludi fortunis.[c] [c] custodiis. Erepta est huic conueniendi facultas, nec mittendis litteris premissa libertas est. Nam et cauponem qui post edes Lucresie viuariam tabernam conduxerat, ex qua solebat Eurialus affari Lucresiam, ac litteras per harundinem mittere, sicut Menelaus suasit, ingratus [d] expulit. Restabat solus oculorum intuitus, nutuque [e] magistratus tantum se consalutabant amantes. Neque istac amoris extrema linea commode perfrui poterant: erat ingens dolor vtrique, cruciatusque morti similis. Quia nec amoris poterant obliuisci, nec in eo perseuerare. Dum sic[e] anxius Eurialus quid [f] si consilii capiat meditatur, venit in mentem Lucresie monitum, quod sibi de Pandalo scripserat Menelai sobrino; peritosque medicos imitatus quibus mos est in periculosis egritudinibus anceps adhibere medicamentum, et ultima potius experiri, quam morbum sine cura relinquere. Aggredi Pandalum statuit, remediumque suscipere quod antea refutarat. Huic ergo accersito, et in penitiorem domus partem vocato: " Sede," inquit, " amice: rem grandem tibi dicturus sum, indigentem his quas in te scio sitas, diligentia, fide, et taciturmitate. Volui hec dudum tibi dixisse, sed non eras mihi adhuc plene cognitus ; nunc et te nosco, et quia probate fidei es, amo et obsecro : Quod si aliud a[f] te [f] de [non] scirem, satis est quia omnes tui conciues te laudant, tum comites mei quibuscum amicitiam conflauisti, et qui sis, et quanti pendendus, me certum fecere : ex

i

lviii APPENDIX.

^a cupere [al. ed.]

^b inescant [Leyden ed.]

^c sis [Leyd. ed.]

^d satis.

^e om.

quibus te capere ^a meam beniuolentiam didici, cuius iam facio participem : Quia non minus illa es dignus, quam ego sum tua. Nunc quid velim, quoniam inter amicos res agitur, paucis exponam [verbis]. Tu scis mortale genus quam in amorem sit pronum; seu virtutis sit, seu vicii, late patet ista calamitas; nec cor est, si modo carneum est, quod amoris non aliquando sentiat stimulos. Scis quia nec sapientissimum Salamonem, nec Sampsonem fortissimum ista passio dimisit immunem. Incensi preteria pectoris et amoris improbi ea natura est, vt si prohibeatur magis ardeat. Nulla re magis ista curatur pestis, quam dilecti copia. Fuerunt plures cum viri tum mulieres, tam nostra quam maiorum nostrorum memoria, quibus inhibitio durissime necis fuit occasio. Contra vero plerosque nouimus, que post concubitum et amplexus passim concessos, mox furere desinerunt. Nihil consultius est, postquam amor ossibus hesit, quam furori cedere: Nam qui aduersus tempestatem nititur sepe naufragium facit. Et qui obtemperat procelle, superat. Hec ideo dixi, quia te scire meum amorem volo, et quod mei causa sis facturus. Tum quod emolimentum hinc sit oriturum nihil tibi tacebo, quia iam mei cordis alteram te reputo partem. Ego Lucresia[m] diligo : neque hoc, my Pandale, mea culpa est factum. Sed regente fortuna in cuius manu est totus quem colimus orbis. Mihi non erant noti mores vestri, nec huius vrbis consuetudines noram. Putabam ego feminas vestrates quod oculis monstrant in corde sentire [sed me stant ^b homines, vestro maritate non amant]. Hinc deceptus sum. Credidi namque amatum me Lucresie fore, dum me luminibus intuebatur placidis, cessique contra diligere; nec tam elegantem dominam dignam putaui cui vices non redderentur amoris. Nondum te noui vel tuum genus : amaui putans amari. Quis enim tam saxeus est aut ferreus qui non amet amatus? Sed postquam fraudes noui, meque [dolis] irritum, ne meus sterilis esset amor nisus sum omnibus artibus illam incendere, vt par pari referretur. Ardere namque, nihilque vrere, tum rubor erat, tum anxietas animi, que me die noctuque mirum in modum cruciabat, et eram adeo introrsum vt egredi nullo pactu valerem. Factum est igitur vt, me continuante, par sit amor amborum. Illa incensa est, ego ardeo, ambo perimus nec remedium protelande vite videmus vllum, nisi tu scis ^c adiumento: Vir custodit et frater; non tam vellus aureum peruigil draco seruabat, nec aditum orci Cerberus, quam ista diligenter recluditur. Noui ego familiam vestram; scio quia nobiles estis inter primores vrbis, diuites, amati, vtinam nunquam nouissem hanc feminam, sed quis est qui possit resistere fatis?^d Non elegi hanc, sed casus dedit amandam. Sic se res habet: tectus adhuc amor est. Sed nisi bene regatur, magnum adhuc ^e quod superi auertant, malum pariet: Possem ego me fortassis compescere, si hinc abirem, quod quamquam esset mihi grauissimum, facerem tamen vestre familie gratia, si hoc putarem ex vsu fore. Sed nosco illius furorem : aut

No. 18. *To face page* lviii.

EURIALUS CONFERS WITH PANDALUS.

APPENDIX. lix

me sequeretur, aut manere coacta manus sibi consciret,^a quod esset domui vestre   ^a conscisceret
dedecus perpetuum, quod igitur te volebam te [que]^b vocabam, vestri causa est ; ^b [al. ed.] al. ed.
vt obuiemus hiis malis: Nec alia via: nisi vt amoris nostri aurigam te prebeas,
curesque vt bene dissimulatus ignis fiat opertus. Ego me tibi comendo,
deuoueo: obsequere nostro furori, ne dum oppugnatur magis incendatur: cura
vt simul conuenire possimus, quo facto magis humiliabitur ardor, tolerabili-
orque reddetur. Tute scis aditus domus; scis quando vir abest; scis quomodo
me valeas introducere. Frater viri aduertendus est qui est ad has res nimium
prospicax; Lucresiam quoque, tanquam locum germani tenet, magnaque cura
custodit: Inuersaque Lucresie verba, euersas ceruices, gemitus, screatus, tussim,
risus, attente considerat. Hunc eludere sententia est, nec sine te fieri potest.
Assis ergo, et quando abfuturus sit vir, me instrue, remanentemque fratrem
diuerte ne custos affixus Lucresie sit, neue custodes adhibeat alios. Tibi credet;
et quod dii faxint, hanc tibi prouintiam fortasse committet. Quam si
susceperis et me iuueris, vt spero, in uado res est. Poteris enim me clam, dum
ceteri dormient, intromittere, et amorem lenire furentem. Ex hiis quot emer-
gant vtilitates, arbitror te pro tua prudentia palam cernere: Seruabis namque in
primus honorem domus; amorem teges qui non posset abs vestra^c infamia mani-   ^c tua
festari. Sobrinam tuam in vita tenebis; Menelao uxorem custodies, cui non tam
obest vna nox mihi concessa nesciis omnibus, quam si sciente populo illam perdi-
derit me sequentem. [Nupta] Senatori romano secuta est Ippia ludum^d ad pharon   ^d Lybdum [al. ed.]
[et nilum] formosaque menia lagi. Quid si me domi nobilem atque potentem
[lucresia] sequi statuat. Quod dedecus vestri generis: qui^e populi risus: que   ^e quis
nedum vestra sed totius vrbis infamia. Diceret forsan aliquis, absumenda potius
ferro aut extinguenda uenenis est mulier, quam id agat. Sed ve illi que^f se   ^f qui
humano sanguine polluit, et maiori scelere vindicat minus. Non augenda sunt
mala: sed minuenda. Nos hoc scimus ex duobus bonis melius eligendum: aut
ex malo et bono quod sit bonum: sed ex malis duobus quod miuus obsit. Omnis
via periculi plena est; sed hec quam monstro, minus habet discriminis; per
quam nedum sanguini tuo consules, sed mihi quoque proderis, qui pene insanio
dum mei causa video Lucreciam cruciari. Cui potius odio esse vellem, quam te
rogare: Sed hic sumus; eo deducta res est. Et nisi tuis artibus, tura cura,
ingenio atque solicitudine nauis regatur, nulla salutis spes maneat. Iuua igitur
et illam et me, tuamque domum abs nota conserua: nec me putes ingratum:
Scis apud Cesarem quanti sim: quicquid petierim impetratum tibi efficiam. Et
hoc ante omnia tibi polliceor, doque fidem, Palatinum te Comitem futurum,
omnemque tuam posteritatem hoc titulo gauisuram. Ego tibi Lucresiam meque
et nostrum amorem, et famam nostram, et tui generis decus committo, tueque

mando fidei: Tu arbiter es; omnia hec in te sita sunt: Vide quid agas, vt seruare potes ita et perdere."

"Vbrisit hiis auditis Pandal*us*, facta q*ue* morula, "noram hec Euriale," dixit, "et utinam non accidissent: sed eu*m* i*n* locum, sicut abs te dictum est, res rediit, vt necesse sit me q*uod* iubes efficere, nisi et nostrum gen*us* affici contumeliis, et scandalum ingens cuipiam exoriri. Ardet mulier, sicut dixti, et impotens sui est: nisi occurro, ferro se fodiet, aut ex fenestris se dabit pr*e*cipite*m*; nec vite iam sibi nec honoris est cura: Ipsa mihi suum ardorem patefecit: Restiti, increpaui, lenire flammam studii; nihil profeci: Omnia pr*e*ter te parui facit: Nihil nisi te curat: Tu illi semper in mente sedes; te petit, te desiderat, te solum cogitat. Sepe me vocitans, 'audi, precor Euriale,' dixit. Sic mulier ex amore mutata est vt non eadem videa*tur*. Heu pietas! heu dolor! Nulla [prius] in vrbe tota vel castior vel prudentior Lucresia fuit. Mira res si tantum iuris natura dedit amori in mentes humanas: Medendum est huic egri[t]udini; Nec alia cura est, nisi quam tu monstrasti. Accingam me huic operi, teq*ue* du*m* temp*us* erit commonere faciam. Nec ex te gratiam quero, q*uia* non est officium boni viri, cum hiis nihil promerea*tur*, gratiam poscere. Ego vt vitem infamiam nostre imminentem familie hoc ago. Quod si tibi conducit, non propterea sum premiandus." At enim Eurial*us* inquit, "Ego vel sic tibi gratiam habeo; et creari te comitem vt dictu*m* est faciam. Tu modo dignitatem istam nihil spernas." "No*n* sperno," inquit Pandal*us*, "sed ne hinc profecta sit volo: Si ventura est, libere veniat: nihil ego co*n*ditionale facio: Si potuisset hoc te nesciente fieri, mea vt opera apud Lucresiam esses, libentius id egissem: Vale." "Et tu vale," retulit Eurial*us*; "Post q*uam* animum redidisti, fac, finge, inueni, effice vt simul simus." "Laudalis,"ᵃ inquit Pandal*us*, "Letusq*ue* abiit q*uod* tanti viri gratiam inuenisset, tum q*uod*ᵇ se comitem fore iam sperabat; cui*us* dignitatis tanto erat auidior, quanto se minus cupere demonstrabat. Sunt enim homines quidam, vt mulieres, que cum se maxime nolle dicunt, tunc maxime volunt. Hic lenocinii mercedem sortit*us* est; Comitatum et auream bullam sue nobilitatis posteritas demonstrabit. In nobilitate multi sunt gradus mi Mariane. Et sane si cuiuslib*et* origin*em* queras, sicut mea sententia fert, aut nullas nobilitates inuenies, aut admodum paucas, que sceleratum no*n* habuerint ortum. Cum enim hos dici nobiles videam*us* qui divitiis abunda*n*t, Divitie vero raro virtutis sunt comites, quis no*n* videt ortum nobilitatis esse degenerem? Hunc vsure ditauerunt, illum spolia, proditiones alium; Hic veneficiis ditatus est, ille adulationib*us*; Huic adulteria locumᶜ prebent, non nullis mendacia pros*unt*; Quida*m* faciunt ex [coniuge questum, quidam ex] natis; Plerosq*ue*

ᵃ laudabilis
ᵇ qu*ia*
ᶜ lucrum

EURIALUS FORCES HIMSELF INTO LUCRETIA'S HOUSE AT THE HALF-OPENED DOOR.

APPENDIX.　　　　　　　　　lxi

homicidia iuuant; Rarus est qui iuste diuitias congreget; Nemo falcem ᵃ amplam   ᵃ fascem
facit nisi qui omnes metit herbas; congregant homines diuitias multas, nec vnde
veniant, sed quam multe veniant querunt. Omnibus hic versus placet; "unde
habeas querit nemo, sed oportet habere." Postquam vero plena est archa, tum ᵇ   ᵇ tunc
nobilitas poscitur, que sic quesita nil est aliud quam premium iniquitatis.
Maiores mei nobiles habiti sunt; sed nolo ᶜ mihi blandiri: non puto meliores ᶜ noli
fu[i]sse proauos meos aliis quos sola excusat antiquitas, quia non sunt in
memoria eorum vitia. Mea sententia nemo nobilis esse,ᵈ nisi virtutis amator. ᵈ est
Non miror aureas vestes, equos, canes, ordinem famulorum, lautas mensas,
marmoreas edes, villas, predia, piscinas, iurisdictiones, siluas; Nam et hec
omnia stultus assequi [potest], quem si quis nobilem dixerit, ipse fiet stultus.
Pandalus noster lenocinio nobilitatus est.

" On multis post diebus rure inter Menelai rusticos rixatum est, et occisi
non nulli qui plus [equo] biberant; opusque fuit ad res componendas
Menelaum proficisci. Tum Lucresia "mi vir," inquit, "grauis es,
homo debilisque; equi tui grauiter incedunt; quin gradiarium aliquem
recipe commodatum." Cumque ille perconctaretur ᵉ vbinam esset aliquis; "opti- ᵉ percuncta-
mum," inquit Pandalus, "nisi fallor, Eurialus habet, et tibi libens concedit. Si   retur
me vis petere." "Pete," inquit Menelaus. Rogatus Eurialus mox equum iussit
adduci; idque sui gaudii signum recepit, secumque tacite dixit," Tu meum
equum ascendes, Menelae: Ego tuam vxorem equitabo." Conuentum erat vt
noctis ad horam quintam in vico Eurialus esset, speraretque bene si cantantem
Pandalum [audiret]. Abierat Menelaus, iamque celum noctis obduxerant
tenebre: mulier in cubili tempus manebat. Eurialus ante fores erat, signumque
morabatur: Nec cantum audiebat, nec screatum. Iam preterierat hora et vt
abiret Eurialus suadebat Achates, delusumque dicebat. Durum erat amanti
recedere, et nunc vnam nunc aliam causam manendi querebat. Non canebat
Pandalus quia Menelai frater domi manserat, et omnes aditus scrutabatur, ne quid
insidiarum fieret, noctemque trahebat insomnem; cui Pandalus; "Nunquamne
hac nocte cubitum ibimus? Iam nox medium poli transcendit axem, et me
grauis occupat sompnus. Miror te cum iuuenis scis,ᶠ senis habere naturam, ᶠ sis [Leyd.
quibus siccitas somnum aufert: nunquam dormiunt nisi paululum prope diem,   ed.]
dum currus voluitur septentrionalis, cum iam tempus esset surgendi. Eamus
tamen iam tandem dormitum. Quid si ᵍ hec volunt vigilie?" "Eamus," inquit ᵍ sibi
Agamennon, "si tibi sic videtur; antea tamen inspiciende sunt fores au satis
firmate sunt ne furibus pateant." Veniensque ad ostium nunc vnam nunc
aliam [seram] ammouit, et pessulum addidit. Erat illic ingens ferrum quod

APPENDIX.

vix duo poterant eleuare, quo nunquam ostium claudebatur: Quod postquam Agamennon admonere non potuit, "iuua me," inquit, "Pandale; admoueamus ferrum hoc ostio, tum dormitum ibimus." Audiebat hos sermones Eurialus, et, "actum est" tacitus ait, "si hoc ferramentum adiungitur." Tum Pandalus : " Quid tu paras Agamemnon? tanquam domus obsidenda sit, firmare ostium paras? An tuta sumus in ciuitate? Libertas hic est et quies omnibus eadem, cum hostes procul sunt quibus-cum bella gerimus Florentini. Si fures times, sat clausum est: Si hostes, nihil est quod in hac domo te possit tueri. Ego hac nocte non subibo onus, quia scapulas doleo, et infra sum fractus, nec gestandis oneribus sum ydoneus; aut tute leua, aut sine." "Vach,[a] satis est," inquit Agamennon, dormitumque cessit. Tum Eurialus, "manebo hic adhuc horam," ait, " si forte aliquis adaperiat." Tedebat Achatem more, tacitusque maledicebat Eurialo, qui se tam diu retineret insonnem. Nec diu mansum est, cum per rimulam visa est Lucresia, parum quid luminis secum ferens; versus quam pergens Eurialus. "Salue mi anime, Lucresia" dixit : At illa exterrita fugere primum voluit: Ex inde recogitans, "quis tu es vir?" ait: "Eurialus tuus" inquit Eurialus. " Aperi, mea voluptas; iam mediam noctem te hic opperior." Agnouit Lucresia vocem; sed quia simulationem timebat, non prius ausa est aperire, quam secreta inter se tantum nota percepit. Post hec magno labore seras remouit. Sed quia plurima ferramenta fores retinebant, que manus feminea ferre non poterat, ad semipedis dumtaxat amplitudinem ostium patuit. "Nec hoc," ait Eurialus, " obstabit," extenuansque suum corpus, per dextrum latus intro se coniecit, Mulierem que mediam amplexatus est. Achates foris in excubiis mansit. Tum Lucresia, siue timore nimio, siue gaudio, exanimata, inter Euriali deficiens brachia, pallida facta est, et amisso verbo ac oculis clausis, per omnia similis mortue videbatur, nisi quod adhuc calor pulsusque manebant. Exterritus Eurialus subito causu,[b] quid ageret nesciebat ; [Secumque] "si abeo" inquit, "mortis sum reus, qui feminam in tanto discrimine deseruerim. Sim[c] maneo, interueniat Agamennon aut alius ex familia, et ego perierim. Heu amor infelix, qui plus fellis quam mellis habes! Non tam absinthium est amarum quam tu! Quot me iam discrim[in]ibus obiecisti! quot mortibus meum caput denouisti ! Hoc nunc restabat vt ineis brachiis feminam exanimares. Cur me non potius interemicti?[d] Cur me leonibus non obiecisti? Heu quam optabilius erat in huius me potius gremio quam istum meo sinu deficisse! Vicit amor virum; abiectaque propria cura salutis, cum femina mansit ; eleuansque altius mutum corpus atque deosculatus, madidus lacrimis, "Heu Lucresia," inquit. "Vbinam gentium es? Vbi aures tue? cur non respondes? cur non audis? Aperi oculos, obsecro mi[e] meque respice : Arride mihi vt soles : Tuus hic assum

[a] vah

[b] casu [Leyd. ed.]
[c] si

[d] interemisti

[e] mi nm [Leyd. ed.]

APPENDIX. lxiii

Eurialus; tuus te amplectitur Eurialus: Cur me [non] contrabasias? Mi cor, abisti[a] an dormis? Vbi te queram? Cur, si mori uolebas, non me monuisti ut occidissem una? Nisi me audis, en iam latus meum aperiet gladius, et ambos habebit exitus unus. Ach[b] uita mea: suauium meum! delicie mee! spes unica! integra quies! siccine te Lucretia perdo? Attolite oculos! eleua caput! nondum mortua es! Video, adhuc cales; adhuc spiras: Cur mihi non loqueris? Sic me recipis? ad hec me gaudia vocas? Hanc mihi das noctem? Assurge, oro, requies mea! respice tuum Eurialum! Assum tuus Eurialus!" Ac si[c] fatus lacrimarum flumen super frontem et mulieris tipona[d] pluit. Quibus tanquam roseis aquis excitata mulier quasi de graui somno surrexit, amantemque videns, "heu me," inquit, "Euriale! Vbinam fui? Cur me non potius obire sinisti? Beata iam moriebar in tuis manibus: Vtinam sic excederem antequam tu hac vrbe discederes."

[a] obisti
[b] Ha
[c] sic [Leyd. ed.]
[d] tempora

"Vm sic inuicem fantur, in thalamum pergunt. Ubi talem noctem habuerunt qualem credimus inter duos amantes fuisse, postquam nauibus altis raptam Helenam Paris abduxit: Tamque dulcis nox ista fuit, vt ambo negarent tam bene inter Martem veneremque fuisse. "Tu meus es Ganimedes, tu meus Hipolitus, Diamedesque[e] meus," dicebat Lucresia. "Tu mihi Polixena," Eurialus referebat; "tu Emilia, tu Venus ipsa." Et nunc os, nunc genas, nunc oculos commendabat. Eleuataque non nunquam lodice, secreta que non viderat antehanc[f] contemplabatur; et, "plus," dicebat, "inuenio quam putaram! Talem lauantem vidit Atheon[g] in fonte Dianam! Quid his membris formosius? Quid candidius? Iam redemi pericula. Quid est quod propter te non debeat sustineri? O pectus decorum! O mamille prenitide! Vos ne tango? vos ne habeo? vos ne meas incidistis manus? O teretes artus! O redolens corpus! te ne ego possideo? Nunc mori satius est quando hoc gaudium est recens, ne qua interueniat calamitas: Anime mi teneo te, an somnio? Vera ne ista voluptas est? an extra mentem positus sic reor? Non somnio, certe vera res agitur. O suauia basia! o dulces amplexus! o melliflui morsus! Nemo me felicius viuit, nemo beatius! Sed heu quam veloces hore! Inuida nox, cur fugis? Mane,[h] apollo, mane apud inferos diu! Cur equos tam cito in iugum trahis? plus[i] graminis edant. Da mihi noctem vt Alcmene dedisti. Cur tu tam repente Titoni tui cubile relinquis aurora? Si tam illi grata esses, quam mihi Lucresia, haud tam mane surgere te permitteret. Nunquam mihi nox visa est hac breuior, quamuis apud britannos dachosque fuerim." Sic Eurialus: nec minora dicebat Lucresia. Nec osculum nec verbum irrecompensatum preteriit. Stringebat hic stringebat illa, nec post venerem lapsi[k] iacebant. Sed vt Antheus[k] lassi

[e] Adonisque
[f] antehac
[g] Actæon [al. ed.]
[h] magne
[i] sine vt plus
[k] lassi

lxiv   APPENDIX.

ex terra validior resurgebat, sic post bellum alacriores isti robustioresque fiebant.
Nocte peracta, cum crines suos ex oceano tolleret aurora, discessum est: Nec
post multos dies rediendi copia fuit crescentibus dietim custodiis; sed omnia
^a repetit superauit amor viamque tandem conueniendi reperit,^a qua se usi amantes sunt.
Interea Cesar qui iam Eugenio reconciliatus erat Romam petere destinauit.
Sentit hoc Lucresia; quid enim non sentit amor, aut quis fallere possit amantem?
Sic igitur Lucresia scripsit Eurialo.

^b miror

"I posset animus meus irasci, tibi iam succensserem, quod abiturum te dissimulasti. Sed amat te quam me magis spiritus meus, nullaque potest ex causa aduersus te moueri. Heu mi cor,^b quid est quod mihi Cesarem non dixti recessurum? Ille itineri separat, nec tu hic manebis, scio; quid, obsecro, de me fiet? Quid agam misera: Vbi requiescam, si me relinquis? non viuo biduum. Per, ergo, has litteras meis lacrimis madidas, per que tuam dexteram, et datam fidem, si de te quicquam
^c meum merui aut fuit tibi quicquam dulce mecum,^c miserere infelicis amantis! non peto
^d me tecum. vt maneas, sed vt tollas te mecum.^d Fingam me vesperi bethleem petere velle, vnicamque recipiam anum: Assunt illuc duo tresve famuli ex tuis; me rapiant. Nihil negocii est volentem eripere. Nec tibi dedecori puta: nam filius Priami coniugem sibi raptu parauit. Non iniuriaberis viro meo; is enim omnino me perditurus est. Namque nisi abducas, mors illi me aufert. Sed nolis tu ess crudelis, meque morituram relinquere, que te pluris semper quam me feci." Ad hec Eurialus in hunc modum rescripsit.

"Elaui te vsque nunc, mea Lucresia, ne te nimium afflictares antequam tempus esset. Scio mores tuos: noui quia te nimis crucias. Nec Cesar sic recedit, vt non sit reuersurus. Ex vrbe postquam reuenerimus Hac iter est nobis in patriam: quod si Cesar aliam viam fecerit, me certe si vixero reducem videbis: negent mihi patriam superi, errabundoque similem me reddant vlixi, nisi huc reuertar! Respira ergo mi anime, sumeque vires; noli te macerare, quin viue potius leta. Quod dicis de raptu esset mihi tum gratissimum tum iocundissimum; Nec maior mihi voluptas prestari posset quam te semper mecum habere, ac meo ex arbitrio potiri: sed consulendum est magis honori tuo quam mee cupiditati. Exigit namque fides tua qua me complexa es, tibi vt consilium fidele prebeam, et quod in rem sit tuam. Tu te scis prenobilem esse et in clara familia nuptam. Nomen habes cum pulchritudine [tum pudicissime] mulieris, nec apud ytalos solum tua fama clauditur, sed et teutones panonii et bohemi et omnis septemtrionis populi tuum

nomen cognoscunt: q*uod* si te rapiam, (mitto dedec*us* meum q*uod* tui causa
flocci facerem,) qua ignominia tuos afficeres necessarios! Quibus doloribus matrem
pungeres! Quid de te dicerent! Quis rumor exiret in orbem! Ecce Lucre-
siam que Brute [a] coniuge castior, Penelopeq*ue* melior dicebat*ur*, iam mecum se- [a] bruti
quit*ur* im[m]emor parentum et patrie! Non Lucresia sed Ippia *est*: vel Jasonem
secuta Medea? Heu me quantus meror [haberet] cum de te talia dici sentirem!
Amor noster clam est, nemo te non laudat: Rapina turbaret omnia, nec unq*uam*
tam laudata fuisti, q*uam* tunc vituperareris. S*ed* mittamus famam; quid q*uod* nos
amore nostro perfrui non valerem*us*? Ego Cesari seruo. Is me viru*m* fecit
potentem diuitem. Nec ab eo recedere possum sine mei status ruina; q*uod* si
eum desererem, non quirem te decenter habere. Si curiam sequeretur nulla
quies esset: Omni die castra mouemus: nusquam Cesari tanta mora fuit
qu*an*ta nunc Senis. Idq*ue* belli necessitas facit q*uod* si te circumducerem, et
quasi publicam feminam in castris haberem, vide q*uam* esset mihi et tibi de-
decorum? Hiis ex rebus obsecro te mi Lucresia mentem vt istam exuas,
honoriq*ue* consulas. Nec furori magis quam tibi blandiaris. Alius fortassis
amator aliter suaderet, et vltro te fugere precaretur, vt te, quam diu poss*et*,
abuteretur; Nihil futuri prouidus dum presenti satisfaceret egritudini. Sed hic
non esset amator verus, qui libidini magis q*uam* fame consuleret. Ego, mea
Lucresia, q*uod* frugi est moneo. Mane hic te rogo, nec me dubita reditur*um*,
quicquid apud etruscos agendum Cesari, mihi committi curabo, daboq*ue* oper*am*
vt te frui abs tuo incommodo possim. Vale: viue: ama: nec meum q*uam* tu*us*
est ignem putato minorem. Aut me non immitissimum [b] hinc abscedere. Iterum [b] inuitissi-
vale mea suauitas, et anime cibus mee." mum

Cquievit his mulier et imperata facturam rescripsit. Paucis post
diebus Eurialus cum Cesare Romam perrexit: Nec diu moratus illic
febribus est incensus. Infelix penitus, qui cum arderet amore,
febriumq*ue* cepit ignibus estuare: cum [c] iam vires amor extenuasset, [c] cumq*ue*
adiectis morbi doloribus parum superat vite. Tenebaturque spirit*us* medicor*um*
remediis, poti*us* q*uam* manebat. Cesar dietim ad eum veniebat, et quasi filium
solabat*ur*, omnesque curas apollinis adhibere iubebat. Nulla *est* [d] valentior medela
quam Lucresie scriptum, quo viuentem illam et sospitem cognouit; que res ali- [d] Sed nulla
quantisp*er* morbum imminuit, Eurialumque surgere in pedes fecit: et coronationi fuit
Cesaris interfuit, ac ibi militiam suscepit et aureum calcar. Post hac, cum Cesar
Perusium peter*et*, is Rome mansit nondum ex integro san*us*. Exinde Senas
venit, quamuis adhuc debilis exterminatusque faciem. Sed intueri potuit, non
alloqui, Lucresiam. Epistole plures vtrinq*ue* misse sunt, Rursusq*ue* de fuga

tractatum est. Triduo illic mansit Eurialus: demum cum sibi aditus omnes videret ereptos, recessum eius amanti renuntiauit. Nunquam tanta dulcedo in conuersando fuit quanta in recedendo mestitia. Erat in fenestra Lucresia; per vicum iam Eurialus equitabat: humedos [a] oculos alter in alterum iecerat. Flebat vnus, flebat alter: ambo doloribus vrgebantur, vt quiuis [b] ex sedibus cor euelli dolenter [c] sentiebant. Si quis in obitu quantus sit dolor ignorat; duorum amantum separationem consideret; quamuis maior hic anxietas: in est et cruciatus ingentior: dolet animus in morte, quia corpus relinquit amatum: Corpus, absente spiritu, nec dolet nec sentit: Ac cum duo ad [d] inuicem conglutinati [per amorem] sunt auimi, tanto penosior est separatio quanto sensibilior est vterque dilectus. Et hic sane non erant spiritus duo: sed quemadmodum [inter amicos] Aristophanes putat Aristophones [e] vnius anime duo corpora facta erant. Itaque non recedebat animus ab animo, sed vnicus amor scindebatur in duos; cum cor in partes diuidebatur, mentis pars ibat et pars remanebat, et omnes iuuicem sensus disgregabantur, et a se ipsis discedere flebant. Non mansit in amantium faciebus sanguinis gutta; nisi lacrime fuissent et gemitus, simillimi mortuis videbantur. Quis scribere, quis referre, quis cogitare posset illarum mentium molestias, nisi qui aliquando insaniuit. Laudomia, recedente Protheselao, et ad sacras ylii pugnas eunte, exanguis cecidit. Eadem, post quam viri mortem agnouit, viuere amplius minime potuit. Dido phenissa post fatalem Enee recessum, seipsam interemit. Nec Prochia [f] post Bruti necem voluit superesse. Hec nostra, postquam Eurialus ex visu recessit, in terram colapsa, per familias recepta est, cubilique data donec resumeret spiritum. Vt vero ad se rediit, vestes aureas purpureasque et omnem letitie ornatum reclusit, pullisque tunicis vsa, nunquam post hac cantare audita est, nunquam visa ridere, nullis facetiis, nullo gaudio, nullisque vnquam iocis in letitiam potuit reuocari. Quo in statu dum aliquamdiu perseueret, [in]egritudinem incidit; Et quia cor suum aberat, nullaque menti consolatio dari poteret, inter multum plorantis brachia matris ac collacrimantis, et frustra consolatoriis verbis vtentis, indignantem animam exalauit. Eurialus, post quam ex oculis nunquam se amplius visuris abiit, nulli inter eundem [g] locutus: solam in mente Lucresiam gerebat, et an unquam reuerti posset meditabatur. Venitque tandem ad cesarem Perusii manentem quem deinde Farrariam, [h] Mantuam, Tridentum, Constantiam, et Basileam, secutus est, ac demum in Hongariam atque Bohemiam. Sed vt ipse Cesarem, sic cum Lucretia sequebatur [i] in somnis, nullamque noctem sibi quietam permittebat. Quam vt obiisse verus amator cognouit, magno dolore permotus lugubrem vestem recepit; nec consolationem admisit, nisi postquam Cesar ex ducali sanguine virginem sibi cum formosam tum castissimam atque prudentem matrimonio iunxit. Habes amoris exitum, Mariane mi amantissime, non

---

[a] humidos
[b] qui suis
[c] violenter
[d] om.
[e] Aristophanes
[f] porcia
[g] eundum— (Al. ed.)
[h] ferrariam
[i] loquebatur

LUCRETIA, HEARING OF EURIALUS'S DEPARTURE, FAINTS AWAY.

ficti neque felicis : Quem qui legerint, periculum ex aliis faciant quod sibi ex vsu sciet.ª Nec amatorium bibere poculum studeant quod longe plus aloes habet quam ª fiet. mellis. Vale. Ex vienna quinto nonas Iulias. Millesimo quadringentesimo quadragesimo quarto. Explicit opusculum Enee Silui de duobus amantibus impressum argentino Anno domini millesimo quadringentesimo septuagesimo sexto.

ÆNEÆ SYLVII OPERA. BASLE, 1551, p. 869, EPISTLE 395.

"Tractatum de amore olim sensu pariterq: ætate iuuenes cum nos scripsisse recolimus, Carole fili dilectissime, poenitentia immodica, pudorq: ac mœror animum nostrum vehementer excruciant : quippe qui sciamus quiq: protestati expresse fuimus, duo contineri in eo libello, apertam videlicet, sed heu lasciuiam nimis prurientemq: amoris historiam, et morale quod eam consequitur, edificans dogma, quorum primum fatuos atque errantes video sectari quamplurimos: alterum heu dolor pene nullos : ita imprauatum est atque obfuscatum infelix mortalium genus. De amore igitur quæ scripsimus olim iuuenes, comtemnite o mortales atque respuite, sequimini quæ nunc dicimus et seni magis quam iuueni credite, nec priuatum hominem pluris facite quam Pontificem : Æncam rejicite, Pium suscipite ; Illud gentile nomen parentes indidere nascenti, hoc Christianum in Apostolatu suscepimus. Porro si quem descripsimus Euriali Lucretiæq: amorem, deuoti, ut accepimus, O miseri, O insipientes, perlegitis, huc propensius iamiam accedite."

The worthie Hystorie of the moste Noble and Valiaunt Knight Plasidas, therwise called Eustas, who was martyred for the Profession of Jesus Christ.

Gathered in English verse by Iohn Partridge, in the yere of our Lord. 1566.

IMPRINTED at London, by Henrye Denham, for Thomas Hacket: and are to bée solde at his Shoppe in Lumbarde strete.

To the worshipfull Arthur Dwabene,

MARCHAUNT VENTURER, his seruante and dayly oratour
JOHN PARTRIDGE wisheth increase of worship,
by his worthy trauayle.

WHAT tyme, right Worshipfull, the moste excellent Philosopher of ye worlde, Democritus was demaunded of a frend, what was the chiefeste beste amongeste men in all the worlde, verely (quoth he) a pacient man in miserie. The other replying, and demaunding the cause of that his assertion, he answered and sayde: eyther he is not in miserie at all, or else armed most strongly and surely agaynste all aduersities what so euer they be, that shall happen vnto him. By pacience, sayth he, of a thousande euilles he is not at all any whit molested. Anaxagoras the Philosopher, borne of a noble stocke, and sonne to Eubullus, who in Philosophie dyd exceede, sayeth that he himself could find nothing more excellent in war, than this one thing, that is, a Souldier to be hardy, and also chiefely aboue all other things, the same to be likewise trustie and pacient to indure trauayle, payne, and other kind of miseries that shall happen or befall vnto him in that conflicte of war in which he then is conuersaunte. Alexander I meane the greate, hauing made war against the Persians and of thē had made gret slaughter, the king of Persia being of a noble corage bolde, stoute, pacient and hardy, hauing taken a castle or hold for his defence, and beeing in tyme brought in subiection to the Macedonians, was demaunded of Alexander in what poynt he sawe himselfe not to be ouercome, to whome the King of Persia answered in this wise: Sir king, in no point at all am I ouercome. Alexander hering him saye so, demaunded if he had not lost both friends, cūtries, castles, townes, and all thinges else, yes verily (quoth he) and yet am I not ouercōe: for though they be gone, yet can I with pacience beare the losse of the same. Oh greate was the pacience of this King, yet verily nothing in comparison of his, whome I haue taken to write vpon. Therefore I deeming nothing more fyt for a good nature than to set forth so notable a fact of pacience, as this was, haue at the request of a speciall friend of mine, drawen the same though rudely yet hoping not without some profite, eyther of myself, or of som other. And bicause that to euery castle, towne, citie, worke or workemanshippe, there belongeth defence: and knowing that defence canne not be made wythout some one defender, I am so bolde (consydering mine owne weakenesse) to dedicate this my simple worke vnto youre worship, that your wisedome may bee the defence thereof agaynst the rancorous Zoilictes, whiche at all tymes from the beginning haue bene readie to breathe the fylth of their cancred stomackes vpon those most famous works of the excellentest clearkes that euer were, whose bokes I am not worthye to beare, knowing likewyse that if those went not fre, mine can not. Therfore I hoping of your worships defence, am boldened the more in prosecuting of the same. Thus trusting to your goodnesse, I end, desiring God to mayntayne your estate, and sende you long life and good health, to his pleasure and your heartes desire.)(

Your humble seruaunt,

IOHN PARTRIDGE.

To the Reader.

Let pacience increase by kinde,
    within thy dolefull breast:
Let that swete dame within thy howse,
    haue hir abyding ncast.
Consider, viewe and vnderstande,
    what liquor doth descende:
Out of hir welles, from perils great,
    the same will thee defende.
The stinking bande of fowle dispaire,
    thy state shall not molest:
Ne slaughter in thy gates shall not,
    to strike be ready prest.
For Socrates doth playne declare,
    no other good to be:
Than wrapt in woes and pinching cares,
    a pacient one to see.
The saincts haue shewed what pacience is,
    howe precious in Gods sight:
In stories we may reade and finde,
    how much they did delight,
For to be founde in miseries,
    in pacience to dwell:
Whereof to vs this story doth
    most playnely shewe and tell.
What patience had Iob I finde,
    such patience is rare:

A thousand Martirs I with him,
    may very well compare.
What was the pacience of those,
    whome flashing firy flames:
Bereft of life, yet coulde it not,
    at all extinct their fames.
For fame for good desert doth rest,
    behinde though they be gone:
Bicause we might pursue the like,
    and oft thinke thervpon.
Therefore let vs pursue the same,
    and then we shal be sure:
For to possesse that glorious crowne,
    that lastes and shall endure,
After that earth, yea birdes and beastes,
    shall be consumed to nought:
Which crowne to vs O Lord do graunt,
    that with thy bloud vs bought.

The Verdicte of the Booke.

Learne here thou shalt one God most hie
To rule the heauens the earth and all :
The Sunne, the Moone, the starry Skie,
Subiect to be vnto his call.
Of pacience likewise reade thou shalt,
Which is a gift of all most pure :
Aboue the rest I thee ensure.

Gods prouidence here thou shalt knowe,
His great good will I doe declare :
His mighty force I playne doe showe,
Reade on therfore and doe not spare.
Though that my skill be very bare,
Yet fruite hereby well take you may :
If it to reade you wil assay.

In whome to put thy trust be bolde,
In whome to ioy here thou mayst see :
A treasure passing any golde,
Or precious stones what that they be.
The same I doe declare to thee,
To reade me therefore take some payne :
And that I count my authors gayne.

Farewell my friendes for for your sakes,
My author hath abrode me sent:
I passe not for all crabbed crakes,
That Zoilus to make is bent.
For all for you my author meant,
When that in hand his pen he toke:
And out this storie first did loke.

      Patienter ferenda quæ mutari
            non possunt.

The Noble History of Plasidas.

Sometyme in Romane lande there was,
    a king of noble fame:
Who was full faire in martiall feates,
    and Trayan had to name.
Who vnder him of lusty knightes
    did keepe a comely trayne:
And ouer them he poynted hath,
    One knight as Capitaine.
This knight to name had Plasidas,
    one whome the king did loue:
For martiall feates that in this knight,
    did shine the rest aboue.
A wife he had of glistering hew,
    of shape both faire and trim:
Of louing minde, of gladsome heart,
    and trusty vnto him.
By her he had two children fayre,
    surmounting Phœbus bright:
Who for their manly courage stout,
    compare with him they might.
The prouerbe olde is verified,
    vpon these babies twaine:
By splendent courage they assay,
    their honoures to maintaine.
The father he before doth striue,
    to runne a happy rase:
The manly children parent like,
    do followe on apace.

And sekes for to obtayne the crowne,
    of honour and of prayse :
Which to atchieue the noble hearts,
    indeuour still alwayes.
They spende their tyme with ioy and blisse
    their labour they imploy :
According to their parentes mindes,
    their hope and perfect ioy.
Such bookes these babes did learn to reade
    as present tyme did giue :
Which might their tender yeares trade vp
    in Mametrie to liue.
Thus they in whom all tendernesse,
    of age did still remaine :
Were taught the labour tedious,
    of study to sustaine.
The parentes eke imploy their dayes,
    good learning to attaine :
And now and then they finde pastime,
    their griefes for to restraine.
Sometime on hunting he doth ride,
    sometyme to Chesse they goe :
Sometime great doutes they do decide,
    that in the Realme might growe.
This was the vse of Plasidas,
    his minde to recreate :
This vsed eke his children deare,
    O blessed happy fate.
The stormy winter dayes hath left,
    with misty cloudes to swell :
And Phœbus bright appointed is,
    more nearer vs to dwell.

Of Plasidas.

And Eolus no pleasure takes
    to dim the ayre with cloudes:
And Phœbus nowe is quite deuoide,
    of fogges his beames that shrowdes.
Then doth Aurora leaue the bed
    Of Titan, and doth bring:
Some ioyes to men, the wished day
    beholding once to spring.
And trees and hearbes with ioyfull heart,
    do shew their pleasaunt hew:
And Knights in Forrests bende their force
    the Bucke for to subdew.
Then Plasidas with comely traine,
    of knightes of royall kinde:
Do enter now the greene Forestes,
    a Bucke foorth for to finde.
At lēgth he came where bucks great store,
    did stande confusedly:
And ech man now doth bend him selfe,
    his lusty Stede to try.
Now here and there the harmelesse Buck,
    assayeth for to runne:
And Plasidas at one faire Bucke,
    to ryde he hath begonne.
The other knightes amongst the Buckes,
    in fieldes abrode do raunge:
But Plasidas followeth hard,
    this Bucke and will not chaunge.
At length in thickst of woods I say,
    the Bucke doth enter in:
And then more fiercely hir to sew,
    this knight doth straight beginne.

Till at the last the Bucke had tooke,
    a Mountaine huge and hye :
And there the huge and lofty Bucke,
    Plasidas did discry.
But as he was addicted sore,
    the Bucke with force to take :
The mighty God in Skyes aboue,
    his seruaunt did him make.
And out from cloudes he called to him,
    his Idolles to detest :
Which by and by fel in a swoune,
    and so he left the beast.
Then there he layde his sprangling corps,
    almost deuoyde of breath :
I am thy God then sayd the Lord,
    which bought thee with my death.
My very bloud doth iustifie,
    in me thou hast thy life :
Go wende in hast the Lorde can say,
    conuert thy Heathen wife.
Thy children eke let them be taught,
    one God to honour pure :
Then thou my kingdome shalt possesse,
    hereof thou mayst be sure.
Where thou shalt liue eternally,
    if thou this life detest :
And shalt if thou fight manfully,
    for aye with me be blest.
Arise therfore go wende in hast,
    this life is but as grasse :
To day full faire (hir glistring hew,)
    to morow quite is past.

Those stocks and stones the which thou doest
    as Goddes adorne with prayse:
Are in my sight Idolatrous,
    therefore eschewe those wayes.
Arise I say and get thee hence,
    make hast thee to baptise:
And see thou do conuert thy wife,
    I say in any wise.
Apalled sore with feare and dreade,
    the Knight straight wayes did say:
Haue mercy Lord, and me forgiue,
    I hartly do thee pray.
Stand vp thou knight then sayd the Lord,
    thy sinnes remitted be:
Do thou not feare for Sathan will,
    thee plague with misery.
Then downe he sat with stretched handes
    to God he gaue the prayse:
And sayde, to thee that sittes on hye,
    be honour due alwayes.
That hast vouchsafe this day to call,
    thy seruaunt gone astray:
Euen as a sheepe by fortune strayed,
    out of the herde away.
I do confesse thou onely arte,
    my comfort and my trust:
And eke my God, and thy promyse,
    thou kepest true and iust.
No part thereof thou violatest,
    thou art both God and man:
These stockes, these stones be Diuels yll,
    do vs no good they can.

Thee therefore I do worship still,
    thou madest the worlde of naught:
And I the Image of thy grace,
    that thou of earth hast wrought.
I do confesse my heauenly king,
    that no good is in me:
But that the goodnesse which I haue,
    doth all discende from thee.
Without thy grace and goodnesse, I
    no day at all can say:
But that I should be ouerthrowen,
    and brought to deathes decay.
But thou O God art my defence,
    my aide, my hope, and trust:
Thou art my king, my God, my Lord,
    my sauiour true and iust.
O Lord I know that Sathan will,
    with cares my soule molest:
But thou O Lord in pacience,
    defende my carefull brest,
Let me with pacience still abide,
    thy gracious laysure good:
And graunt also to me full hope,
    in thy most precious bloud.
That what so euer illes do hap,
    vnto thy seruaunt here:
With willing minde the burden huge,
    with pacience I may bere.
Graunt also that dispayre do not,
    molest my quiet state:
Ne that I should in any wise,
    incurre thy heauy hate.

But give me Lord a minde alwayes,
    obedient for to bee ;
Unto thy hest, and to submit
    my will alwayes to thee.
So shall I be a most fitte braunch,
    ingrafted in the tree :
Of liuing dayes, and at the last,
    shall euer raigne with thee.
To whome be prayse eternally,
    both now and euer more :
One only God though persons three,
    as I haue sayd before.
Then at the last this noble knight,
    from Forrest made returne :
And thought within his hunting race,
    no longer to soiourne.
But home he commes in posting wise,
    The knightes they after hye :
And some the chase will follow on,
    the ende thereof to trye.
The mighty Buckes lye dead on launde,
    the Palfrayes they do sweate :
And from their frothy mouthes they breath
    the inward partching heate.
Now here now there with launce in hand,
    the marshall knightes do runne :
And at the last they haue espyed,
    how Plasidas did come.
From out the groues so greene which was
    beset with many a tree :
With heauy chere much like vnto,
    a man in miserie.

When they pérceyued well that he,
    with sorrow was infect:
They mused much, yet of that hapte,
    they nothing did suspect.
Then home they go and some doe lade,
    the pray that they haue slaine:
And other some for their repastes,
    in Forrestes do remaine.
At length Plasidas doth ariue,
    before his Castle gate:
His wife to welcome home hir Loue,
    is ready sone thereat.
From gate to Hall they do ascende,
    and there the bourdes be spred:
The sunne is downe, and time it is,
    for men to goe to bed.
The chamberlaynes the bed downe lay,
    and fier in chamber make:
And nowe Plasidas he is come,
    his corporall rest to take.
When he in bed had layne a while,
    great griefes he did sustayne:
And so at length his minde to breake,
    he purposeth certaine.
At length his wife perceyuing that,
    no rest her Mate could finde:
She did procure him for to shewe,
    what dreade was in his minde.
At length he sayde, oh louing mate,
    the cause sith thou wouldest know:
Of these my cares so huge and fell,
    to thee them I will showe.

Of Plasidas.

This day (quoth he) as I abrode
    In Forrest thicke did runne :
A mighty Bucke his race to take,
    before me hath begunne.
At whom I sued with all my might,
    and force that I could make :
At length the Bucke for his defence,
    the densid woodes doth take.
And there the Bucke I do pursue,
    on loftie steede amaine :
Till that the toppe of one great hill,
    he seketh to attaine.
And there from out the skyes did breake,
    A voyce like thunders cry :
For feare wherof almost my breath,
    to Skyes away did fly.
Quoth he I am thy very God,
    ne made but being still :
Both heauen and earth, yea Skyes and al
    obeyes vnto my will.
I made them all, and thee O man,
    as Lorde of earth to bee :
The fishe, the foules, the birdes, the beast,
    shall all obey to thee.
And for the loue which I thee bare,
    my Image I thee made :
A liuing soule the life wherof,
    away shall neuer fade.
Thus art thou now my Image pure,
    and I thy Lorde and king :
Thou art the shepe whom I do loue,
    aboue all earthly thing.

By this my loue I did declare,
    when thou wast vtterly :
Condemned for thy wickednesse,
    eternally to dye.
I loued thee so that I did take,
    a seruaunts shape on me :
For to be slaine euen as a sheepe,
    at Sacrifice we see.
And thou vnkinde forgetting quite,
    what I for thee haue done :
Hast made thee Goddes, and of vile earth,
    a God is now become.
Yet I bicause I tender thee,
    And rewe thy heauy fall :
Vouchsafe againe thee to the folde,
    once more from sinne to call.
Repent therefore and learne to knowe,
    thy God, thy Lord, and King :
So shalt thou with him eterne liue,
    where Angels holy sing.
Forsake thy Idolles and become,
    a Christian now at last :
And Ile remitte and quite forgiue,
    thy wickednesse forepaste.
Arise therefore go wende in hast,
    make speede for to conuert :
Thy gentle wife, that honour shee,
    may me with all hir heart.
O Lord (quoth I) if Sathan do,
    with care my corps molest :
Be thou my ayde, let pacience still,
    abide within my brest.

Do thou defende our sinfull corps,
   O Lorde we thee desire :
That by thy death vnto the crowne
   of life we may asspire.
Then sayd the Lorde with troubles great,
   Sathan shall thee anoye :
By fraude in frendship such as erst,
   with thee were wont to toye.
And speake thee faire, with cap and knee,
   at euery worde do make :
Now in thy fall and miserie,
   their flattering leaues shall take.
And not content with rayling voice,
   reprochfull wordes to say :
But eke are bent to spoyle thy Tent,
   thy goodes to beare away.
Which thou shalt by my grace diuine,
   with pacience beare thy losse :
And at the length when I see time,
   Ile take away this crosse.
And will againe in former state,
   thee place with ioy and blesse :
With double folde, and shalt againe
   possesse thy lost rychesse.
Then downe I fell in swouning there,
   and loud and shirle I cryed :
Oh Lord thy seruaunt will I be,
   hap me what will betide.
These were the wordes when sacred tops,
   of mountaines great and tall :
He left, O Plasidas go home,
   thy wife see that thou call.

Then sayd his wife, my louing Lord,
    O Plasidas so true :
He is the God of heauen and earth,
    that did appeare to you.
For yester night as I did lye,
    in bed with heauy minde :
Me thought before me one most faire,
    in chamber I did finde.
Appalled sore twixt feare and dreade,
    at length to me he spake :
And sayd, O Theapis from slepe,
    and drousinesse awake.
To morrow shall thy husbande dere,
    what I am well perceaue :
I am thy Christ and went his way,
    and thus he tooke his leaue.
This for to shewe my louing Lord,
    I durst no whit to thee :
Least happely thou mightst haue thought,
    in me some iniury.
But now I knowe and well perceyue,
    that that was Christ in deede :
He is of God coequall mate,
    and eke of Dauids seede.
To him therfore with thankes giuing,
    on Flutes and Pypes full shrill :
Our Sacrifices vnto him,
    on Aultars will we kill.
This is the Prophet which to vs,
    full long was prophecied :
This is the very sonne of him,
    who Starres in Skyes doth guide.

Therefore my Lord if that thee please,
    of baptisme let vs take:
The sacrament, and then let vs,
    our Country soyle forsake.
Then sayd the knight, faire dame at hand,
    Doth rest a clarke of fame:
A Minister of sacred rightes,
    who Buno hath to name.
A comely man, of fayth most pure,
    to him straight we will wende:
For rightes of Baptisme to receyue,
    I verily do pretend.
Our children eke he baptise shall,
    according vnto right:
And thus to him they went in hast,
    in middest of the night.
And when they baptisme had receyued,
    as now the maner is:
Plasidas, Eustas had to name,
    his wife is Theapis.
His children eke whom nature made,
    of beauty passing faire:
Were tender ones, thone Agapite,
    Theospite was the heyre.
Thus baptisme done vnto their house,
    agayne they do repaire:
And there in peace a while they liue,
    both honestly and faire.
At length the sturdy boystrous blastes,
    of Sathan gins to rore:
Euen as the water from a hyll,
    or as a myghty Bore.

Which of some wight receyued hath,
    a wound both huge and great :
Or as the flashing waues of floudes,
    that craggie rockes doth beate.
With hurling here and there hir streames,
    indeuoring for to weare :
The ragged bankes which of their floudes,
    the crabbyd rage doth beare.
Much like vnto a battayle made,
    a Citie for to get :
And munition with burning strokes,
    to sacke the walles is set.
And breach is made, and houses burne,
    and souldiers nowe beginne :
For ioy of spoyle, by vitall breath
    not for to set a pinne.
Or else when as a Lion great,
    doth range with angry moode :
With hungrie chawes amid the woods,
    doth seeke to haue his foode.
And he that first within his sight,
    appeares that he may see :
With gasping mouth on him he runnes,
    deuoured for to bee.
So Sathan now in roving wise,
    on Plasidas doth runne :
His sheepe and cattell for to slay,
    already hath begunne.
Then Plasidas to pouertie,
    is brought the ready way :
And eke when that his fayned friendes,
    perceyued his decay,

They runne his house to spoyle and sacke,
    his goodes they beare away:
Euen those whom he had feasted earst,
    before his great decay.
These pampered churles that sit all day,
    at tables dayntie fed:
Who by all mischieuous crabbed guiles,
    with stinking heart is led.
Whome neyther loue ne hate can driue,
    from out the Castell dore:
They learned haue so for to rowe,
    with the Athenien oare.
I may such persones well compare,
    vnto a pype or tonne:
That hath good wine to outwarde sight,
    in which there is poyson.
For they themselues so beautifie,
    their wordes in inward showe:
But poyson much is hyd therein,
    as afterwardes we knowe.
Thus Plasidas from great renoume,
    to pouertie is brought:
And where he was a royall Knight,
    nowe is he worse than nought.
Thus then when shame had ouertoke,
    this worthy knight, then loe:
In midst of all the darkesome night,
    from house and friends they goe.
To water side, and there doe wayte,
    when lofty ship shall glyde:
On foming seas, the winde is good,
    for them on seas to ryde.

They do inquire if any ship,
 to countrey farre will wende:
To whome the Master aunswere made,
 that straight they did intende,
To hoyse their sayles and to departe,
 to Egipt in all hast:
Agreed they are, they hoyse their sayles,
 to sayle away at last.
The lande they leaue, into the deepe,
 they launce with winde at will:
The mighty shippe the hollowe waues,
 at euery surge doth fill.
The night is gone and day is come,
 wherein eche thing doth ioy:
And here the lusty fish begin,
 at paynted pupe to toy.
With fetching frischoes here and there,
 with spready finne in sea:
And seemeth who fastest should swimme,
 some wager for to lay.
They sayled haue and now at length,
 neere Egipt they ariue:
The Master of the ship doth like,
 the beautie of the wife,
Of Plasidas, and doth delight,
 his wauering wanton minde:
With rolling in his diuelish brayne,
 the beautie of hir kinde.
She pleased hath his lothfull eyes,
 with beauties shining beames:
Fro whence sometime did yssue out,
 of teares abundant streames.

Of Plasidas.

Then at the last when vnto land,
    they drewe, and playne did see:
The touret tops, and knewe full well,
    how far from lande they be.
The Master of the ship did say,
    yon passangers we see:
That nere to land our ship is come,
    therefore nowe ready be.
For that you haue your fraught to pay,
    as due it is by right:
Come on sir boy, launce out this boate,
    the towne is here in sight.
The anker then through flashing floud,
    a way doth make for holde:
And there to ryde from daungers great,
    the Master is full bolde.
The Master and the Mariners guide,
    the cocke boate vnto lande:
Then he his fraight for to receiue,
    he stretcheth forth his hande.
Yet nought at all from Plasidas,
    might hap in any wayes:
For all was gone, and naught was left,
    before he toke the seas.
Why Plasidas the Master sayd,
    thy wife Ile haue away:
If that thou wilt not out of hand,
    my duetie to me pay.
Then out of hande he toke his wife,
    Plasidas being on shoare:
And sayd, y^u friend thou shuldst haue sought
    thy frayght to pay before.

Therefore I say thy wife with me,
    away from hence shall wende :
With whome Plasidas all in vayne,
    did labour and contende,
To kepe hir still, the Master straight,
    His Mariners bad to bring :
Plasidas loe in midst of seas,
    by furious force to fling.
So that his wife the Master he,
    at will might then possesse :
His wilfulnesse brought him his death,
    in thende as I doe gesse.
Well Plasidas must needes departe,
    whether he will or nay :
For money none at all he had,
    as then, the frayght to pay.
But from the shoares of surging seas,
    with heauy minde doth wende :
And for to liue in Egipt lande,
    he verily doth intende.
With his two babes of tender yeares,
    so faire in natures grace :
The one on fathers armes hanging,
    both followe on a pace,
The other he doth runne afore,
    with euery grasse to play :
His father mery for to make,
    all meanes he doth assay.
At length wher flashing streames of flouds,
    the shoares doth cleane deuide :
They are ariued, and there they stande,
    the maner to decide,

How for to passe those troublesome waues
    for needes that way he must:
Unto the towne, O Fortune thou
    to good men neuer iust,
Who earst a loft in chaire of state,
    was wonte in peace to syt:
Is now in floudes of miserie,
    and thou not leauing it,
Doest adde more care vnto his payne,
    thy fashion it is so:
Bycause thou wouldest that all men shuld
    take thee for friend nor foe.
What mourning makes ye wight good lord
    whome wife is borne fro:
And taking vp his yongest sonne,
    from dolefull shoares doth go,
To thother side where woodes and trees,
    on fertile ground doth stande:
He is ariued, and there doth set,
    his tender childe on lande.
And entring nowe the rushing waues,
    that soundes with noyse so shrill:
He doth approch the hollow waues,
    in myddest thereof to fill.
When he in myddest was thereof,
    there came a Woulfe and tooke:
The tender childe who late before,
    was borne ouer the brooke,
And bare away, but God who made,
    the heauen the earth and all:
Did so prouide that once no hurt,
    vnto it should befall.

He seeing then his childe was gone,
   with dolefull minde he cride :
Oh wicked wretch and miser vile,
   what shall of me betide ?
And comming nowe to the other side,
   his eldest sonne to catch :
A Lion huge from wood doth come,
   and thother vp doth snatch.
Which straight doth trudge from thence away,
   vnto the wood agayne :
A heauy sight for Plasidas,
   in this his dolefull payne.
But Plasidas pore soule doth striue,
   his childe to get againe :
But he pore wretch of very truth,
   laboureth all in vayne.
When that he sawe no helpe there was,
   good Lorde he doth lament :
But mighty God the childe to saue,
   hath rescue ready sent.
The countrey men that were as then,
   a plowing in the fielde :
The heard men eke that sheepe did kepe,
   did stand and all behelde.
Where as a Lion huge did runne,
   and eke with him did beare :
A manly childe, and loked as though,
   in pieces he would teare.
Then out they sent their hungry dogs,
   the Lion to ouertake.
And so at length the Lion he,
   the childe did quite forsake.

The Woulfe likewise to beare the childe,
    already hath begunne:
Through mydst of the plow men there,
    and they at him do runne
With battes and staues, the praye he left,
    and there the childe they founde:
A comely wight, no hurt he had,
    But was both whole and sounde.
The plowe men and the heard men both,
    are ioyous of this thing:
That chaunced hath, and to the towne,
    the children both they bring.
There they declare how that they toke,
    these tender babes of age:
From beasts ful fierce, and how they brought
    them home to their village.
These men they were both of one towne,
    and set the babes to schole:
To learne such things as after they,
    thereby their life might rule.
Nowe leaue we here a while and stay,
    and let vs furder heare:
Of Plasidas how he doth range,
    in dolefull heauy cheare.
He passed is the watrie streames,
    of that vnhappy shoare:
With sobbes and teares his cares and smart,
    increaseth more and more.
And then at last vpon the ground,
    prostrate on face he lies:
Haue mercy Lord on me vile wretch,
    continually he cries.

Thou god that madest both heauen and erth,
    the sea and eke eche thing :
Which al the windes from out their caues,
    and hollowe rockes dost bring.
That madest the world and eke eche beast,
    that liueth now therein :
Who makest pore, and eke dost cause,
    of pore to ryse a King.
Who made the Sea, the fish, the foule,
    that flies vnder the Skies :
Who rules the very iawes of beastes,
    in whom all force now lies.
Who placed first the heauenly throne,
    of thy Godhead diuine :
Who eke hath made within the world,
    both houres, dayes and time.
Thou that didst make the firmament,
    with Stars shining so bright :
Thou that for day didst make the Sunne,
    mens steps to guide aright.
Thou that hast made the planets seauen,
    in spheares to runne their race :
Thou that next to the croked Moone,
    the burning flame doest place.
And next to it a vacant place,
    where aire doth all abounde :
The water eke which compasse doth,
    the heauy massiue grounde.
That hast to man such power giuen,
    thy noble workes to knowe :
And yet on him of thy good grace,
    dost dayly more bestowe.

Graunt vnto me thy seruaunt here,
    one sparke of thy good grace:
That in this land I may now finde,
    some ioyfull resting place.
Euen I that wretch who is denoyde,
    of wife and children twaine:
Giue pacience Lord, to me pore wretch,
    though languished in payne.
Haue mercy upon my children deare,
    where so their corps shall lie:
Haue mercy on their parent eke,
    who liues in miserie.
This sayde, vnto the towne he goeth,
    and ceasseth not to weepe:
For children twaine, at last he commeth,
    in middest of the streate.
And there the men of that same towne,
    do Plasidas desire:
To kepe their sheepe, and so he should,
    of them receyue his hire.
Agreed they are, and Plasidas,
    his sheepe full well doth knowe:
And now forthwith vnto the fieldes,
    his sheepe and he do goe.
Now leaue we heare of Plasidas,
    in shepheardes weede for gayne:
Sometime he was a noble Lorde,
    but now more pore certayne.
But now we forth will shewe the meane,
    how God did all prouide:
For mother and the children eke,
    as it may well be spide

In ende, for loe, the fatall wretch,
    hath his rewarde with gayne:
His great desire was once the cause,
    why that his corps was slayne.
For when on lofty roaring waues,
    he was with winde at will:
He then in hast would strayght assay,
    his lust for to fulfill.
But as he would by force of armes,
    haue wrought the deedely acte:
The mighty God with death repayde,
    this his purposed facte.
And there in shippe all deade he lies,
    whose lust did cause his woe:
The mariners lament this case,
    and eke to lande they goe.
With hir, on shoare to set, and eke
    more victuals for to buy:
When winde is faire to cuntry soyle,
    againe that they may hye.
And much they prayse hir constancie,
    hir beautie and hir grace:
Hir faithfulnesse vnto hir Loue,
    in this hir heauie case.
The Lorde they praise and honor him,
    with all their might they haue:
That so of his benignitie,
    his blessed flocke can saue.
Then when to shore their boate was come,
    she there hir leaue doth take:
And willingly not with them any
    longer soiorne to make.

Doth wende vnto a towne thereby,
    intending there to liue:
Untill that God shall see his tyme,
    hir from hir cares to meue.
Thus fiftene yeares all desolate,
    she liues in widdowes ray:
Hir honest life not one there is,
    in all that towne that may
Distaine. And loe it so befell,
    since Plasidas was gone:
That enimies the Romane lande,
    do vexe and warre vpon.
At whome the King enuying sore,
    doth warre on them beginne:
But all in vaine his trauell was,
    he lost, and nought could winne.
Then of his Knight good Plasidas
    to thinke he doth beginne:
And wishing alwayes that he were,
    in Romane land with him.
At length the King doth sende abrode,
    through many a place and towne:
His lusty Knightes in hast to seeke,
    Plasidas of renowme.
And bring him home to Romane lande,
    where earst he was the Knight:
That did most harme vnto his foes,
    by mortall dint of fight.
And who that findes the same in ende,
    the king would honour giue:
With riches eke in honour great,
    all dayes of life to liue.

Within the armie of the King,
    two Knightes there were certayne:
Who euer under Plasidas,
    in warres did much remayne.
They into Egipt land do goe,
    some newes for to heare tell:
Of Plasidas, and loe they chaunce,
    in streate where he doth dwell.
And Plasidas from field doth come,
    as they were entred in:
Then to inquire of Plasidas,
    the Knightes doe now begin.
If that he knewe not one, within
    that towne that had to name:
Plasidas, who of chiualrie,
    did beare away the fame.
He aunswered them, and sayd forsooth,
    no such man I doe knowe:
But yet he doth the Knightes desire,
    vnto his house to goe.
And take such things as he poore soule,
    vnto them then might giue:
Which might their weary faynting lims,
    from wearinesse relieue.
With whom they went with al their harts
    and their repastes did take:
With such small cheere as he good man,
    at that time could them make.
But when he did reuolue in minde,
    the state that he was in:
Sometime with them, good Lord therefore,
    to weepe he doth begin.

Then went he out from chamber where,
    the Knightes did then remaine:
To wash his face, and afterwardes,
    returne to them againe.
But whilest he was from them a time,
    they thought that it was he:
Whome they appoynted were to seeke,
    and so agreed they be,
At his retourne for to demaund,
    some licence and some leaue:
To see a wounde which sometime he,
    in battayle did receaue.
At length he commes, and they to him,
    with gentle wordes doe speake:
Good sir sayd they, much like thou arte,
    to him whome we doe seeke.
Therefore of thee we do desire,
    this one thing for to loke
Upon thy head, for such a wounde,
    that he in battayle toke.
They then behelde the wound, and knewe,
    full well that it was he:
No tong can then expresse their ioy,
    fulfilled so they be.
With stretched armes they him embrace,
    desiring him to tell:
Where that his children are become,
    and where his wife doth dwell.
Then aunswered he and sayd his sonnes
    were refte of vitall breath:
And as he thought, his wife likewise
    tasted of cruell death.

And howe the Master had his wife,
    vnto the Knightes he tolde:
And how by force of armes from him,
    his wife he did with holde.
This done, in hast throughout the land,
    reporte doth blowe this thing:
The neyghboures then do hast vnto,
    Plasidas pore lodging.
With maruelling, much like vnto
    A swarme of bees they goe:
About the house, and there the knightes,
    their message forth do shew.
And then they ray sir Plasidas,
    with vestementes of price:
Then from their seates to walke a while,
    the lusty Knightes arise.
In hast they leaue that ioyfull soyle,
    and homewarde do they wende:
They are ariued in Romane lande,
    ere fyftene dayes were ende.
The Emperour then when that he heard,
    that Eustas was at hande:
Doth ioy that God hath sent this Knight,
    agayne vnto his lande.
Now Trayan he doth ryde in hast,
    Plasidas for to meete:
And ioyfull Trayan Plasidas,
    his louing friend doth greete.
Then Trayan with Plasidas,
    vnto his court doth goe:
With great frequent of people that,
    behind them did followe.

When he came there, of al his happes,
    he doth declare and tell:
Of all the woes and miseries,
    that vnto hym befell.
How his wife was taken him fro,
    how children both were slayne:
And how himselfe nowe fyftene yeares,
    did liue in dolefull payne.
From thence they goe to banketting,
    to reuels and to play:
In dauncing and in minstrelsie,
    they spend that lucky day.
And Plasidas is made I say,
    Lieutenant of the bande:
And all the ordering of the warres,
    is put into his hande.
He then before him calles the Knightes,
    and doth their number take:
Intending vp an armie great,
    in hast forthwith to make.
And doth commaund that strayght,
    eche towne to him should sende:
Two lusty men with Plasidas,
    vnto the warres to wende.
It happened so that that same towne,
    two souldiers forth must make:
Which from the Lion and the Woulfe,
    those tender babes did take.
At length the townes men do agree,
    that both these children should:
Goe with the Knight, with willing mindes
    and heartes, euen so they would.

The countrie men these souldiers twayne,
    did bring vnto the Knight:
Their maners and their comelie shape,
    did much his minde delight.
Wherefore with first at table he,
    hath placed the same to be:
Bycause in them such noblenesse,
    of maners he did see.
The day is come, to battayle they,
    must wende euen out of hand:
And now they must the great assault,
    of cruell foes withstande.
The battayles great on eyther part,
    the flames do reach the Skie:
The roaring sound of Canons shot,
    the force of walles doth trie.
The Knightes with launce in hand I say,
    do pearce throughout the throng:
The souldier doth assay to lay,
    his enimie all along.
The battayle standes in doubt of truth,
    which side shall other beate:
Here martch they on amayne and there,
    they blowe agayne retreate.
Here all along on ground they lie,
    and here from tourets hie:
The deadly shaft through mistey cloudes,
    aloft in Skies doe flie.
And here in flesh it lightes full deepe,
    and giues a deadly wound:
And in an other parte there is,
    a thousand brought to ground.

Of Plasidas.

Here fighteth Plasidas ful harde,
    in midst of all the throng:
And here the children parent like,
    slay enimies along.
They forwarde doe retire in hast,
    and men afore do lacke:
And Plasidas assayles his foes,
    behinde vpon their backe.
The wings that were the ayde and helpe,
    of foote men, goe their way:
The battayles lost, all through defacde,
    of keping their aray.
The wings are fled, and battayle must
    by footemen stand awhile:
The battayls great, but at the length,
    they are brought to exile.
The enimies flie from fielde amaine,
    and Romanes followe styll:
Upon the chase, for they did minde,
    their cruell foes to kyll.
Retreate is blowen, and home agayne,
    to campe the souldiers hie:
That willing were, eyther their foes,
    or they in chase to die.
The towne is made full strong and sure,
    with rampiers for shotte:
And eke eche syde of all the towne,
    with munition is hotte.
The scaling lathers downe to throwe,
    they haue their iron staues:
They haue their hatchets for to cut,
    in sunder all their raues.

Some stand with slings from far to strike,
    the Romane armies great :
Some stand with billes those that assault,
    with furious force to beate :
The pike men they on walles doe stande,
    their towne for to defende :
And some from towre with bow in hande,
    the graygoose wing do sende.
The labourers do mende the walles,
    with gonshot all to shake :
The townes men all within the towne,
    do seeke defence to make.
And sluises al are opened,
    to stop the enimies way :
Least that to scale their walles by night,
    the enimie doe assay.
The night is come, and it doth parte
    the armies for that time :
The watch man he aloft in towre,
    beginneth for to clime.
The warde at gate is kept all night,
    the souldiers stand in ray :
That when the onset shall be giuen,
    resist their foes they may.
The night is gone, and breake of day,
    beginneth to drawe nie :
By which the watch man in the towre,
    the armie may discrie.
And see from farre howe Plasidas,
    doth order all his bande :
How that he telleth them the way,
    their foes for to withstande.

Of Plasidas.

He doth declare, as he can deeme,
    what number that they be:
And doth espie if any troupe,
    of horse men he may see.
That doth aproch vnto the towne,
    for to increase their feare:
Plasidas sent horse men forth,
    to range both here and there.
To see if that they enter would,
    from towne, and would descend:
In open fielde by force of armes,
    their citie to defende.
But they within did kepe themselues,
    in order for to fight:
Then had the day quite droue away,
    the lothsome mystes of nyght.
And Plasidas his comely trayne,
    vnto the walles doth bring:
The which the watch man well perceyued,
    and al arme out doth ring.
To walles they goe both tagge and ragge,
    their Citie to defende:
And euery man his businesse,
    doth duely nowe intende.
The pushing pikes stand next the walles,
    their enimies downe to fling:
The stelly boyes the heauy earth,
    on shoulders thither bring.
The sunne from depth of Occean sea,
    did scarce himselfe areare:
When as the Romane armie did,
    before the towne appeare.

And then the gonnes the way doe make,
    through walles of stone and bricke:
And eke the flames of fiers do,
    the tops of houses licke.
The Romanes, they bring to the walles,
    their scaling lathers hie:
With iron hookes, vnto the tops
    of houses for to tie.
Now all the walles of Romanes stout,
    is filled to the ende:
And more and more continually,
    vpon the walles ascende.
The towne is wonne, and Plasidas
    in midst thereof is set:
And all their labour is as nowe,
    the spoyle thereof to get.
The towne to dust is quite consumde,
    and burnt with scorching fire:
The trumpets sound triumphantly,
    to cause their men retire.
Then after when the towne is wonne,
    and all was brought to ground:
A resting place for all his bande,
    there in a towne he found.
In which his wife did dwell, and kept
    a house for hostage there:
To whome hir sonnes for harbor then,
    vnto hir do repaire,
Not knowing what she was, in deede,
    they there their restes doe take:
And for their noble victories,
    great ioy they oft do make.

Of Plasidas.

At last the yonger doth desire,
    the elder for to tell :
His yong estate, and what to him,
    in childehode oft befell.
Whose talke the silly mother oft,
    did listen much to knowe :
Some newes by warriers stoutly done,
    and afterwardes might showe.
The same vnto hir friendes that list,
    oft times of warres to talke :
Therefore full oft I say she doth,
    before the chamber walke.
At last the eldest sayd, good friend,
    I doe remember well :
Howe that my father rulde the Knightes
    of Rome that did excell.
And eke a Lady faire I had,
    to mother well I knowe :
Two children eke they had full fayre,
    I well remember so.
My yonger brother was full faire,
    surmounting in degree :
All other men, so rich he was,
    with giftes of dame beautie.
Long did they liue in ioy and blisse,
    within that lande I know :
But yet by night he toke a shippe,
    and from that lande did goe.
Unto a countrey not farre thence,
    the name I doe not knowe :
The shippe is come vnto the porte,
    and then to land we goe.

My mother she behinde was left,
 but howe I can not say :
But as I iudge, the Master he,
 my mother there did stay.
And then from thence we did depart,
 vnto a towne thereby :
With heauy minde, vntill he came,
 vnto a great ferry.
And there he set me downe on ground,
 and ouer strayght he bore :
His yonger sonne ouer the floud,
 vnto the other shore.
And entring now the floud agayne,
 me thither for to fetch :
A cruel Woulfe my brother yong,
 vp in his mouth doth catch.
And wendes his way vnto the wood,
 my brother loud doth cry :
My father still he striued harde,
 agayne to me to hie.
But out alas, a Lion huge
 came from the wood amaine :
And snatcht vp me, and to the wood
 he did returne agayne.
But when the Lion great and tall,
 the heard men they doe see :
Their dogs they set vpon the beast,
 and so they saued me.
The yonger sayd, my brother deare,
 euen as I heard it tolde :
The plowmen toke me from a Woulfe,
 which had me in his holde.

By that thou saydst, coniecture I,
    thy brother that I am:
Loe happy day they both doe say,
    that vnto warres we came.
The ioy that they doe make forsoth,
    no tong can it expresse:
No heart can thinke, no eye hath seene,
    such blessed ioyfulnesse.
The mother then hath heard their talke,
    and ponder it well doth she:
And doth reuolue within hir minde,
    if that hir babes they be.
Then vnto Plasidas she goeth,
    and doth desire him sone:
That he would let hir goe with him,
    for she was borne at Rome.
And as to him these wordes she spake,
    in sounding she oft fell:
And cried at length, O Plasidas,
    I knowe thee very well.
I am thy wife pore Theopis,
    which taken was thee fro:
In midst of floudes, when thou from ship,
    vnto the land didst goe.
The mighty God of heauen and earth,
    for thee hath kept me cleane:
The Master he for his deserte,
    by darte of death is slayne.
Then Plasidas doth well perceyue,
    his wife, his loue and make:
His heart, his life, and vnto him,
    in armes he doth hir take.

What ioy was there I can not tell,
　　my fingers weary be:
To write the same, my eyes like that,
　　in world did neuer see.
The wife the husband doth embrace,
　　the man the wife likewise:
The ioy to shewe, the teares doe gushe,
　　like streames from out their eyes.
And in their ioy, the wife demaundes,
　　where that hir children be:
Then he did say, my louing wife,
　　their deaths myselfe did see.
Two cruel beastes with foming mouthes,
　　our children both hath slayne:
Then sayd his wife be of good cheere,
　　aliue they both remaine.
For loe, the God which vnto vs,
　　this ioyfull meeting gaue:
By his good grace and power diuine,
　　did both our children saue.
Then him she tolde how souldiers twaine,
　　their infancie did showe:
And strayght he sent for those yong men,
　　the truth of them to knowe.
The children both vnto him come,
　　and eche of them doth tell:
His infancie, by which he knoweth,
　　they be hys sonnes full well,
He then doth kisse and eke embrace,
　　those tender babes of his:
The armie then for newes hereof,
　　in heart right ioyfull is,

They spende those dayes in ioy and blisse,
    and after do intende:
To Romane lande triumphantly
    his hoste and he to wende.
But whilest in warres he did abyde,
    good Trayan was deade:
And Adrian in the Empire,
    succeeded in his steade.
Who in all mischieues did abounde,
    as stories vs doe tell:
For persecuting of the truth,
    he did the rest excell.
When Plasidas to Rome was come,
    and did a time soiourne:
Then Adrian did him commaund,
    his Idols to adourne.
For that the Romanes did possesse,
    so great a victorie:
But Plasidas would not so doe,
    he playnely did deny,
That they were Gods, and unto him,
    they nought at all could giue:
He said by Christ, in Christ it was,
    that he in world did liue.
Then Adrian commaunded that,
    deuoured they should be:
Of a Lion in Church, whereas
    his Goddes the facte might see.
And so it was as he commaunde,
    perfourmed eke and done:
The Lion he most ioyfully,
    vnto their feete doth come.

And there doth lie much like a dogge,
   cum caude that doth play:
And from their feete no man ywis,
   can get the beast away.
But there he lies and mery makes,
   he doth no hhurt at all:
Then Adrian doth strayght commaunde,
   his men them forth to call,
And doth commaund that they be put,
   in Oxe of brasse to die:
But nought they care, in Jesus Christ
   they had their trust wholly.
The Oxe with flame is thorow hote,
   and they are put therein:
And ioyfully in Christ they all,
   to sing do then beginne.
Thus ended they their mortall race,
   their file was at an ende:
That we may so indure good Lorde,
   to vs thy mercy sende.

       FINIS.   John Partridge.

The most famouse and worthie Historie, of the worthy Lady Pandauola, daughter to the mighty Paynim, the great Turke.

Imprinted at London, in Paules churchyard at the signe of the Lucrece, by Thomas Purfoote.

1566.

¶ The historie of Pandauola.

Sometime in Turky there,
    A famouse lande by name,
Did dwell a kīg whose daughters fare
    Deserued immortal fame :
So bewtifull she was,
    So fette of lymme and ioynte,
That sure a worlde it was to see,
    Her shape from point to point.
So comly to be knitte,
    For witte she bare the bell,
Her comly shape all other wightes
    For bewtie did excell :
Her grace is such to see
    That heauen it was to heare
And see, what suters was to get
    This worthy royall peare :
As thicke as starres in skies
    So thicke the people be,
In euery place the comly corps
    Of this Princes to see.
The lusty gentell knightes,
    On foaming steades on hie,
Her loue to wynne, their manly force
    Full often there doe trie.

And demyng in their myndes
    That he that once should haue
The victory, auaunce more nede not
    Of her, her loue to craue.
Therfore they haue decreede
    A tournament to crie,
In which they thinke with dynte of sworde
    Their harnes for to trie.
Then to the king they go
    With one assent, and saie :
We thee desier most royall Lorde,
    To graunt without delaye.
A tournament to be,
    Our forces for to trie,
Your presence likewyse there we craue,
    The playe to bewtifie.
This is all our request,
    This is that we doe craue :
Thus shall you doe a gratefull thing,
    If our requestes we haue.
The king foorthwith doth graunte,
    To their request in deede,
And biddeth them prepare them selues,
    To trie them selues with speede.
And thus their leaue they take,
    And homeward take their waye :
And euery oure they thinke a yeere,
    Before that come the daye.
The daie then being come,
    In glistring armour bright :
One might beholde on coursers tale,
    Full many a manly knight.

With speare and lannce in hande,
    I clad in plate of steele,
Naught wanting there, that might become
    A manly knight so wele.
But first of all it doth
    Behoue for to descriue,
The maner of the place, wherein
    These lusty knightes should striue.
Without the Palaise great
    Of Sylewma the king,
Appointed was the field, which was
    Made compasse like a rynge;
In ether ende whereof
    Was mightie pillers sette,
To which the parties ouercome,
    By forse of armes were fette,
And there the lawe was so,
    That then they must abide,
Untill such time that other were
    Toke of the other side.
And at one ende there was,
    Appointed for to stande,
Pandauola for whom this broile,
    They first had tooke in hande.
And all the companie
    Of Ladies of great prise,
Stoode there beside, within a place
    That was made there likewyse.
At thother end the king,
    Did sitte with all his traine:
And in the middes were Judges sette,
    Indifferent for them twayne.

Thus passed was the night,
 And daie began tappeare :
And trompettes blew in euery place,
 The sound eche wight might heare.
Then first in field there came,
 The king and tooke his place :
And afterward Pandauola,
 Came with her fathers grace.
And tooke her seate where as
 She, pointed was and then
The harrauldes foorth are sent to shew
 Unto these lusty men
How that the king was set,
 And wayted them to see,
Wherefore the trompettes are commaunde
 Foorthwith I bloun should be,
The Martiall seas that none
 Doe come within the rayle :
Then comes the knightes and to their king,
 Their bonettes they doe vayle.
But one among the rest,
 That Alfine had to name,
Is chalenger and must beginne
 To showe this royall game.
A comly knight he was,
 Pandauolas one deare :
And she to him did speake these woordes,
 Euen with a mery cheare,
My Lord (quod she) you see,
 That naught can here auayle,
But stripes with courage bold and stout,
 Your foes for to assaile.

And for your party I
    Am sure good knightes to haue :
And nought there wantes but courage bolde,
    From daunger you to saue.
And courage stoute I knowe,
    Doth you possesse and holde,
Wherby your foes neuer so stoute,
    May easy be controulde :
Go wende in haste therfore,
    Prepare your selfe to fight :
And for to honor you the more,
    We will giue you the sight.
To whom he aunswered,
    If that I so might craue :
Your gloue or sleue, then might I thinke,
    The victorie to haue.
Oh Lady deare therfore,
    Graunt this my small desier :
And then I thinke for my desert,
    I am repaide my hier.
This saide, her gloue she drawes
    From of her fingers small,
And giues to him and eke a ringe,
    She giueth there withall.
Who nowe doth ioye but he,
    Who els desires to fight
But he, then straight the defendant,
    Is come redy in sight.
Who Flaccus had to name,
    And after him doth ryde,
The brother of this Alfine looe,
    A man of litle pride.

When as before the kyng
 They came, they license craue,
That they the field as doth behoue,
 May full possesse and haue.
To trie their lusty steedes,
 Their hartes and harnes strong,
And eke to trie which of them all
 Should lay other along.
The king hath graunted them,
 The trompettes straight doth blowe,
With speare in reste these manly knightes
 Thone at thother goe.
He that in fielde then was,
 Must learne his head to saue,
Or els may chaunce appointed be,
 To lie full long in graue.
Their speares that well were whette,
 On harnise chrasshing crie,
And other some how swoordes will holde
 Upon their helmettes trie.
But Flaccus Alfine markes,
 And straight at him doth ronne,
But Alfine falling on his men,
 This worthy knight doth shonne.
But he with cruell hate
 Aloude in fielde doth crie :
Oh Alfine, Alfine, where art thou
 That pointed hast to trie?
With me by force of armes
 The gloue and ringe to haue,
Come forth I saie, both the and thine,
 Against me se thou saue.

When Alfine harde him crie
　　After this kynde of wise,
His harte for Ire began to quake,
　　His bloud began to rise.
And setting sporres to horse,
　　He brake his foes araye,
And smyteth Flaccus in the shelde,
　　That on the grounde he laye.
Then Alfine striues to drawe
　　This Flaccus lacking breth
Unto the piller there beside,
　　But Brennus rescueth
This Flaccus, and vpon
　　His brother Alfine falles,
With mortall dynte of sworde,
　　Aloude to him he calles.
O brother tourne thee nowe,
　　I doe thee here defie,
And if thou be a gentill knight,
　　Seeme not for to denie,
To meete me here in fielde,
　　Sithe that fortune hath so
Appointed vs, then both at once,
　　Togeather they doe go :
And rushing here and there,
　　How for to sytte they trie :
And thone at thother ranne so sore,
　　Their speares in peeces flie.
But by this time Flaccus,
　　His selfe was come vnto,
And armed now his foes in field,
　　Doth mortaly pursue.

But meting once againe,
    With Alfine in the field,
Of courage and of ire he doth
    Unto the soldiers yield,
Such bloes that none before,
    His swoorde durst once to stand,
And hauing made a way by force,
    He ioyneth hand to hand,
With Alfine and they both,
    At once to ground are caste :
And then they both agreed are,
    Retrete to blowe at laste.
The rest for to deferre,
    Untill the sunne began
For to descende possessing earst,
    His place Meredian.
The king vnto the court
    Anone doth take his waye,
Pointing an our or two I wis
    Within his place to staye.
And then for to retourne,
    The ende hereof to see,
Agreed they are and in the court
    To dinner gone they bee,
But lo Pandauola,
    Hath caught a mortall blowe,
Euen with a shafte that was shot foorth
    From out dame Cupides bowe.
Her harte was set on fire,
    And she began to burne,
The rosis in her ruddey cheekes,
    Began awaye to turne.

Pandauola.

Her senses doe denie,
  Their offices to doe :
Her breath doth fayle and men doe looke,
  But death for to insue.
She eates no meate at all,
  But downe on bed is laide :
But at the last her eies out brast
  With teares, and thus she saide.
Oh Gods that rule the skies,
  In whome my trust doth lie,
And thou O God whiche chiefest arte
  Aboue the golden skie.
And thou oh Lady deare,
  Oh Venus by thy name,
Vouchsaue my wofull crie to heare,
  Thy captiue doe not blame :
Though that alwayes I sought,
  Thy forse for to withstande :
Yet nowe I feele the mighty stroke
  Of Cupide thy sonnes hande.
Take pitie now therefore
  Sithe that a captiue I :
Can not preuaile, yet giue me salfe
  To helpe my misery.
And take me to thy grace,
  Sythe that my selfe I yelde,
And graunte to smyte him with that shafte
  Thou hittes me in the fielde.
Oh Cupide I the praie,
  This whyle the knightes are gone
Them selues to dine and rest their corps,
  But Alfines layd vpon

His bedde, and doth complaine,
    Of heuy woes and smart,
Which for Pandauola his dere,
    Doth vexe him at the harte.
The king hath heard hou that
    His daughter doth not well,
And sendeth for Phisitians
    In conning that excell,
To knowe the cause of griefe,
    That doth her so molest,
And eke of them to knowe what kinde
    Of medicines are beste.
Her health againe to gette,
    The messengers are gone,
Whome the Phisitions aunswere,
    That they will wayte vpon
His prudent grace, as fast
    As possible they may:
And with the messengers they all
    To court doe take their way.
The game is then deferde
    Untill an other tide :
And postes for Phisitians yet,
    About the countrey ryde.
In meane space she with paine
    Is vext, and greuous smart :
And cruell cares with great anoye,
    Tormente her gentill harte.
At last the Phisitions,
    Are come her grace to see :
But oh alas there is none can tell,
    To cure her maladie.

The king doth weepe and wayle,
    His daughter thus to see:
At last of them he doth inquire,
    If any helpe there be?
To whom they aunswere made,
    With heuy pending cheare:
That naught but death in her at all
    To their sight did appeare,
For liuely bloud was gone,
    Her poulses did not beate
Her limmes waxt starke for want of bloud,
    And of her liuely heate.
Her sensis all are dull,
    And death approched nye,
But this they said vnto the kyng,
    Their cunning they would trye:
Her health againe to get,
    Hir Ladies sitte her by,
And doth beholde how now and then,
    She tournes her heuy eye:
As though that Atropos
    Should ende her vitall race:
And eke that nature quite and cleane,
    Her worke should so deface.
The place with waylinges great,
    Is filde vnto the ende,
The Phisitions the company
    Out of the chamber sende.
Then they their medicines,
    Unto this lady giue:
The whiche opprest with cares beginnes
    Againe for to reliue.

The king is this meane while
    Within his chamber set,
To whom a messenger is come,
    And thus the king doth greete.
The Gods thee saue O king,
    Thy seruaunt still doth praye,
Alfine thy knight desireth thee,
    To graunt without delaye,
A phisition with speede
    His maladie to cure:
Or els oh king that he shall die,
    Thereof thou maiest be sure.
To whome the king thus spake,
    What greater griefe can be,
Unto a king then for to lose,
    So good a knight as he.
Ah fortune that doest beare,
    A double face in hood
Ne knowest thy frende ne fo, but doest
    Unto them equall good.
And him thou settest on hie,
    Euen him thou laiest alowe:
As to thy friend suche frendlines,
    Thou showest vnto thy foe.
With weping teares he saide,
    And then he foorth doth call
His Phisitions, and doth commaunde
    That they go with him all,
Unto Alfine his knight,
    With that Pandauola
Began to speake to one that stoode
    Her by, and thus did saye.

Pandauola.

And is it true I heare?
    Is Alfine sicke also?
She called then a Phisition,
    And bad him straight to goe
To him in all the haste,
    And tell him this that she
Is ready nowe for to departe,
    But lackes his companie.
To whome she might as mate,
    With him take paine in waye:
The Phisition did thinke that she
    These woordes of feare did saye.
And like a wise man then,
    He aunswered by and by,
Be you content ho lady deare,
    Thinke not that he will die
But if you will commaunde,
    I will your will obay,
And willingly will doe the thing
    That it shall please you saye.
And if that death should carpe
    My vitall thread atwaine,
Your secretes I will keepe still close
    Though that I should be slaine.
With that she drew her breath,
    But fainting nowe and then,
Ah God (quod she) Alfyne Alfyne,
    The truste of all men:
With that as men perceiue
    By little streames that ronne
The place, and cause that first their course
    Of water hath begonne:

Or as one might perceaue
    Where eaco doth resounde,
That in that place though touching skie
    It is their hollowe grounde.
So he when as he harde
    Her clamor and her crie,
Knewe well in ende that such streames would
    Their fountaine head discrie.
And as the man that hath
    By trauell and by payne
Founde out, where as of golde there is
    Some riche and costly vaine:
Doth digge and delue the more,
    The ende therof to finde:
So he a conning workeman doth
    Reuolue within his mynde
Whereof their wordes should ryse,
    He then perceiueth plaine
The cause of grief and seketh meanes
    Her woes for to restraine,
And then beginning newe
    His tale to her he said,
Oh Lady, of my woordes be not
    One whitte at all dismaid.
For I in ende I hope
    Will fynde you for to ease,
So that my seruice may not once
    Your gracious minde displease,
My frend (quod she againe)
    No whit shall me displease.
What that it be, saye what you will
    So it be for any ease,

And I the truth will tell,
 But see you trusty be
Of all the cause and where I am
 Thus vexte with malady,
To whom he aunswered,
 The Gods by whome eche thing,
Was made, quighte me confounde,
 And vnto ruine bring,
Euen at that instaunt, when
 Your secret I bewray :
And bring my soule where furis fell
 Shall it moleste I pray,
That I may with him gape
 That sekes the floudeds to drinke,
And for my plague from yarning lips
 The same againe may shrynke,
Or els that carping gripe,
 That eates the groing harte
Of Titius, in sonder may
 My faithles harte departe.
And if in hell there be
 One that surmountes the reste
For breache faith, then let it all
 Be iudged for my breste,
As due rewarde and eke,
 If naught in hell there be,
Sufficient, then mighty Joue
 Against me thus decree,
That I with those may haue
 My towme, whome Joue most hie,
Did fling to ground by thonder boltes
 That flew from forth the skie.

And now their toumes possesse
    Where as their corps doth boyle
With fier and brymstone scalding hote,
    Their corpes for to tourmoyle.
This saide he thus began,
    No Phisition (quoth he)
Can minister vnto your health,
    Unlesse that perfeitly
The cause of griefe he knowes,
    His labour is in vaine,
And lost is all his study, for
    To ease you of your payne.
Therfore of you I craue
    The principall to knowe
Of all your griefe, and then I will
    Some phisick therfore showe.
Your vryne doth declare
    That you in deede are ill,
A cause the same doth showe also,
    But not contentes my will.
For further cause I must
    Of you here vnderstande,
And then I may giue medicines
    To you, ende out of hande.
As when the gentill Buck
    Hath take a mortall blowe,
Doth runne about to seke some ease,
    So she about doth goe.
With sugered woordes to tell
    Howe she at harte was prest
With greuous panges, and afterwardes
    In order all rehearst.

What maladie she felt
 Within her selfe, but she
Did not declare what was the cause,
 Of her great maladie.
At last she cries Alfyne,
 And there her voyce doth staye.
The Phisition perceiued the cause,
 And thus began to saie :
Oh Lady mine take cheare,
 The cause of all I finde
To be the loue of Alfyne, which
 You so doe beare in mynde,
Therfore take you no thought,
 For I will woorke the waye
That shall you ease, therfore your self
 In quiet state doe staie.
I will to Alfyne go,
 Your minde to him to breake,
And if your graces will be so
 I beseeche you to speake.
With that she tournes and toste
 As though she straight will die,
And thus at last to him she spake
 With heuy dolefull eye.
O syr (quoth she) you knowe
 The cause of all my care,
For Alfyne low it is, that I
 This greuous sicknes bare.
And sithe you nowe doe knowe
 What is the cause of wo,
As for my frende I doe you take,
 My secretes doe not showe.

Content your selue a whyle
    Quoth he, and let me worke,
To Alfyn I will straight wayse wend
    To ease him of his hurte:
And afterward I will
    Againe come vnto you,
And as for me, oh Lady deare,
    As friend doe thinke me true,
Well then (quod she) syth that
    You must be gyde, of gayne
Take here this gold the which I giue
    For part reward of paine,
And sithe to him you go,
    To him this ringe doe giue,
And tell him that without his loue,
    I desire not to liue,
And if to doe him good,
    My death could ought auaile,
To haue the same without delay,
    Sure, sure, I would not faile.
This saide, the Phisition
    To Alfyne straight doth goe,
Who whē he came straight to the kinge
    This ioyfull newes doth showe.
That he did hope in time
    His daughter well to see,
Wherof the king exceading ioyse
    To Alfyne gone to be.
And telles the king that he
    His disease well doth see,
And will in time without all doughte
    Finde out a remedy

For him, and then he doth
　　Them all with harte desire
For to depart, the king and all
　　Doth that he doth require.
When all was foorth of dores,
　　He thus his tale began :
Right worthy Syr, I doe perceiue
　　That you are a sick man,
And sore torment with paine,
　　But be you of good cheare,
For from a frende of yours I haue
　　A message good to heare.
The worthy knight then said,
　　Good syer welcome to me,
And for her sake that hath you sent
　　Right welcome syr ye be.
With that the Phisition
　　Began on this same sorte,
The Gods confounde me, if my tonge
　　Shall forder false reporte.
Good syr (quoth he) eache thing
　　Obedient needes must be,
Unto the will of him that made
　　Those thinges, as thinges to see.
And as the hounde which is
　　His maisters great delight,
Unto the hare by nature made
　　Doth daily worke despight.
Or as the sylley doue
　　No greater ioye can finde
When as she in loue is macht
　　With one of selfe same kinde.

K

So mortall man though he
    Be kinge and lorde of all,
Yet in this point w' him eache beast
    Is to their Lorde equall,
And thus beside we see
    As Cupide shaft doth fall,
So oftentimes the feruent loue
    Departeth there withall.
And for because that loue
    Is cause of your vnreste,
Therfore I thinke the principall
    To shewe it were the best.
Oh sier said Alfyne then,
    My honor doth not craue
That though my loue so feruent be,
    That I the same should haue,
And if so be that I
    In byrth her grace might mate,
Yet doe I thinke that worthy I
    Were not for such a state
As she, but would be glad
    If I were king of kinges,
Euen for her sake, to leaue my state,
    And eke all royal thinges.
And if I might haue hope
    To craue I could not sease,
If I were sure my sute to gaine,
    No happier is the peace
That with a tound is made
    When warres indured hath
Ful long thē were with me, I swere
    Of knighthod by the faithe.

But out alas her witte
    And iudgement sage is so,
That of my sute when I beginne
    To faile, in ende I know.
Therfore maister Doctor,
    I you desire and praie,
In any case of her no more
    Unto me for to saye,
But let me in destres
    Now end my dolefull dayes
And let me die remediles
    Sithe I haue bene alwayes.
To whome the Doctor spake
    And bad him quiet be,
For so he saide that somewhat might
    Ease him of maladie.
And if he would a whyle
    His talke giue eare vnto,
He might haue ease, and Alfyne he.
    Is willing so to do.
With that he thus began,
    And saide, I maruell much
That for to shew such one as you
    For feare so sore should grutche,
To doe the thing wherby
    To you comes all the gaine,
And it were so, why should you shrinke
    To take so small a paine,
Sithe labour can not lose,
    Parhappes she does to trie
Your faithfulnesse, and other whyles,
    Perhappes she doth denie

To graunt you that you craue,
    Because she would that ye
Should not suppose in your conceit
    Her person light to be,
Therfore this would I wyshe,
    That you should courage take,
And in the walles with manly hart
    Should seeke a breache to make
For once the citie which
    Can scarse there defence make,
Doth giue vnto the conquerer
    A hope it for to take,
And where they willing are,
    No treate ought to be:
The Sea to ebbe and flowe so oft
    Is not constrainde we see,
Yet doth it so therfore
    Of courage take some part,
And do assaie yet once againe
    To breake her flinty hart.
For as the litle droppes
    That oft fall from on hie,
The hardest stone with falling on,
    Both thorowe weare and trie,
So she with praiers fayre,
    May be obtainde I knowe,
Therfore good syr, and if you please
    my counsell do folowe.
To whom Alfyne answerd,
    Good syr as you do saye,
I doe intende the chaunce to proue
    Without any delaye.

And for your great good will,
    I giue you thankes certaine,
And if it lie in me one daye
    I will rewarde your paine.
And sitting then vpright
    Within his bed, he saide,
That for to prosecute his mynde,
    He would not be afraide.
And geuing thankes as then
    The Phisicion vnto,
He purposeth as he hath saide,
    Forth with end so to doe,
The Phisition perceiued
    That then he might haue time
To shewe his mynde, and thus he said,
    If not committing crime,
I might my message showe,
    So bould then I would be
To speake in few, to whome ye knight
    Did aunswere courtously
Saie on, oh Doctour myld
    With willing harte certaine
We will you heare, if to declare
    That you will take the paine.
Then with a mery cheare,
    On this wyse he did say :
I haue (quoth he) before I came
    Haue ben that part of daie.
With faire Pandauola
    The daughter of the king,
Which vnto me before I came
    Hether, gaue me this ring

With this in message to
    Declare vnto your grace,
That you would be of a good cheare,
    She prayes in any case :
And as a token of
    Her faith she this hath sent,
To you protesting that she hath
    As yet no other ment,
Ne neuer tendes to doe
    While life she doth possesse,
And so that you will like protest
    She verely doth gesse,
As when a man hath lost
    Some Juell riche of pryse,
With heuy hart and painfull mind
    He ginneth for to ryse,
And so the Juell great
    He seketh round about,
And neuer scaseth till that he
    The Juell hath founde out.
And when that he hath founde
    The same, vp to the skeyse
He liftes his handes, the Joyse whereof
    Makes streames runne downe his eyes,
So plaieth Alfine nowe,
    With teares he blotes his face,
And stretching out his heuy armes,
    The Doctor doth imbrace.
And kissing twyse the ringe,
    Upon her name doth call,
And eke beholde he feles him selfe
    Reliued therewithall.

Pandauola.

And willing with his harte
    The equall will to be
Equaly macht, sithe her goodwill
    To his will so did gree.
And douting nothing nowe,
    He thinkes him well at ease,
Minding the Doctor for his paynes
    With golde and fee to please.
Then doth the Doctor saie,
    That he would also wende
Unto Pandauola, and askes
    If ought that he would sende
As token vnto her,
    To whiche he doth consent,
And vnto her a chaine with ring
    Withall his hart hath sent.
The Doctor goes his waes,
    Well rewarded for paine :
And wished that he were daily
    So set a woorke againe,
Who nowe doth Alfyne loue,
    But Pandauola bright,
Who is to him coequall mate
    Who ioyeth nowe in light.
What payne doth Alfyne feele,
    Ne all is fled away,
He of his griefe is reliued,
    To ryse he doth assaie :
And taking courage bolde,
    To walke he doth assaie :
And feling not him selfe at ease,
    Againe on bed he laye

With ioyfull cheare I wis
    He sate as any wight,
He taketh then his pen in hande,
    And thus began to wrighte.
And seking for to feede
    His flinging fancies so,
Purposith in some pretty songe
    His Ladies praise to showe.
And thus he doth beginne,
    Desiring helpe and ayde
Of Musis nyne, and thus at last
    With pleasaunt voyce he saies.

The song made by the Translator.

You Musies nyne that sisters be,
Helpe now my dolefull voyce to singe,
The prayse of her whose comly gle
Surmounteth nowe eche vitall thing,
    The same whiche so Appelles sought,
    At once in her is trimly wrought.

Appelles O thou happy man,
Whose daies to short were for to see
The floure that of dame nature came,
So faire, so trimme, and eke so free,
    Whose shape doth passe all in the time,
    Much more then snow doth passe the slime.

If thou hadst liued and sene the wight
Which now doth liue in Turky lande,

As one deuoyde of life and sight,
Before her grace thou wouldest stande,
    Such wōdring would haue toke the there
    Her worthy shape in minde to beare.

Pigmalion for all his arte,
So faire a peece once could not graue,
Nor if they both should take a part,
By conning so their fames to saue
    Yet should they eare and not come nere
    My Ladies grace that royall peare.

To whome I wishe eternall ioye,
With healthfull state and happy dayes,
And eke to passe without anoye,
These euill times and perilous seas,
    And I my selfe what euer betide,
    With her in shippe on them may ryde.
        Finis.

This done he layes him downe
    Some rest on bed to take,
And afterward within an houre,
    He ginneth for to wake.
The Phisition is come
    Pandauola to see,
But lo, the king and all his Lordes
    Within her chamber be,
To whome the Doctor ginnes
    To drawe him selfe vnto,
And coming in, Pandauola
    He asketh howe she doe.

To whome she aunsweres then,
    The better him to see:
And of the same she asked then
    Wheare he so long hath bee.
He aunswered straightwaye,
    He was for to prouide
For certain things that nedes he must
    For her haue in that tide,
But then she ginnes to saye
    The weather hote to bee,
The Phisition that her intent
    Did well perceiue and see.
And did the Lordes desire,
    A while them selues to keepe
Abroade in chamber there beside,
    To see if she could slepe.
The king then doth departe
    And all the Lordes are gone
According to their duties,
    The king to wayte vpon.
When all was foorth of doores,
    The Phisition doth tell
The order of his being there,
    And howe eche thing befell.
And vnto her doth giue
    The tokens that were sent
By him to her, and afterwards
    He showes the whole intent
Of Alfynes sicknes then,
    She him desires againe,
That early on the morowe he
    To come will take the payne,

To her, and then he shall
    Knowe more of her intent.
To whose requeste, the Phisition
    Doth thorowly consent,
And then his leaue doth take
    Till time of her request :
And she her selfe doth laie her down,
    And there doth take her rest.
The sunne from height of heauen
    Into the sea doth fall,
And rūning through the flashing flods
    Ascendeth there withall:
And being weary then
    Of his iourney God wote,
He putteth out the monstrous hores
    From out the chariot.
And comming now where as
    Aurora hell her see,
To make the night somewhat longer,
    They both agreed be :
At length Aurora doth
    The bed of Titan flye,
And ginnes to shewe her cristall face
    Throughout the syluer skie.
And Phebus he him selfe
    His goulden head doth showe :
Lifting him selfe from out of the waues
    Our orisont belowe.
And with his fyrie chaire
    Is flowne into the skie
An houre long, the Phisition
    Perceiueth by and by,

That time it is to go,
 And foorth straightwaies he went
Unto Pandauola, and she
 Unto his house hath sent,
But at the last he comes
 And vnto her doth go,
Desiring that he may foorthwith
 Her graces intent knowe.
To whome she straight did saye,
 That he forthwith must beare
A letter vnto Alfyne, whiche
 You after all shall heare.

¶ **The Letter of Pandauola to her louer Alfyne.**

As to the heuy wight
 Tormented sore with paine,
All thinges are ioyfull that doth seeke
 His tormentes to restraine.
So it is vnto me
 O Alfyne, this to heare,
That life with health y^u dost possesse
 That art to me so deare.
Which all the gods I praye
 For euer to maintayne,
And good successe in all assaies,
 I wishe to the certaine
The cause why that to you
 My letters I indighte
Is this, because you may suer thinke
 My promyse to be right,

Pandauola.

And that the Doctor hath
    Unto your goodnes tolde,
To be the thing which I doe meane
    Therof you may be bolde.
And for your sicknes lo
    I rew, this thing is plaine,
But yet suppose that much more ill
    Then you, I was againe.
As well my father could
    Declare, and Doctor to,
Who as you know for me in deede
    Hath had somewhat to doe.
And sithe the Gods doe so
    Graunt our requestes to be:
This is the cause that you foorthwith
    Come hether me to see,
And thereof myne intent,
    The ende shall you perceiue:
And thus because of leasure I
    You to your selue do leue.
Fare well therfore my knight,
    Good health the Gods the sende:
And thus from the kings manor place
    My minde and wryght I ende:
Fare well oh Juell deare,
    Fare well my owne delight:
Fare well also of knighthoode thou
    The chiefe and truest knight.

This letter she doth geue
    The Phisition vnto,

And bad him that in all the haste
    He should his labour doe
The same in haste to beare,
    Alfyne to vnderstande :
And afterwardes to bring to her
    An aunswere out of hande.
The Phisition is gone
    Alfyne her knight vnto,
According to her graces wyll,
    The message for to do.
The meane spase she from out
    Her wery bed doth ryse,
And deckes her selfe in trimme aray
    After her wonted gyse.
And walking up and downe
    Within her chamber, she
Beginneth in her minde to roull
    Of him the great bewty,
And doth his state compare
    With Paris comly gle :
And yet within her selfe she saies,
    Much fairer loe is he
Then Narsissus so faire,
    Or mystus lo is he :
And by and by, she thinkes fairer
    He is if there may be,
Fairer then Narsissus
    Or Mystus that haue bene
The fairest and the comliest wightes,
    That euer earst were seene.
At last her father comes
    To see howe that she doe,

Pandauola.

With many a Lorde and lusty knight
    That come her grace vnto.
Her father, he doth aske,
    If she her helth possesse:
To whome she aunsweres by and by,
    For all his great richesse,
She would not feell suche paine,
    As she not past eight daies
Did feele ago, but to the Gods
    She gaue immortall prayse.
Her father then doth ioye,
    And doth declare how that
The noble knight Alfyne, is nowe
    Recouered of late
Of his disease, and doth
    Sit up, and walkes about,
And saith that Alfyne would lyue,
    Therof he had no doubte.
Wherto she saies Amen,
    Though yet were there vnknowne
The fame then of her health abroade,
    About the cities blowne.
As sone as once the health
    Of her the people knowe,
On aulters of the Goddes they all
    Their offringes bestowe.
And bond fyers they doe make
    For ioye of this good chance:
In euery streate they mery make,
    They singe, they leape, and daunce.
And as the wight that is
    From death deliuered late,

So ioyeth she and father eke,
　　Oh thryse and happy fate.
They all this daie therfore
　　For holy doe suppose,
And then their myndes to eleuate
　　The hearmony they chose.
The Phisition approched is
　　Syr Alfynes house vnto,
And vnto him his message then
　　He ginneth for to doe.
And then declares that she
　　His comming would abide
Within the court of Sylluma :
　　Then takes he him aside,
And vnto him doth giue
　　The letter that he bare,
Desyring lo an aunswere straight,
　　For he to court would fare.
To whome Alfyne doth tell,
　　That he straightway would frame
An aunswere and he should forthwith
　　To her go beare the same.
Then to his closet he
　　Doth go, and penne doth take,
And on this wyse the aunswere he
　　Therof to her doth make.

¶ The aunswere to the letter of Pandauola.

The Gods whom we accompt
    As iust and blest to be,
Preserue thy life oh Lady deare
    The chiefest ioye to me,
As to a captiue naught,
    Is ioye but libertie.
Euen so likewyse, there nothing is
    More ioyfull vnto me,
Then thus by your goodnes
    Although a captiue I,
And as it were one rescued nowe,
    Once iudged for to die:
And as for demyng lo,
    Unworthy I me fynde
The least good gift of your good grace
    That you to me haue syn.
I thinke those famous men
    That liued haue eare this,
Could not deeme other, but that ye
    Are chiefest cause of blisse.
Or els I deeme that they
    Would neuer vndertake
Suche perilles, as full often they
    You to obtaine, doe make.
Achilles champion stoute,
    What tyme in Troye he sawe
Polyxena, he did desire
    To be the sonne in lawe

Of Pyramus, that king
    Of Troye of renowne,
Syr Parys eke the worthiest knight,
    That was in Illyon towne.
His brother Hector saue
    To Grece his passage tooke :
His Aunt the faire Exiona,
    Within their courtes to looke.
But being taken with
    The fyry cleuing darte,
Of Helena the Queene, whose syght
    Did strike him to the harte.
That maugre all their heades,
    To shippe this dame he bare :
And hoisyng vp his mery sailes,
    To Troye began to fare.
So if that Cupide durste
    These champions stoute assayle,
What boutyd them him to resiste,
    When naught they could preuayle.
To striue against the streame,
    Is labour lost in vayne :
The more he striues, the more increase
    His dolour and his payne.
The noble Pyramus,
    Him selfe for Tysbe slew,
Because he thought that he was cause
    Of breaking faith so trewe.
Thus if these did as heare,
    Full oft we haue heard saye :
Then maruell not oh Lady dear,
    Why that as quighte awaye,

My senses all were fled.
 Sythe you doe passe them all,
Then all the reste, it doth behoue
 That I should lower fall.
And that you haue your health,
 I ioye therof to heare,
The which I praie the Gods to holde
 Full many daies and yeare.
If life or death you should
 Commaunde, I would obey:
Be life or death, or what thing els,
 If that it please you say.
And whyle that life this corps
 Should full inioye and haue:
I am the knight that shall performe
 What thing your grace shall craue.
And here I bynd me to
 Your grace, your man to be
At all assaye without delay
 To doe that pleaseth ye,
Thus here I take my leue,
 Desiring Gods to sende
The wyshed ioyes that we desire,
 Our griefes to make an ende.

This done, the letter he
 Unto the Doctor bringes,
Desiring that the Doctor would
 Before all other thinges,
Deliuer that his deede
 Unto her graces hande.

The Phisition doth straight departe,
    He will no lenger stande
With him to talke, but goes
    Awaye from him apace,
And then within a whyle he is
    Ariued in the place
Of Syluma the king,
    And forward straight doth goe
Unto the faire Pandauola,
    His message for to showe.
And coming in where as
    The Lordes a daunsing be,
He makes a signe, the which thing lo,
    Perceiued soone had she:
And from her place doth ryse,
    Taking him by the hande,
Desiring him, that she might there
    His message vnderstande.
The letter foorth he drawes
    And giues it her vnto,
And saith that Alfyne is preste
    Her bidding for to doe.
With that he goes awaye,
    And saieth then that he,
At one time or an other, will
    Returne her grace to see.
And now the pleasaunt dewe
    Of heauen beginnes to fall
And eache man loe, his reste to take
    Perswadeth there withall.
The syluer skye of hew
    The darkesome shades of night

Doth couer cleane the sunne and daye
    Descended out of sight,
And glistring starres do decke
    The pole of heauen so hie,
And nature ginnes her rest to craue
    With heuy pensiue eye.
Thus-then Pandauola
    Her rest to take doth go,
And wisheth that Alfyne her knight
    Weare there so none might knowe.
She roules, she tournes, she tosse,
    With dreaming often, to
One while she thinketh on their loue
    An other while to doe.
Some prety feate so that
    They their desire may haue,
An other whyle she counteth on
    Her honor for to saue.
Thus on this wyse she spendes,
    And driues the night awaye,
Untill such tyme as Phebus did
    His banner foorth displaye,
With clearsome light aboue,
    Our Horisonte in east.
And with his praunsing horse drewe foorth
    His chaire into the weste.
Then Alfyne comes vnto
    The court of Sylewma,
And enters into the chamber
    Of fayre Pandauola,
Who when she sawe, then straight
    With stretched paulmes awid

She giues the Gods most harty thankes,
    That so for her prouide.
And then about his necke
    Her gentill armes she caste,
With kissing swete, a thousand foulde
    She welcomes him at last.
And there he doth abide
    With her his Lady bright,
His life, his health, his ioye, his trust,
    And eke his hartes delight.
Unto the king they go,
    And he in chamber is,
Who for to welcome Alfyne, doth
    With frendly hart him kisse:
And eke Pandauola:
    Whose kisses were more swete
Then fathers were, Alfyne her knight
    Againe with kisse doth grete.
Then downe to meate they go,
    For dinner drewe full nie, ioyfull
So they consumde that ioyfull daie
    With pleasaunt hermony.
But Alfyne and the mayde,
    (The dinner being done)
Unto their chamber richely decte,
    To talke are thether gone.
Thus haue they past the daye,
    And Alfyne sees that night
Is come, for to departe as then,
    He sheweth that it is right.
But lo Pandauola,
    This parting ill doth take,

Pandauola.

And doth desire him that he will
    As then his soiorne y make.
But he desiring lo
    Paredon, doth her denie,
(For those his wordes) and sayeth more,
    Her father he will trie,
As concerning the thing
    That they haue greede upon,
They take their leaue and Alfine he
    Unto his place is gone,
The gliding starres perswades
    Eche thing vnto his reste
And darkesome shades the pole of heauen
    Do compas to the west,
And pleasaunt sleape doth creepe
    By stealth into their eies,
In meane while the golden pole
    Of heauen about earth flies,
And gilding starres doe fall,
    Then shone Aurora cleare,
And Phebus bright with glistring beames,
    Unto vs he doth appeare.
Then Alfyne doth arise,
    And to the king doth go,
In purpose of the king the ende
    Of his intente to knowe,
Who when he comes he gretes
    The king likewyse againe,
Doth welcome him and geues him thankes,
    That he would take the paine
As to come him to see,
    With that a knight full faire

Came to the king and said, that he
    For this cause did repaire,
To tell vnto his grace
    Some newes, wherby he might
Some helpe forsee, for him and his,
    As due it was be tright.
To whom the king commaund,
    That he without all shame
Should tell his tale, and said that he
    Therfore should haue no blame.
The knight then thus begonne,
    Oh king, the Christian knightes
Inuade thy lande, and daily yet
    They worke vs more despights.
The Spasyardes doe possesse
    Almost thy countrey rounde,
And Hungarians doe like wise
    Thy people quight confounde,
Helpe therefore nowe O king
    With spede we thee doe praye,
Or els they quighte will ouerronne
    This land without delaye.
For now from this same place
    They be but iourneyes small.
Helpe nowe oh king, sith we as nowe
    For helpe to thee doe call.
This saide, the king straght way
    Doth for his counsell call,
The which doe come, and then they do
    Enter the counsell hall.
When they were set, Alfyne
    Doth foorth his matter breake,

But lo, the king doth him commaunde
    No woorde therof to speake.
And thus he saide, syr knyght,
    You knowe the royall rase
Of Pandauola, and she ought
    In suche a kinde of case
For to be matcht with one
    Whose birth is somewhat like :
Therfore syr Alfyne wey this well,
    And yours is farre to seke.
Therfore your selfe content,
    For I doe tell you plaine,
She shall not yet be maried,
    Yet muse I more againe,
Sithe that you being but
    A Duke of lynage poore,
Should seme to craue in mariage
    So ryche and fayre a flowre.
When as syr Flaccus, who
    Is next me in this lande,
Will not presume her for to craue :
    Therfore thus it shall stande,
That when a time shall come
    Better we will prouide
For her then so, therfore (quoth he)
    Set this your talke aside.
And then he doth declare
    The fine of this intent,
As concerning the warres in hand,
    And this was their iudgement :
That Syluma him selfe,
    An army great should make,

And shall descende in battell and
    Should Alfyne with him take.
So thus they haue agreed,
    And there the counsell brake,
And Alfyne he doth from the king
    His iourney forthwith take
Unto the chamber of
    The daughter of the king,
And vnto her recounteth all
    Of euery kinde of thyng
That hath bene saide or done,
    Within the chamber lo.
She vnderstandeth euery white,
    Alfyne then thence doth go
With heuy cheare and then
    Pandauola doth wayle,
And afterwards her maydes she calles
    With them for to counsaile
Wherof one Palyne,
    Suche one as she may truste
She calles to her, and so her mynde
    At last she hath discuste
From point to point, and then
    For counsell she doth craue,
To whome Palyne aunswered,
    'This sorte (quoth she) I haue
Oh noble Lady deare,
    Byne trusted nowe ear this
About suche cures, wherfore I hope
    That nowe I shall not misse,
But will you ease certaine,
    Of good chere therefore be,

And for a tyme let fortune woorke,
　　The ende your grace shall see
To be profitable,
　　When he at warres hath bene.
We can not tell but happely
　　May chaunce some kinde of thing,
Or iust deserte of his
　　Upon our enemies tride,
That may vnto this euill chaunce
　　Some better waye prouide.
Therfore my counsell is,
　　That he with willing mynde
Shall doe the thing what that it be
　　To him that is a synde.
Therby full soone he may
　　Obtaine your fathers grace
To be his friende, more faithfull then
　　He nowe is in this case.
And when some noble feate
　　He shall haue complishd so,
A daily friende the king will be
　　To him, this well you knowe.
Then may he seme to craue,
　　And also iustly may
You, to obtaine be the bolder
　　Your father for to praye.
Therfore my counsell is,
　　That you with spede and might
Shall him perswade for to be stoute
　　According vnto right,
Your fathers foes to quell
　　And true subiect to be,

Regarding not your fathers woordes,
    But his faith and dutie.
The daye is come, and they
    Their armies great haue chose,
And Alfyne with his armie, he
    Unto the Palayse goes
Of Syluma the king,
    And mousters him before
With colour pale and angry harte,
    Much like vnto a Bore.
He castes his holowe eyes
    Now here, now there about,
With frothing lips his dedly thoughtes
    With colour black flye out.
The king the mouster sees,
    For Alfyne he doth sende,
And doth cōmaunde that he forthwith
    Unto the fielde do wende,
The Christians they prepare
    Defence with spede to make,
And Alfyne he beginnes forthwith
    Thether his waye to take.
The armie of the king
    Is ready in this tide,
The which to Flaccus he committes
    Unto the fielde to guyde,
But yet before they go,
    Alfyne his leaue doth take
Of Pandauola bright and shene,
    His loue, his deare, his mate,
To whome she on this sorte
    Began her tale to tell,

(Quoth she) O Alfyne this my deare,
    You know full sure and well,
That when by prowes great
    Some thing you shall achiefe,
Then bouldly may you aske i wys
    Me for to be your wife.
Therfore my counsell is
    All rancor layde asyde,
That you my fathers heastes to doe
    With spede shall runne and ryde.
Neither that you should take
    Suche griefe, of that he saide,
Be of good chere, fortune hath now
    Her worste at first displayde.
Then rounde about his necke
    Her gentell armes she caste
With teares she brwes her gētil chekes
    And takes her leue at last.
Now Alfyne and the king
    Unto the army goes,
The king the conduct of the warre
    Nowe vnto Alfyne shoes,
And him exhortes to striue
    Victorie to obtaine,
And then he sayes in end he shall
    Him well rewarde for paine
This wordes to Alfyne gaue
    Some hope his praye to wynne,
For ioye whereof his heauy harte
    Reioyseth now within.
The Sunne hath entryd now
    The waues that shine so bright

And Luna spreades her beames abroade,
    Now procheth on the night.
The king and Alfyne they
    Unto the campe are come,
Before the waues haue coucred
    The golden shining Sunne.
The Souldiers busy be
    Their campe to fortifie,
Some go to reste, the glistring starres
    Fulfilling all the skie.
The night is gone and all,
    The armie plaine Apeares:
Then all the Christians foorthwith
    Their standardes tall vpreares.
The Turke is nothing slowe
    The Christians to mete,
With chrayshing swoordes, the other they
    With lusty bloes do grete
Upon the name of Christe
    Full loude the Christians call,
The Turkes vnto their Mahomet
    With prayer ginnes to fall.
The Turkes haue lost that daye,
    Of men a nomber great,
But yet for that they do not seace,
    The Christians heads to beate.
The gonstones through the ayre
    With dolefull voyce doe crie,
And fautall arrowes through the cloud
    Into eche armie flie.
And here in fleshe it lightes,
    And geues a deadly wounde:

And in an other parte there is
    A thousand brought to grounde.
The battaile standes in doubt,
    At last the Christians, they
Haue wonne the fielde, the Turkes apase
    From thence doe flie awaye.
Thus pleased God to graunte
    The victorie as then
By force so gotte, end for to fall
    Unto the Christen men.
The night departed hath
    The armies for that tide,
And misty cloudes eche others campe
    Asunder doth deuide.
When that the daie was come,
    And Phebus shone full bright,
The Turke beginnes to incourage
    His souldiers for to fight.
And thus to them he saies
    With cruell angry cheare:
As by the wordes that he did speake,
    May very well appeare.
Oh catiues quight undone,
    You traytours to your king:
You enemies to Mahomet,
    What got you by flying.
This other daie nowe paste
    Before your enemies hande,
And for your cowardnes durst not
    Before their swordes to stande.
Why should not they possesse
    That earst our fathers wanne,

And why, haue they not quite destroide
    Of vs both childe and man ?
What could their force withstande
    When you began to flie.
Thinke you that stones for our quarel
    With them would seme to trie.
The honour of our name,
    Through you is gone and lost
The fame of oure olde aunceters
    Is topsy touruy toste
By Mahomete (quoth he)
    Nothing doth make me muse,
That then to spoyle our tentes also,
    The Christians did refuse,
But that I thinke some god
    Our ruen did porpende
And therfore would not suffer them
    Their fury to extende.
With that he paused awhyle,
    His souldiers full bould
Did giue a showte as heauē and earth
    As then together would
The whiche he marked well,
    My thinkes (quoth he) I see
The hartes and willes of men which woulde
    Not so accompted be,
But that they would reuenge
    Their shame committed so
They crie, desiring of the king
    That they to fielde may go,
And then he should perceiue
    Their hartes and willes the more,

How they would reuenge the iniurie
    Done so the daie before.
Then saide the king, sithe that
    Amendes you tende to make,
I am content forthwith the fielde
    Against our foes to take.
Then to the fielde he goes
    With all his Turkishe trayne:
The Christians forthwith also
    Descende vnto the playne,
The battaile then beginnes
    Full fiers on ether side.
The Christians striue the bodies of
    The Turkes for to deuide.
But Alfyne he doth so
    With sworde the Christians checke,
That some he makes lower to be
    By head and eke the necke.
Then when the Christian kynges
    On that sorte so beholde.
Euen with a winge of horsemen they
    Syr Alfyne doe infolde.
There they him prisoner take
    And led him to their tent,
The Turkes ye while to win the felde
    Or els to die are bent.
Thus standes it all the daye
    The Christians are full faine
For to retire they hauing so
    Almost their armie slaine.
Then Syleuma the king
    Unto their tentes doth go,

And by and by, a messenger
 Comes and to him doth showe,
Howe that the noble Duke
 Syr Alfyne him doth praye,
In all the haste that eare he came,
 His raunsome he will paye,
And also this beside,
 The Christians require
To haue a peace confirmde of him,
 For the space of three yeare.
When nues did come to him
 That Alfyne did abide
With the Christians as prysoner,
 He calles his Lordes asyde.
And asked them what they
 Would counsell him to doe:
To whom syr Flaccus answered
 That sithe it came so to
Passe, as he looked for,
 He thought it best, that he
Should as a prisoner with those
 Of Christendome still be,
For he that would your grace
 To them haue deliuere,
In my iudgement he ought not now
 So to be raunsomed.
But for the peace he saide,
 He thought it good to be
Concluded vpon for so small time,
 As farre as he could see.
And lastly ye shall fynde
 Full well (quoth he) I knowe,

Pandauola.

That he for a litle or naught
    Againe shall be let go.
That I haue saide (quoth he)
    I will proue it to ende,
Therfore (quoth he) oh king you may
    If please you answere sende
Unto the Christians, that
    Sithe that they peace doe craue,
You are content that for three yeares,
    A peace that they shall haue.
The counsell all doe like
    This Flaccus counsell so
That thereupon they doe agree
    Before the truthe they knowe.
The messenger they call
    His message to receiue :
Who hath the peace graunted to him,
    And so they take their leaue.
But as for Alfyne, he
    Should not his raunsome haue,
And with this floute he bad that they
    That iuell riche should saue.
The messenger is gone
    The Christen kinges vnto :
When he was come, he thus at last
    His message gan to doe.
The kinges and Lordes once set,
    His tale he thus began :
(Quoth he) I haue most royall Lordes
    As farre forth as I can
Requested of the king
    A peace for three yeares space,

The whiche he hath graunted to vs,
    But yet thus saith his grace,
That as for Alfyne he
    Sall still your prisoner be.
And this condicion that
    You all his lande must leaue
Within eight monethes vpon this same
    Your peace ye must receiue :
This message being done,
    They straight them sport and playe
With ioye and myrth, and some of them
    To Alfyne take their waye,
Who mourning ginnes to wayle,
    And thus at last he saide.
And hath my Lege denied me
    My raunsome to be payde,
I some time was a Prince,
    But now a captiue vile,
A slaue, a drudge, a beaste, no man,
    But drouen to exile.
Oh would (quoth he) to God
    My Lady fayre and bright,
Did knowe my case how my true hart
    Hath brought me this despight.
Oh Sylewma (quoth he)
    Haue I so trusty bene
To thee and thine, and yet by me
    Thou settest not a pinne.
These Christian knightes I know,
    Would haue sone raunsomed me
If theirs I were and had bene tooke
    Of thee mine enemy.

Muche gentlier be these knightes
    Unto me, I doe fynde,
Then thou oh Tyraunt fierse and fell
    Unto me in this kinde,
Wherfore I praie the Goddes
    Some good lucke then to sende.
That once they may of thee and me,
    Both see some euill ende :
Fare well my Lady deare
    Pandauola the fayre,
That art to Sylewma the king,
    His daughter and his ayre :
Fare well I saye, for now
    Thou shalt some other haue.
And Flaccus now myne enemy,
    May boldly seeme to craue
Thee of thy father now,
    I can not him withholde,
For lo, the king doth not esteme
    Me worth a strawe of golde.
Oh knightes, alfyne beholde
    For Ladies bright and shene
That wonted was with you to iuste
    With speres both sharpe and kend
Lo, now in chaines he lies
    Fast bounde, both foote and hande :
Oh Pandauola that for thee
    With Flaccus oft did stande.
But thus why doe I wayle,
    Come death and ende my dayes,
Sythe that vyle wretche I can not be
    Relieued, by no wayse.

But yet would God my harte
    She might inioye and haue
Before my corps intumyld were
    Or put into the graue.
This saide, he wepes and wayles,
    And so his talke did ende,
The whiche the Christian kinges haue heard
    And for him straight did sende.
The king of Spaine doth rewe,
    The king of Hungary
Doth also wepe to heare how he
    Lamentes his destenie,
At last Alfyno is come
    Before them, and they all
Of him inquier what he would doe,
    If so it might befall,
That if so be at libertie
    As then that he should wende,
Wherto he aunswered, that this
    As then he did intende
That is, he neuer would
    Take sworde in hand to fight
Against the Christians, but that he
    With all his power and might
Would them defende he saide.
    Wheron they doe agree,
That without any raunsome he
    Forthwith shall losid be
To go where that he please,
    Or els there to abide.
They gaue him eke a lusty steade
    To Uardam for to ryde.

Where after foure monethes space
    Unto the court he came
Of Syleuma which then was held
    Within the towne Uardam,
But when he would haue prochte
    Syleumase court vnto,
He was forbode by the porter
    So on that sorte to doe.
Wherfore he doth departe
    Unto his mansion place,
To whome a messenger doth come
    From old Syleumas grace.
With this message in hande,
    That he his house should holde
Untill he knewe farther, and not
    Once for to be so bolde
As once abrode to go
    From that his house certaine.
The messenger doth then departe
    Unto the king againe,
And Alfyne he this while
    As the rewarde of payne,
Unto the Christian Kinges hath sent
    Twelue cartes lodid with graine,
Which thing when Flaccus knew,
    He forward straight doth goe
To Syluma the king, and he
    Therof his grace doth showe.
Then Syleuma doth sende
    His messenger to areste
Syr Alfyne, of such treason as
    Before it is exprest.

The messenger hath done
    He was commaunded to do,
The officers syr Alfync bringes
    King Syleuma vnto.
Who when he comes, then straight
    The king to iudgement goes,
And Flaccus he doth enter in
    And the accusement showes,
Whiche Alfyne doth denie:
    But Flaccus doth desire
According to the lawe of armes,
    To trie it with his speare.
Wherto the king doth graunt,
    The our of fight is set:
And now the Lordes and Ladies do
    About their places get,
The houre being come,
    The king with all his trayne,
Are come and take their place
    In middest vpon the playne.
Then Flaccus commeth in,
    The king once being set,
And then the Harrauldes are cōmaūde
    Alfyne to fielde to fette:
Pandauola she sittes
    Hard by her fathers side,
The Harauldes are come, and Alfyne
    Into the fielde doth ryde
To Syluma the king:
    Flaccus doth come also,
And there the accusation
    Againe Flaccus doth showe,

For proufe wherof he is
    Contented for to trie
The combate, but Alfyne
    Syr Flaccus wordes deny,
And saieth that he will
    According vnto right,
Proue y' he hath spoke al these wordes
    Of falshod and despight.
The Harraulde then beginne
    Therof to make the crie,
With speare in hand like lusty knights
    They runne immediatly,
When speares were broke, they then
    Vnto their swordes them take
And laiyng on such lode, they teache
    A medicine for head ake.
Suche bloues Alfyne doth deale
    As he that had bene there
Would not haue thought, that Flaccus shold
    So many bloues haue beare.
But lo as thinges are set
    So oftentimes they fall,
Their swordes are broke, and they
    For other swordes doe call,
The which when that they haue,
    With courage bould and stoute,
The manly knightes vnequall macht,
    Doe lay them rounde about,
But Flaccus to Alfyne
    Hath such a blowe him lent,
That maugre all his force, to grounde
    He Alfyne downe hath sent:

P

But Alfine being quicke,
    He getteth vp againe,
And such a blowe Flaccus he lent,
    That Flaccus he hath slaine.
Which when the king behelde
    With heauy dolefull cheare,
He parted thence, much like a man
    Full mad he did appeare.
Then Alfyne did commaunde
    His body to be drawne
Throughout the citie round about
    According to the lawe.
Then Alfyne to the court
    Of Syleuma doth come,
And Pandauola in her armes
    Her Alfyne hath up num
And kisseth him full ofte,
    With geuing thankes certaine
Unto her God, that so Alfyne
    His enemy hath slaine.
The king with ier possest,
    No lenger can abyde,
But drawes his fatall blade, and it
    In Alfynes throte doth hyde.
Whiche when his daughter sawe
    That murdring cruell dede,
She tooke him vp, and euen then
    She to her father yede,
Desiring him that she,
    For all his raging spytes
Might geue the body of buriyng,
    The solome kinde of rightes.

To which thing he doth graunte,
    But saies, she shall not be
At the buriall, but she should stande
    Where as she might it see.
So straight a fyer great
    Under the toure was made
Where she did stande, and Alfyne
    Into the fyer was layde.
When she behelde this corps,
    Alfyne she loude doth call,
And sodainly from of the toure
    She flong her selfe withall,
Disdaining lo that so
    Her father did presume.
And there in fyer two louers
    Did quight and cleane consume.
The Ladies they runne in
    Her father for to tell
Who when he harde of his daughter
    What mischiefe had befell :
Upon his fatall sworde,
    He fell and so was slayne,
Not leauing any issue there
    As king for to remayne.

        Finis.   quoth J. Pertridge.

¶ **To Thomas Baynam**
his friende, John P.
wysheth health.

Amicus est quasi alter idem.

Vnworthy is that wight
    A benefite in deede,
Which will not once requite
    A gift that did proceede
From such a one whose will
    Indeuour and intent,
To pleasure him in very deede,
    From time to time was bent.
But like a crabid churle againe
    Naught wayeng that they payde
But for thy gentilnes foreshoude
    Requites it with disdaine.
As is the prouerbe olde,
    Wherfore least I should be
Acoumpted as vngratefull nowe
    To such a frende as ye;
I haue this story brought
    Unto our vulgar speche
To pleasure you, wherfore accept
    The same, I you beseche.
And as a recompence
    Though that the gift be small,
Yet doe accept the louing hart
    The giuer giues withall.

        Finis.

¶ De amore inter Amicos.

As loue is chiefest thing
    That common is to all,
So faithfulnes is rariste thing
    That to louers doth fall.
For many frendes there be
    In outwarde kinde of showe,
But faithfull friendes as wyse men saye
    There is a very fewe,
Suche friendes I meane, as will
    Not hault with hound nor hare
But for the profite of his friend,
    Nor friend ne foe will spare.
Nor he who heate nor colde,
    Ne tempest, wynde, nor rayne,
Can cause to flie but in all stormes
    Still constant doth remaine.
Such one a Juell is,
    Excelling golde and fee :
And he is riche that hath a friende
    So sure a one as he.
The gredy yauning iause
    Of vipers flattring taile
Do what they cã, against such friendes
    Can naught at all preuaile.

¶ In blanditia adulatorum.

As he is blest in deede
    That hath a trusty friende,
So contrary is he on whome
    Flatterers doe much intende.
For as the trusty friende
    No paine can call awaye,
Euen so doe flatterers flie apase
    When that no more they may
Obteine that they desire,
    But in his paine and griefe
They do him leaue whē their frēdship
    Of ioyse should be the chiefe.
But as the Scorpion doth
    As those that trye doe knowe
No hurt at all, so long as you
    In quiet let them go.
But when she once shall feele
    You, to disturbe her ease
Neuer so smal then straight she seekes
    Againe you to displease :
By pouring out of her
    Her poysoned styng, wherby
She stynges so sore, that out of hande
    The party stong shall die,
Vnlesse that the selfe same
    That stong him so before
Be slayne, his health againe
    He cannot get no more.
And yet it standes in doubte
    Though that the same they get,

If that the Scorpion to the hart
    The poyson so hath set.
Hermes, a flattring man
    Doth lyken well certaine
Unto a Camell, which saue white,
    All colours doth retaine.
And as he wantes the same,
    So like wyse may we see
A flatterer, all pointes to haue
    Saue only honestie.
No dagger strikes more depe,
    Nor Uiper poysones so
As doth the flattring parasite,
    A swete destroiyng to.
Therfore if you be wyse,
    Learne to escewe the snare
Of flatterers, or els perhaps
    They make your purse full bare.
And warning take by him
    That therof feeles the payne
If you be wyse, and from such men
    Your footesteps do you frame.

        Finis. quoth J. Par.

Imprinted at London
in Paules churcheyarde
at the signe of the Lucrece
by Thomas Purfoote

COMET EURIALUS ESCOUTOIT LA LAGUE
DES S'UITEURS, ET FUT MIS EN LA CHAMBRE PAR LA FENESTRE, ET
DE CE Q' FUT FAIT LA.

The goodli

Hiſtory of the moſte noble & beau-
tifull Ladye Lucres of Scene
in Tuſkan, and of her louer
Eurialus, verye
pleaſaunt
and delec-
table
vnto the re-
der.
(*)
*
* *

* Inno Domini.
M.D.LX:vii.
E.V.

THE Emperour Sygismonde enteringe into the Towne of Scene in Tuskane what Honours he receyued: is al redy euery where published. His palace was prepared at Saynote Marthyes chapell in the strete that ledethe vnto the Strete, called Tophore. After the Cceremonys finyshed, when Sigismond was come thyther, foure ladyes in noblenes, facion, age and apparell semblable dyd mete hym not lyke mortal women: but as goddes, to euery mans iudgemente and yf they hadde ben but thre they hadde been too bee rekened theym that Parys sawe in his dreme. Sigismōd (though he were aged) was prone vnto luste, and delyted muche in deuysinge with ladyes, and reioysed in blandismentes of women, nor nothinge was to hym more plesaunt, then to behold goodly women. Then in aduysinge them (vnlyke to the rest) he was receyued from his horse among them and turnīg to his familiers sayd, saw ye euer any lyke to these women I am in doubt whether these faces be mankynde, or aungels, but surely they are heauēly. They casting their eyne to the ground in blushynge became fayrer, and that ruddy flushynge in theyr chekes, gaue suche a colour to their countenaunce, as hath the ynde euery stoined wᵗ the scarlet, or the whit lilies amōg the purple roses: But amōg al: Lucres the yong Ladie not yet of twenty yeres, shone in great brightnes yong maryed in the famyly of the Camilis, vnto a very rich mā, named Menelaus vnwortheie to whome suche beutye should serue at home, but wel worthye of his wyfe to be deceyued. The stature of the Lady Lucres was more hygher than the other. Her heare plenteous and lyke vnto the gould wyre, which hanged not downe behinde her, after the manner and custome of maydēs: but in goulde and stone, she had ēclosed it, her forhed high of semely space, wythoute wrynkell, her browes bente facioned, wyth fewe heares, by due space, deuyded, her eyne shininge wythe suche bryghtnes that lyke as the sonne, they ouercame the beholders loking with those she might whome she woulde, flee (and slayne) whē she wold reuyue. Strayt as thriede was her noose, and by euen deuision parted, her fayre chekes, nothinge was more amiable, then these chekes, nor nothing more delectable to behold, wherein (whan she dyd laughe) appeared two proper pytes, whiche no man dyd see, that wished not to haue kissed. Her mouth smal and comely her lippis of corall coloure, handsome to byte on, her small tethe wel set in order semed Cristal, throughe which the quyuerynge tonge dyd send furthe, (not wordes) but mooste pleasaunt armony. What shall I shewe the beautye of her chynne, or the whitenesse of her necke? Nothynge was in that bodye not too bee praysed, as the outwarde aparaunces shewed token of that was in warder no man beheld her that dyd not enuye her husband, she was in speche as the fame is, that the mother of Gracchus was or the doughter of Hortentius. Nothyng was more sweter, nor soberer, than her talke. She pretended not (as doth mani) honestie by heui countenaunce: but with mery vysage, shewed her sobernes, not fearefull nor ouer heardye: but vnder drede of shame, she cared in a womans harte. Her apparell was diuers, she wanted, nether broches, borders, gyrdels, nor rynges. The abilymentes of her head, was sumptuouse, many pearles, many dyamantes, were on her fingers and in her borders. I thincke the day that the Greeke Menelaus feested Parys, Helen was no fayrer: nor Adromaches no more gorgeus when shee was married vnto Hector. And amonge those was Katheryne of Perusia that shortelye after dyed, in whose funerals the Emperoure was presounte (and thoughe he were but a chylde) made her Sonne knyght at her sepulchre, and of her the beautye was also merueluse: but no thinge so greate, as of Lucres. her dyd the Emperoure Sigismonde and all other, prayse and beholde, but one among theym, more than ynoughe was sette vppon her.

¶ Eurialus of the contre of Francony, whome neyther shap nor rychesse caused to be vnmete to loue hee was of the age of two and thyrty yeres, not very hyghe stature, but of gladsome and pleasaunt facion, with noble yene, his chekes ruddy and fayre, as the whyte lylyes amonge the purple roses hys other membres (as who sayed) w^t a statelines of shape correspōdent to his stature. The other courtyers by lōg warre, were but poore Hee besydes his owne substaunce, by famylyarytie wyth the Emperoure, receyued daylie rewardes. He was more and more gorgeouse in sighte of menne, and leade a greate trayne of seruauntes after hym. And he hadde suche a horse (as the tale reporteth) as Mennō hadde, whan he came to Troye. Nothing he wanted to prouoke ye same hete of the mynd, called loue but onlye ydlenes, yet youth lust, and the glade goodes of fortune, with whiche thynges Hee was well nouryshed, ouer came hym out of his owne power, Eurialus as sone as he had sene Lucres, he brent in the loue of the Lady, and fyryng his eyne in her face, neuer thought he to haue sene ynoughe, yet loueth he not in vayne, it is a wounderouse thynge, there were manye goodly yonge men but Lucres had onely chosen thys, there were manie goodly women : But Eurialus had chosen her onely. Neuertheles, not at the tyme knewe Lucres the fame of Eurialus towarde her, nor he hers, but eche one of theym thought to haue loued in vayne.

The ceremonyes vnto ye Emperoure finished, she retourned whome, hoole vowed vnto Eurialus, and Eurialus clene geuen vnto Lucres, remaynethe, Who nowe should maruell of the tale of Pyramys and Thysbe ? betwyxte whome, bothe ,acquayntaunce and neyghbourehode myghte be entre of theyr loue, and in tyme grewe theyre lowe. These louers Eurialus and Lucres, neuer sawe nor hearde afore eyther of other, he a Franchonyen, and she a Tuskan, nor in these busenes they occupyed not theyr tongues : but it was all done w^t eyne, sythens that the one so plesed the other. Lucres then wounded

with greuous care, and takē wyth they blynde fyre forgeting all
readye that shee is maryed, hateth her husbande, and wyth woundes
nouryshynge the wounde holdethe fyxed in her breste the countenaunce and face of Eurialus, nor geueth no maner reste vnto her
lymmes and wyth her selfe saythe, I wote not what lettethe me that
I can no more companie with my husbande nothyn̄ge dèlytethe me
hys embracynges no thynges pleaseth me bys kysses, his wordes
anoye me so standeth alwayes afore myne eyene the ymage of the
straūger that to day was nexte vnto the Emperour. Caste halas, oh
vnhappye, oute of my chaste breaste that conceyued flames, yf thou
maye, yf I myght, halas, I shoulde not be, as I am, euell at ease.
A new kind of strengthe agaynste my wyll, draweth me. My desyre
and my reson meueth me dyuerslye, I knowe the best, and the
worste I folowe, Oh Noble cytezen, what hast thou to do with an
vnknowne mā whye brennest thou in straungers loue ? whye seekest
thou thy luste, in a straunge countrye ? yf thy husband louethe the
thyne owne coūtrye may geue thee that thou loueste, Oh, but what
a maner of face hath he ? what woman woulde not be meaued wyth
his beautye, youth Noblenes, and vertue ? surely I am, and withoute
hys helpe, I despayre, God graunt vs better Shall I betray halas,
the chaste spousels, and be take me too a straunger, I wote not
whence ? which when he hath abused me, shall departe, and shal be
an others and so leaue me behinde, but by his countenaūce, it is not
lyke to be so and the noblenes of his mynde semeth not to be suche
nor so pretendethe not the grace of hys beuty that I should fere
disceit or his forgeting of loue. And he shall promise a forehande
assured, whye do I dread I shall apply it without ferther abrode,
parde, I am so fayre that hee will no lesse desyre me, than I hym,
hee shall be myne for euer, yf ones I may receyue hym to my kysses.
How many do wo me where so euer I go ? how many ryuals do
watche afore my dore ? I shal entende to loue, either he shal tarye
here or at hys departinge cary me with hym. Shall I than forsake,

my mother my husbande and my countrye my mother is frowarde and alwayes againste myne appetites my husbande I had rather wante, than haue, my countrye is there as I delyte to dwel, but shal I so lease my Fame? whye Not? what haue I to do wyth mennes wordes which I shall not here? Nothing shal he dare, y⁺ feareth the theratninge of fame, many other haue, done the same, Helena woulde be rauyshed. Paris caryed her not away against her wil What shal I tel of Dyana or Media? no mā blameth the fauter that fauteth wyth many. Thus sayd Lucres, nor within his brest, nouryshed Euryalus no lesse flames.

In the myd way, betwyxt the Emperors courte, and Euryalus lodgynge was Lucreses house, and Euryalus myght not go vnto the pallace, but showing her self out of the highe wyndowes, was in hys eyne, but always Lucres blusshed, whan she sawe Eurialus, which thyng gaue vnto the Emperour knowledge of the loue For as by custome he vsed to ryde here and there, passynge often that way, he saw the woman chaunge countenaunce, by Eurialus comynge, whiche, was as next vnto hym as Mecena to Octauyan to whome the Emperour lokynge asyde, sayde doste thou bren women on thys facion Euryalus? that woman surely loueth the, and ones in maner as though he had enuyed his loue, whē he came before Lucres house he put Eurialus cappe ouer his ayne, thou shalte not see· quod he that thou louest, I wyll myselfe vse the sighte. Eurialus aunswered, sir what meanethe this? I haue nothinge to do with her, but take heede what ye doe least ye bringe suspecte in them that bee here about vs Eurialus was mounted vpon an hygh rayned couler, wyth a small heade, whose shorte bely and fayre here caused him to shewe, goodly, well brested, lusty, and courageous so that herynge the trumpet he could no where reaste he receyued the fury of the noyse, hys fayre manie honge vppon y⁺ ryght side, And the grounde resowned, beten with his fote, and not much vnlike him was his maister, whē he had espied Lucres who beinge alone, as sone as She hadde sene him, coulde neyther temper the flame nor her selfe so the vnhappy Lucres did burne. In mene houses dwelleth chastetye, and onely Pouertye vsed good affection and Chastye that hanteth small cotages, knoweth not the policies for ryche mene who that haboundeth in prosperytie lightlye desyreth, vnaccoustomed thynges, Fyers, luste, companyon to fortune hathe chosen dylicate Howses and statly mancions. Lucres, that aften times beholdynge Eurialus passing by, might not asswage her ardaunte desire, busely thinckinge to whome she might her selfe discouer, for who that secreatlye brenneth, more greuouslie suffreth.

There was amonge the seruauntes of her husbaunde, one Zosias an Almaine olde and faithfull to his maister : whome he had longe serued, verye honestlye, him doth she go vnto trustiug more to the nacion than to the man.

The Emperour accompanied with manye Noble menne, wente solacyinge throughe the towne, and euen nowe did he passe by the house of Lucres whō whā she knew that Eurialus was ther Come hether quod she Zosias I would speke with thee, loke heare out of the windowe, where in the worlde is there onye youthe lyke this, seest thou how vpryght and fayre sprede shoulders they haue, behoulde theyer bushes and well kempte heares Oh, what faces, what fayre neckes. What noble hartes theyr countenaūces dothe pretend this is an other kynde of people than our Countrye dothe brede, they seme Goddes or of heauenlie kynde. O that fortune had giuen me an husbande of one of these, yf myne eyene had not senc them I woulde neuer haue beleued thee, yf thou hadde toulde me of them, Yet the fame is that the Almaynes excelleth all other people, and surelye I beleue that the colde geueth to them great whitnes, the countries so drawyng towarde the Northe. But dooste to knowe anye of them. yea many quod Zosias Than quod

Lucres, Eurialus the Franconyen, dooste thou know him? Ye as mine owne selfe, sayth Zosias, but why doste thou aske? I shall tell thee quod shee. I knowe it shall not be disclosed, thys hoope hath thy goodnes gyuen me. Amonge all them that are about the Emperoure, none pleaseth me lyke hym. In him mi mynde is meaued. I wotte not wyth what flames I burne, I canne neyther forget hym, nor yet my selfe apease, excepte I maye make my selfe acquaynted wythe hym. Go therefore I beseche thee Zosias, seeke Eurialus, tell him I loue him, nothynge elles I desyre of the, and yet this shalt thou not do in vayne, what is thys quod Zosias? shall I eyther do suche outrage, or ones thynke it Madame, shall I betraye my Maister? shal I nowe olde begyne too deceyue, which I haue hated in my youth Rather mooste Noble Ladye of thys Towne caste fourthe the wicked furoure out of thi chaste breste, folowe not thy cruell hoope, but quenche the fire, Hee doth not painefullie put backe loue, that resisteth the firste assautes, but thee that the sweete yll flatering doth nourishe, geueth hym to bondage of a right harde and cruel maister, nor whan hee woulde, maye not forsake the yocke, whiche yf thy husbande should knowe, halas vnder what facyon woulde he tormente the? no loue can longe lye hyddene.

¶ Houlde thy peace quod Lucres, there is no fcare at all, nothynge he feareth that feareth not death. I am content to suffer it what soeuer happeneth, what oppynyon dooste thou houlde? Oh vnhappie quod Zosias, thou shalt shame thy house, and onlye of all thy kynne thou shalte bee adulteresse, thinkest thou the deade can be secreate. A thousand eyne are aboute thee. Thy mother, yf shee do accordinge, shall not suffer thy outrage to be preuye, not thy husbande, not thy Cousyns, not thy maydens ye and thoughe thy seruauntes woulde holde theyr peace the bestes would speake it, ye dogges the poostes, and the marble stones, and thoughe thou hyde all thou canste not hyde it from God that seeth all, Understande that payne is presente vnto a Gyltye thoughte, and the mynde fylled with offence, feareth hym selfe. Faythe is denied in great crimes Asswage I beseeche thee, the flames of wycked loue, feare to mengle straunge makes in thy husbādes bedde, I knowe quod she it is accordinge as thou sayste, but the rage maketh me folow the worse My mynde knoweth howe I fall hedling, but furour hath ouercom and reygneth and ouer all my thought ruleth loue. I am determyned to folow the commandement of loue. Ouermuche alas haue I wrestled in vaine, yf thou haue pytie on me, carye my mesage. Ful heauie was Zosias with this worde, and sayde to her thus, for these hoore heares on my heade, by age, and for the faithful seruice that I haue done vnto thy kynne humblye I beseche thee leue thys furour and helpe thy selfe, a great parte of helthe is to wyll to be heled. To whome sayth Lucres, all shame hath not forsaken my mynde, I wyll obeye thee Zosia, in the loue that cannot bee hyd only the exchuynge of this yll is by deathe to preuent the offence. Zosias affeared wyth thys sayinge moderate quod hee my ladye the rage of thi vnbrydeled mynde, tempere thy thoughte, nowe arte thou worthi lyfe, when thou iudgest thy selfe worthye of deathe, I am determined quod Lucres to dye. Collatinus wyfe the faute committed, venged with a swearde. I more honestye shall preuent it, I studye but the kynde of my deathe, a cord swearde, fall or poyson, shall reuēge chastitie one of these I shall assaye. I wyll not suffer thee quod Zosias, quod Lucres who, that determineth to dye, cannot be let. Perria, at the deathe of Bruthus, whan weapon was taken frome her, dyd eate hote coles, If the furoure bee soo frowarde in thy minde quod Zosias, thy lyfe is rather to be socoured, than the fame, deceytful is fame that to the yll, better and to the good worser, is oftē geuen, Lette vs assaye thys Eurialus, and lete vs intende to loue the laboure shall be myne, and as I thyncke, I shall bringe it to effecte :

With these wordes the kyndled thought hee enflamed and gaue

hoope to the doubteful mind but his minde was not to doe as hee sayde, hee thought to deferre the mynde of the woman, to aswage the desyre, as often times time quencheth flames and sufferaunce healeth diseases, Zosias went with fals truste to dryue her forthe tel the Emperoure shoulde departe, or shee shoulde chaung her minde leaste yf hee hadde denyed it, yf another messanger shoulde haue bene founde, or els the woman shoulde haue slayne her selfe, oftentimes therefore hee fayned hym selfe to goo and come and that he reioyced in her loue, and sought a cōuenyente tyme that they myghte talke together, sometyme he coulde not speake with hym, some tyme he soughte to be sente oute of the towne, and tyll his retourne deferred her glad dayes, so manie dayes he did fede the sicke minde and because he shoulde not lye in al thinges, once onelye he brake vnto Eurialus, sayinge O howe thou arte here beloued, yet whan he asked what that mente, he answered not. But Eurialus strikē with the secret darte of Cupido, gaue no rest nor sleape to his lymmes, the fyre so crepte in hys vaynes and vtterly wasted his marie yet knewe he not Zosia, nor thoughte him to be the messēger of Lucres, so haue we al lesse hope then desyre, He whan he sawe him selfe burne, a greate while with thys wisdome wōdered and vnder this facion oftentymes blamed him selfe, Lo Eurialus, thou knoweste what the rage of loue is lōg plaintes, and shorte laughters, few ioyes and manye dredes, alwayes he dyeth and is neuer deade that louethe, what doste thou meddle in vayne at laste quod he, and for noughte, O wrech, whye stryue I againste loue? May not I do that Julius that Alexāder, that Hanybal dyd and these were worthie warryoures. Loke besydes vpon Poetes, Virgyll drawen vp by a roape, honge in the mydwaye to the windowe, trustyng to haue embraced his loue. If anye man wyll excuse the Poet, as a folower of a more dissolute lyfe, what shall we saye of Philosophers, maysters of lernynge, and rulers of good lyuing. A woman dyd ryde Aristotle like a horse, and ruled hym with a brydle and spurred hym. It is not

R

true that is sayde comonlye honoure and loue accorde not together the Emperoures power is equall with the goodes, and who is a greater louer then hee ? They say that Hercules, that was strongest of all menne, and of the race of Godes the disroyl of the lyon and his quyuere layde a parte, toke in hande roke, and trymmed rynges for his fyngers, and sette in order his rudde busshe, And with hys hande, where with hee wonte too carye a mace by tyrlinge of a spindell he drewe a threde, it is a naturall passyon. Berdes are brente with this fyre. The turtull and the doue dothe loue. What shall I saye of beastes ? The horse meueth battell for loue. The feareful hearte sekethe to fyghte And by beleuynge shewethe his furoure, the fyers Tegre, and the cruell Boore, whettyng his teath, doth vse it. And the Lyons of Lybya set vp theyr roughe manes, whan loue mouethe. The monstures of the sea do fele this heate, nothing is free, ne nothing vnto loue denied. Hate gyueth place vnto it. It styrred the fyers flames of youth, and vnto very age it reuokethe the deade heate, and strikethe the brestes of maydens with a breninge fyre. Whye then doo I stryue againste the lawes of loue ? Loue ouercommeth all thing and let vs gyue place vnto him.

¶ Whan these thynges were concluded, he seeketh a bawde too whome he mighte take her leters to carye to her, Nisus was his faithfull felowe, and vnderstode muche in suche matters. He takethe the busynes in hande, and hyrethe a woman to whome the letters were taken, writen as foloweth,

¶ **Eurialus bnto Lucres.**

I wolde sende the greatynge and helthe with my letters yf I had any my selfe, but surelye bothe of my healthe and lyfe, the hope hangeth in my handes, more than my selefe I loue the, And I weene it is not vnknowne vnto thee, my face ofte moysted with teres, maye shewe token of my woūed breste, and the sightes which in thy presence, I haue cast fourthe Take it well I beseche thee that I discouere me vnto the, thi beautye hath takenne me and the grace of godlye hede, wherein thou passest al other, houldeth me, what loue mente vnto nowe I neuer knewe, but thou haste subdued me to thy power of thy desyre, longe did I stryue (I confesse) to escape so violente a maister, but thy brightnesse hath ouercome myne endeuoure, the beamys of thine eyne passynge the sonne hath ouercom me. I am taken and am no more myne owne, the vse of meate and drincke thou takest fro me contynually. I the loue, the I desyre, thee I call, thee I awayte, thee I thyncke on the truste in, and with thee I delyte mee, thyne is my mynde, and with the it is hole. thou onlye mayste saue me, thou onelye mayste lefe me, the one of these chuse, and what thou intendest, wryte it vnto mee. Bee no more harde in thy wordes in answering me, than thou was with thine eyne in byndyng me, it is no greate thynge that I aske. To speke conuenyentlye wyth the I aske, this onelye desyreth my letters. That that I wryte, I maye saye afore the this if thou graunt me, I lyue, and well happe I lyue yf not thou sleest my harte that ye more then me loueth. I recōmend me vnto thy good grace, and too the trust that I haue in thee. And thus farewell the delyte and resydue of my lyfe.

These letters sealed, when the woman had receiued, hasteli she wente vnto Lucres, and fynedynge her alone, sayde vnto her thus, The mooste Noble of the Emperoures Courte. Thy louer sendeth these letters, and prayeth thee instantlye to make him vnto thy grace. This woman was noted for a baude, And that knewe Lucres and tooke it verye dysplesauntlye to haue a naughtye womanne sente vnto her, and to her she sayde, what madnesse hathe meued the to come to my presence arte thou so boulde to entre in the houses of noble men dareste thou prouoke greate Ladyes too vyolate sacred marriage ? skance canne I holde my handes frō thy eare. bringest thou letters vnto me ? speakest thou vnto me ? darest thou loke me in my face ? If I regarded not more what becōmeth me thanne what thou deseruest, I shulde so order thee that thou shouldest after this daye neuer carye more letters of loue, entre out of my sighte abhomynable queane, and take thy letters with thee. ye rather gyue them mee, that I maye caste them in the fyre, and snatchinge the paper from her, tare it in peaces and trode vnder her fete, spittinge at it, caste it in the asshes, so should thi selfe be punished Baude quode she more worthy the fyre, than thy lyfe, pycke thee hence shortly leaste that my husbande, fyndynge thee heare gyue thee that that I remitte vnto thee and whyle thou lyuest neuer come in my syghte. A nother woulde haue bene afrayde, but she well acquaynted with the maners of women, thoughte to her selfe, nowe wouldest thou mooste, when thou shewest mooste the contrarye, and sayde vnto her forgeue me madame, I thoughte I had not done amysse, And that it should haue stande wyth thy pleasure, yf it be otherwyse, pardone myne ignoraunce, yf thou wylte not that I retourne vnto thee, I shall obey thy commaundemente, but take thou heede what a louer thou forsakest, and with these woordes departed from her, and when she had found Eurialus : Be of good conforte quod she, thou louer, the woman louethe more thee, then she is loued, But nowe it is was no tyme to wryte vnto thee, I founde her sad, but whan I named thee, and gaue her thy letters, She made good countenaunce, And kyssed the paper a thousand times, doubte not thou shalte shortelye haue an aunsweare, and thus the olde woman departynge, she was well ware no more to be founde leaste she hadde suffred for her lyinge.

¶ Trulye Lucres, after the woman was departed, soughte vp y⁰ peeces of the letter, and sette eche in theyr place, and ioyned soo the torne wordes that she made it legeable, whyche when she hadde

redde it a thousand tymes, a thousande tymes she kyssed it, and at
the last wrapped it in a fayre napkyne, and pute it amonge her
Juels, and remembringe nowe thys worde, nowe that woorde, contynuallye she sooked in more loue, and determined too wryte to Eurialus, and sent her letter on thys fashyon endyted,

¶ Lucres to Eurialus.

O Eurialus, leue to hope after that thou canste not attayne, leue
to bere me wyth thy letters and messangers, thynke not that I am
of that sorte that sell them selues, I am not shee that thou takest
me for nor vnto whome thou shouldest send a bawd, seke for thy
luste another, No affeccione but chastitie shall folowe, wyth other
doo as thee lyketh, but of me aske nothynge, for bee thou sure I am
vnmeete for thee. Farwell.

Thys letter (thoughe it seemed vnto Eurialus verye harde, and
contrarye too thee womannes woordes) yet dyd shewe hym the redye
waye howe too sende hys letters, for hee douted not too truste
whome she trusted, but the ignoraunce of the Italien toungue combred hym, therefore with busye studye he learned it and bee cause
loue made hym dyligent, he was in shorte whyle counnynge, and
hym selfe alone endyted hys letters, whyche afore hee was wonte to
borowe, whan he shuld write anye thynge in Italien.

He aunswered than to Lucres, That she shulde not be dyspleased
wyth hym, Bycause he sente an vnhoneste womanne to her, sythē
hee as a straunger knewe it not, and could vse none other messan-
gere. The cause of hys sendynge was hys loue, desyrynge noo dys-
honestye. Hee beleued her verye honeste and chaste, And so muche
more to bee beloued, and that vnhonest womenne and ouer lyberall
of theyr honour he dydde not onelye not loue : but also greatly hate,

for chastitye loste, nothynge is a woman not to be praysed, for bautye is a delectable pleasure, and a frayle, and nought to be estemed wythoute honestye, and that she that honesty wynneth with beautye, passethe in both gyftes, And that therefore he dyd honoure her and onelye he desyred to speake wyth her, that he myghte by hys wordes declare hys mynde, that he coulde not by hys letters.

With suche manere of letters hee sente a tokene, not onely ryche in value, but excellent in the workmanshype.

¶ To these letters Lu-
cres thus an-
swered,
***

I haue receyued thy letters, nor it is not the womanne nowe I blame thee for That thou loueste mee I esteame not greatlye, For thou arte neyther alone, nor the fyrste whome they saye my beauti hathe deceyued.

Manye haue loued me, and do loue mee, but thy laboure as well as theyres shalbe in vayne : I nether can nor wyll talke with thee and excepte thou were a swalow thou canste not fynde me alone.

The houses be hygh, and the gates be kepte. I haue takene thy token for that the facione pleasethe me, but because I wyll nothinge of thyne for noght, and that it shall not be as a tokene of loue, I sende the rynge, whiche my husbande gaue my mother, that it maye be to the as pryce of thy Juels for it is of no lesse value than the gyfte.

Farewell.

To these letters Eurialus replied. Great confort wer thy letters vnto mee that thou complaynest no more of the womane. But that thou settest thi loue so lyght greueth me sore, for though many do loue thee, none of theyr loue is so feruente as myne, but thou beleueste it not, for that I may not speke with thee, but yf I might thou shuldest not wey it so lyght. Would to god as thou sayest, that I might be a swalowe, ye, or a lesse thinge, that thou myght not shitte thy wendowe agaist mee, but my most grefe is not that thou can not, but that thou wylte not. Ah my Lucres, what meaneth that thou wylte not, yf thou myght woldeste thou not speake wyth mee that am all thyne? and that nought desireth so muche as to please thee. If thou byde me go into the fyre, I shall soner obey thē thou shalte commaunde. Sende me worde I beseche thee, that yf thou myghte thy wyll were good Geue me not death with thy wordes, that mayste gyue lyfe vnto me wyth thyne eyene. If thou wylte not speake wyth me because thou may not I am contente, but chaunce that woorde I praye thee that sayest my laboure shall be in vayne, God forbyde in that suche crueltye, Be I beseche thee the more genteller to thy verye louer, yf thou Contynue so, thou shalte slee mee, And bee thou sure, soner thou with a word then another with a sworde. I aske thou haste none excuse, no man canne forbyde thee that, saye thou louest me, and I am happye that my tokene remayneth with thee, howe soeuer it be I am glade of it, it shall sometyme remember thee of my loue, But it was to symple, and that that I sende thee now is lesse, but refuse not thou that thy louer sendeth the, I shal haue out of my countrye dayly beter when they come, thou shalte not lacke them, Thy rynge shall neuer part from my fynger, And insteede of the I shal moyst it with cōtinual kysses. Farewell my healthe, and in that thou maye healpe me.

¶ At the last after mani writings and answeres Lucres sente hym suche a letter.

¶ Lucres to Eurialus.

I wolde fayne Eurialus doo the pleasure, and as thou desireste, rewarde thee with my loue, for that asketh thy Noblenes, and thy condicions descruethe it, that thou shuldest not loue in vayne, besides thy beautie and goodlye face, but it is not for mee to loue thee. I knowe myselfe, yf I begin to loue I shall neuer keepe measure nor rule. Thou canste not longe be heare, and yf I fall vnto the I canne not lacke the, thou wouldest not to take me withe thee, and I surelye woulde not longe tarrye behynde thee. Many examples do meue to refuse a straungers loue. Jason that wanne the golden flece by Medeas counsell, forsoke her. Theseus hadde bene caste too the Minaturs had not the councell of Adriana healped him, yet dyd hee leue her behinde him in an Iland. What became on the vnhappye Dido, that receyued the wanderinge Eneas Was not her loue her deathe? I knowe what pearyll it is to receiue a straungers loue nor I wyll not put me into suche hasardes, yong menne are of more stronge mynd, and soner can quence the fyre. A womanne whan she beginneth to loue, onely by death maketh an end. Women rage thei doe not loue, and excepte they bee aunswered with loue nothinge is more teryble, after the fire be kindled, we neither regard fam nor lif The onelye remedye is the obtaininge of the louer, for that that we moost lacke, we moost desyre Nor we feare no daunger for our appetytes, I than synce am maryed and vnto a noble riche man, am determined to exclude all louers, and speciallye thyne, whiche cane not be continually laste, I bee noted as Philis or Sapho. Therefore I desyre thee no more to aske my loue, and lyttle by lyttle to asswage and quence thyne, for it is more easy to menne then to womē, nor thou yf thou loue me, as thou sayest, woldest not desire that ye shoulde bee my destruccion. for the token I sende thee a crosse of golde, wyth pearles, whiche thoughe it be litle is of some value. Farewell.

¶ Eurialus to thys Letter helde not his peace, But as he with the newe writing kindeled, so toke he the penne in hande, And vnder this forme folowynge endyted a letter.

¶ Eurialus vnto Lucres.

Honour and helth be vnto my dere hart Lucres she y^t geueth me helthe with her leters, though they be medled some what wythe galle, yet I truste when thou hast heard mine thou shalt withdraw it. Thy letters are come to my handes sealed, whiche I haue red oftentimes and kissed as oft. But it semeth to meane another thing than thy minde wolde. Thou desireste me to leue to loue, because it is not mete for thee to folowe a straungers loue, bringinge examples of such that hath bene so deceiued (so eloquentli) that I must rather wōder of thee, thē forget y·. Who woulde then leaue to loue, when he seeth suche wyte and lerning in his maistres? yf thou woldeste haue swaged my loue, thou shuldest not haue shewed thyne eloquence, for that is not to quēch the fyre, but to make it rather flame, the more I reade it, the more I burned, seynge thy beautie and honestie so ioyned with lerninge, but it is in vayne to desire mee to leaue to loue the, Desire the hilles too be come plaine and the riuers to retourne into the springes, For aswell may I leaue to loue, As the sonne his course, If the highe mountanes maye wante snowes, or the sea fysshes, yf the forestes maye wante Dere, then may Eurialus forget thee. Men ar not so prone as thou wenest Lucres, to quenche theyr desires, for that that thou geueste vnto our mynde, men do ascribe it vnto youres, but I wil not vndertake that to debate, to that must I answere which toucheth me neare for the deceites of other, thou brīgest in exāples wherby y" wylt not rewarde me w^t thy loue. But more are to be brought mi lucres, whō women hath deceyued, Troylus by Cresyde, Deiphus by Helena, and Circes by her enchauntementes deceyued her louers.

But it were not accordynge, by yͤ dedes of a fewe, to iudge all the rest. Souldest thou for a certaine yll man abhorre and accuse all menne? Or I for manye yll women hate all the rest? nay, rather lette vs take other examples, as was of Anthonius and Cleopatra, and of other whome yͤ shortnes of my letters letteth too reherce, but it is red yͭ the Grekes retournynge frome Troy haue bene holden by straungers loues, nor neuer haue come to theyr countries, but taryed with theyr loues, contente rather too wante theyr frendes, theyr houses, theyre reynes, and other deare thynges, of theyr countrye, than too forsake theyr ladyes. This I beseche thee my Lucres remember and note those few thinges that be against our loue.

So do I loue thee, to loue thee alwayes, and euer to be thyne. Nor call me not straunger, I pray thee, for I am rather of this countrye, thā he that is borne heare, sithens hee is but by chaunce, and I by mine owne choyse, no Countrye is myne but where thou arte. And thoughe I departed at anye tyme my retourne at all bee shorte, nor I shall not retourne at all into mi countrie, But too sette ordere in my businesses, that I maye dwel longe with thee, wherefore, occasion maye be found sonne inough The Emperoure hathe muche to doo in these partyes the charge whereof I wyll sue to haue sometyme as ambassadoure, And he muste haue a Lieutenaunte in Strucia, and that wyll I optayne, Doubte not my delyte, my herte, and my only truste. If I maye lyue yet pytie thy louer that melteth lyke snowe afore thee.

Sone consyder my trauailes, and nowe at the last set an ende to my tormentes, whye punisheste thou me so longe? I wonder of my selfe howe I haue suffered so many euyles howe I haue waked so manye nyghtes howe I haue forborne my meate and my drynke soo longe; beholde howe lene I am, and howe pale, a small thynge it is yͭ holdeth the lyfe within my bodye; yf I hadde slayne thy Parētes or thy chyldren, thou couldeste punyshe me no sorer, yf thou so handle mee for that I loue thee, what shalte thou do too them that haue offended thee? Ah my Lucres, my Lady, my healthe, and my socoure take me vnto thy grace, and at laste wryte vnto mee that I am thy beloued. nothynge I woulde els but that I myghte saye I am thy Seruaunte. Pardy both Kinges and Emperoures loue their faithfull Seruauntes, nor the Goddes disdayne not to knowe them that loueth theym, Farewell my trust and my dreade.

¶ Lyke as towre craked wythin sowndynge outewarde imprenyble, yf a piece of ordonaunce be shotte againste it, furthe withe it rente in peces: So was Lucres ouercom with Eurialus wordes, for after shee hadde perceiued the diligēce of yᵉ louer, her dissembled loue she declared with such letres.

¶ Lucres to Eurialus.

I may noo more my Eurialus resiste thy requestes nor longer withold my loue from the I am ouercome vnhappy woman by thy letters, whiche yf thou obserueste nat, accordynge to thy wrytynge, thou shalt be of all periured traytours the worst It is easy to deceyue a Woman, but soo moche Is it the more shamefull now that I am come into thi loue, and as a woman can considre but lytle, thou that arte a man, take charg bothe of thy selfe and of me Thyne I am, and thy faythe I folowe, and thyne wolde I nat bee, excepte it were for euer, Farewel the staye and leder of my lyfe.

¶ After thys were manye letters wryten on both partyes, and Eurialus wrote nat soo vehementelye, as Lucres dyd answer feruentlye, and that had both one desyre of theyr metynge, but it semed harde, and almost impossible, sithens the eyne of euery body dyd behold Lucres, which neuer wente forth alone, nor wanted a keper, Nor argus neuer kepte Junos Cowe soo dylygently as Menelaus caused Lucres too bee kepte. Thys vyce is of property to the

Ytalyens, to shytte vp theyr wyues as theyr treasure, and one my faythe (to my iudgemente) to lytle purpose, for the mooste parte of womenne be of thys sorte, that mooste they desyre that mooste too them is denyed, and whan thou woldest they wyll not, and whan thou woldest not, they wolde, and yf they haue the brydle at lybertye, lesse they offende, so that it is as easy to kepe a woman agaynst her wyll as a flocke of flyes in the hete of the sonne, excepte shee bee of her selfe chaste. In vayne dothe the husbande set kepers ouer her, for who shal kepe those kepers, She is crafty, and at them lyghtely she begyneth, and whan she takethe a fantasy, she is vnreasonable, and lyke an vnbrydeled mule.

¶ Lucres had a brother in lawe he caryed her letters, and was of councell in her loue with him, shee hadde appoynted to shyt priuely Eurialus in hys house, and he dwelled within his stepmother, y' was Lucres mother, whome Lucres dyd oftentymes vysyte, and was also of her oftentymes vysyted, for they dwelt not farre asonder. Nowe thys was the order of it, Eurialus shulde be shyte in the parler, and after the mother was gone to the Churche, Lucres shulde come as it were to speke with her, and nat fyndynge her, shulde tarye for her returne, in the meane tyme she shulde be with Eurialus, this shulde be within two dayes, but these two dayes were too yeres to the louers, for to them y' hoppe well, the houres be longe, and to them that truste lytle they be as shorte, but fortune folowed nat theyre desyres.

The mothere mystrusted, and at that daye whan she wente forth, shyt her sone in lawe oute, which broughte too Eurialus the heuye newes, to whome the displesour was noo lesse than too Lucres, whiche whan she sawe her crafte perceyued, let vs go quod she another waye to worke, yet shall not my mother lette my appetyte.

One Pandalus was her husbandes cousyn, whome shee had also made pryuy of her secretes, for y' flaminge mynde myght no where reste. She aduertysed Eurialus to speke with him, for he was trusty and could fynde well a meane for theyr metynge, but Eurialus thoughte it nat sure to truste hym, whō he sawe alwaye wᵗ him. Menelaus fearinge therby deceyt. In takynge deliberacion, he was sēte by the Emperoure to Rome, to determyne wythe the Pope for hys Coronacyon, whiche was boothe vnto him and her greuous, but it must be obeyed, so was his Journeye two monethes longe: In the meane tyme Lucres kept her house, shytt vppe her wyndowe, pute on sadde apparell, And no where went she forth, euery body marueled and knewe nat the cause, sythen the wyndowes of yᵉ towne shewed thē selfe, and they of yᵉ house thoughte them selfe in darkenes, as though they hadde wāted the sonne, seynge her often on her bed and neuer merye, thoughte it sicknes, and sought all remedes that myghte be, but she neuer neyther laughte nor came oute of her chambere, tyll tyme shee knewe that Eurialus was come to the presēce of the Emperoure, for than, as waked out of a slepe she layde a parte her sade clothes, and dressed wᵗ her former gorgeousnes, opened her wīdowes gladli lokīg for him, whome whan yᵉ Emperoure sawe denye it no more quod Eurialus, the matter is perceyued, neuer mā in thy absence myght see Lucres, nowe that thou art come we may se in the brighte mornonge what measure is in loue; it can nat be cloked nor hydden with hemmes.

¶ Ye mocke syr quod Eurialus, and finde your laughter at me. I know nat what it meaneth, the naythinge of your horses hath peraduenture wakened here, and whan he haddo sayde, pryuelye he behelde Lucres and fixed faste his eyne in heres, and that was theyr fyrste salutacion after his retourne.

Shortely after Nysus Eurialus trusty frende dilygently pursuyng his frendes cause, founde a Tauerne, which behynde Menelaus house hadde a wyndowe toward Lucres chambre, He maketh the Tauerner his frende, and whan hee had voyde the place bringeth thyther Euryalus sayeng, out of this wyndowe maiste thou speke with Lucres, betwyxte bouthe houses was a darke caneil, which no man came too, deuydynge Lucres windowe from the chambre, by the space of three elles. Here satte the louer awaytinge if by chaunce he might see her and he was nat deceyued, for at the laste she came to the wyndowe and lokynge here and there, what doost thou quod Eurialus, the nouryshe of my lyfe, whethere tourneste thou thyne iyene, my dere harte? hyther tourne theym I pray thee, loke hether mi helth, beholde, thyne Eurialus is here, I my selfe am here.

Art thou here quod Lucres? Oh my Eurialus, nowe maye I speke with thee, and wold god I might embrace thee, It shall nat nede no great busynes quod Eurialus, I shall sette too a ladder, opene thy chambre, to longe haue we dyfferred the inioyninge of oure loue, Beware of that quod shee my Eurialus, yf thou loue my lyfe, heere is a windowe on the ryght hande and a verye yll neghbour, and the tauerner is nat to be trusted, that for a lytle money wolde peraduēture betraye bothe thee and mee, but let vs worke otherwyse, it is inough yf here we talke togither. But this is death to me sayethe Eurialus, wythoute I myght in mine armes embrace thee. In this place dyd they talke longe, and at the laste rechid ech to other tokēs uppon a rede, and Eurialus was no more liberall in his gyftes, than Lucres. Zosias perceiued the crafte, and sayde to him selfe. In vayne do I resiste the mynd of the louers, and excepte I prouide wysely, my maistres is vndone, and the house shamed for euer of bothe these; elles, it is best to withstand the one, my maistres loueth, yf it be secrete, it maketh no mater, she is blynde for loue and seethe not well what she doeth.

¶ yf chasteytye can not be kept, it is inoughe to hyde the noyse, leest the hoole house bee slaundered, or leest there bee any murdre done, surelye, I wyll goo to her, and helpe her whyle I myghte. I dyd withstande that no offence shoulde bee doone, and because I myghte nat, it is nowe my parte to hyde that that nedes wyl be, leest it be knowen. Luste is an vniuersall reygnynge myschief, nor

none there is nat infected wythe this syckenes and he is Judged
mooste chaste y^t is mooste secrete. And thus thinkynge wyth hym
selfe, Lucres cam out of her chambre, and Zosias metynge here,
sayde thus, what meaneth it that thou deuyseste w^t me no more of
thy loue? and neuertheles Eurialus is beloued of the? take hede
whome thou trustest, The fyrst poynte of wysdome is, nat to loue at
all. The nexte that at the leest it be secrete, and thou alone withoute a messanger canst nat doo it. In what truste thou mayste
putte me in, by longe tyme thou hast lerned, yf thou wylte trust
me, tell me, for my most care is, leeste thys loue, yf it be knowen,
thou shalte suffre, and thy husbande most of all. To this answered
Lucres, it is as thou sayeste Zosias, and I truste thee mooche, but
me thought I wote not howe neglygence, and agaynst my desyre,
Nowe that thou offerest thyselfe, I wyll vse thy diligence, and I
feare nat to be deceyued of thee. Thou knowest howe I burne, and
longe, I may nat endure this flambe, helpe mee that wee maye be
togythere, Eurialus for loue languisheth, and I dye Nothing is to vs
worse than to lette our appetyties, yf wee may ones mete togyther,
oure loue shall be more temperate, and it shall well be hid. Goo
than and shewe to Euryalus the only waye to come to me, yf he
wyll within these foure dayes, whan the vyllaynes bringe in whete,
disguise him like a portur, and clothe him selfe in sake clothe and
carie the corne in too the garner. Thou knoweste my chambre hath
a backe dore by the lader, tel all vnto Eurialus, and I shall wayte
for hym, and whan tyme is, I shalbe alone in my chambre, and
whan he is alone let hym put opene the dore and come into me.
Zosias thoughte it were a hyghe mater, ferynge a worse, taketh in
hande the busynes, and fyndynge Eurialus, appoyntethe with hym
ye order of euery thinge whiche hee as lyght thinges gladlye ac-
cepteth, and makethe hym redy to this message and nought plaineth
but of longe abode. O insensible brest of a louer. O blynde
thoughte. O hardye mynde and vnfearefull hart. What is so

vnaccessyble that thou thynkeste nat open inoughe? what way so sharpe that the semethe nat playne? what is so close that is nat to bee vnclosed? thou settest lighte all daungers, thou findest nothinge too harde, vaine is the Jelousie of husbandes against the; neyther lawe no feare doth holde thee, to no shame arte thou subiecte, to al labours is but playe.

Oh, loue, subduer of all thynges, a noble man derelie beloued with the Emperoure, rich, of good age, wel lerned, and of gret wite, thou bringest in that case, that purple layde a parte, he clothes him in sake clothe, he dissembleth hys owne face, and of a mayster is he comen a seruaunt, and he that deliciouslie hathe bene nourished, nowe dresseth hys sholders for the burdone, and letteth hym selfe to hyre for a comon portour. Oh maruelouse thynge and almooste vncredyble, to se a man, in other thynges a graue counceller, amonge the companye boystous portoures, pressynge hym selfe among suche raskal people, who wyll seke a greater charge? This same is it that Ouide meaneth in his transformacions, whan he telleth howe women became beestes, stones or trees, that same is it that the nooble Poete Uirgyl meaneth whan he telleth howe circes enchaunted her louers into beestes for so fearethe it by loue, so is the mynde of man thereby chaunced, that lytle hee differeth from a beest.

The mornynge forsakynge the golden bed of Titan, reduced the desyred day, and shortelye the sonne declarynge the coloure of eche thyng reioyced the wayfer Eurialus, that thought him than happye and fortunate, whan he sawe hymselfe among the vyle portours, so goeth he furth into the house of Lucres charged hym selfe wyth whete and settynge it in the garner, discended last of the cōpany. and as he was taught, the dore of the chambre, that was put to, he thrust opē, and wente in, and shyttynge the dore after hym he foūd

Lucres aboute sylkworke and comyng towarde her, god spede quod hee my dere herte and the onely helpe and hope of my lyfe. Lucres, thoughe she hadde appoynted his matter, at the firste sight, was some what abassed, and thought that it hadde bene rather a spyryte, than her louer Eurialus, for she coulde nat well beliue that suche a man as he wolde aduenture suche perrylles, but after warde in kyssyng and embracynge she knewe wel Eurialus and sayde, Arte thou here quod shee poore portour, arte thou here myne owne Eurialus, and than she straynynge hym strayter lokynge in hys face, began her wordes agayne thus Alas quod she my dere herte Eurialus, what daungers haste thou aduentured, what shall I saye now, I perceyue I am mooste dere vnto thee, I haue made profe of thy loue, and thou shalte neuer fynde me none other wyse vnto thee. God sende vs only good lucke at in our loue, and whyle the spyryt shal rule my lymmes, none shalbe before thee wythe Lucres, no, Nat my husbande, yf I call hym ryghte. My husbande that was gyuen mee agaynste my wyll : where too my minde neuer consented. But nowe I beseche thee my Eurialus, caste a waye this sacke cloth, and shew y⁰ vnto me as thou arte, put a waye this portours garmente and laye awaye these ropes, Let me see my Eurialus. than he caste of the fylti apparell and shone all in gold and purpull, and began to entende busely to the offyce of loue, whanne Zosias scrapynge at the dore, sayd take hede ye louers, Menelaus sekinge I wote nat what, comethe hyther, hyd al thynge pryuely for oute ye can not scape. Than quod Lucres there is by the bedde a derke closette where bee Juels, thou woteste what I wrote vnto thee, yf my husbande came in, while thou were wythe mee goo thou thyther, there thou mayste be sure in the derke, and neyther styrre nor spytte. Eurialus beynge in doute what he shulde do folowed the womans bydding, she set opē the dore, and went to her worke. There came Menelaus, and one Bertus a scryuener with him, to seke thynges that belonged to the comon weale, whiche whan they

T

were nat in dyuers boxes founde, they are parauenture quod Menelaus in the closet. Goo Lucres, and fetche a lyght for to seke here. With this worde Eurialus was sore afrayde and beganne strayte to hate Lucres, and to hym selfe sayde, Ah foole that I am. Who caused me to comme hether, butte myne owne lyghtenes, I am takenne, I am shamed, I shall leose the Emperoures fauour: what for fauour? I wolde God my lyfe were safe. Howe shall I scape alyue? I am sure too dye. Oh vayne, and of all fooles mooste foolyshe, I am fallen in to theese bryeres wylfullye, to what purpose is the enioynyng of loue, yf it be bought soe deare? the pleasures be shorte and the doloures infinite. Oh yf we woulde endure these thynges for heauen, it is a maruelous folyshenes of men that forsakethe lyghte laboures, for longe ioyes auef or loue, whose ioyes bee comparable to smoke, wee putte oure selfes into extreme daungers, Loo, my selfe nowe shall I bee a tale and example to euerye bodye and knowe not what ende shall become of it, yf anye Good sainte woulde healpe me hence, neuer agayne shall suche laboure deceyue. O good Lorde healpe me hēce and pardon my youthe. Remember not myne ignoraunces, but saue me to repente me of thys faute. She hath not loued me, but as a dere hathe takene me in the net, my daye is come, no man maye healpe me, but thou good lorde. Ofte haue I herde the deceytes of women, and I coulde nat eschew it. yf I escape nowe there shall neuer no crafte of women deceyue me. But Lucres was all yll combred, that fearyd as muche hys healthe as her owne, and as womens wyttes is more redye than mannes in sodeyne peryles, hadde founde a remedye. Come hether quod she husband, here is a caske in this wyndowe, wherin I haue sene you putte dyuers thynges of charge, let vs see yf the wrytynge be there, and runnynge as it were to opene it, ouerthrewe it into the strete, and as it had bene by chaunce; alas quod shee come hethere husbande leest we lese any thynge, the casket is fallen oute of the wyndowe, go quyckely, leest anye Jewels or wrytynges fall oute, goo goo for goddes sake, why tary ye I wyll loke oute that no man take nothynge. Se the desceyte of the womane, nowe trust them hardelye, no man is so circumspecte, that cannot be deceyued, he was neuer kyndelye deceyued whome his wyfe neuer assaied to deceyue, we are ofte more fortunate thene wyse. Menelaus and Bertus abashed with this same ranne bothe hastely into the streate, the house was high after the Italyan facion and manie steppes downe, whereby Eurialus had space to chaūge and putte hym selfe by her coūcell into a nother darcke corner.

They whē they had gathered the writinges and the iewels, because they founde not that that they sought, wente into the closette, wher they founde it, and so byddyng her farewel, departed, and she barred the dore, Come forthe quoth she Euryalus, come forthe my dere harte, and the summe of my ioyes, come the well of my delytes, and sprynge of my gladnes, all thynge is sure, we may talke at lybertie, and now is the place sure for our embracinges, Fortune woulde haue letted oure kyssynges, but God hath fauoured oure loue, and hath not forsaken so faythfull louers, whye taryest thou? here is thy Lucres, whie lettest thou to embrace her. Eurialus at the laste forsakynge hygh feare, clapseth her wyth his armes. I in my lyfe quod he, was I neuer so feared, but thou arte wel worthy for whome suche thīges shulde be suffered. These kyssinges and swete embracings quoth he noo manne shulde haue for noughte, nor, I (to saye trouthe) haue not boughte deare ynoughe soo greate a pleasure. If after my deathe I might lyue, vsynge thy company, a thousand times wold I dye too bye thy embrachynges so oftene. O howe happye and howe blessed, is it a vysyon, or is it in deede? do I holde in mine armes? or do I dreme? surelye it is thyselfe, and thee I haue. Lucres was in a lyghte garmente, that wythoute plyght or wrynkell shewed her bodye as it was, a fayre necke, and the lyghte of eyne lyke the bryght sonne, gladsome countenaunce and a merye face, her chekes lyke lylyes medled wyth roses, swete and sober as her laughynge,

her breaste large and the two papes semynge apples, gathered in
Uenus gardeine meued the curage of the thoucher. Eurialus coulde
no longer suffer the spurre, but forgettynge all feare, and sobernes
layde a parte, sayde vnto the woman: Let vs nowe tast of the fruyte
of loue, hee pressed her soore, and she to the contrarye rested,
shewynge howe shee cared for her honestye, and that her loue desyred nothynge but onely woordes and kysses: Unto whych Eurialus smylynge dyd answere, It is knowne quod hee that I am here or
it is not knowne, yf it bee knowne there is no manne that wyll not
iudge the reaste, yf it bee not knowne, noo moore shall this be, it is
the rewarde of loue, and lette me dye rather than want that. O but
offence quod Lucres. It is offence quod Eurialus not too vse pleasure whan thou mayst, should I forsake such occasion graunted and
desyred so greately? and taking her garmente, The stryuynge
woman y^t wolde not bee ouer comen he ouercame, yet dyd hee not
quenche the desyre of Uenus: but rather prouoked a greater thyrste,
but Eurialus fearinge a further daunger, after he hade a litle ban-
getted, departed, soumethinge agaynste her will and minde, and no
man suspected, because he was as one of the portours. As hee
wente throughe the strete, Eurialus wonderinge on him selfe said
Oh yf the Emperoure shulde now mete with me, and knowe me.
what suspecte wold this garmēt brynge hym in? howe wolde hee
mocke mee. I shulde bee a tale for euery body, and euer a
laughter for him. Neuer wolde he leue me tyll tymee that hee
knewe all, and neades tel him I must what this apparell meanethe,
but I woulde saye y^t it were for another woman than thys, for perauenture hee loueth her, and also it were not mete too declare hym
my loue, for I woulde neuer so betray Lucres, that hathe bothe
receiued and saued me. And thus as he thought he sawe Nisus,
Achates, and plynius, and goth afore and was not knowne of them
tyll he came home, wher as chaungynge hys clothes, vnder coloure
of other names, he telleth the chaunce of the matter, and as hee

remembreth the feare and the joye so dyd he in tellynge feare and reioyce, and in the myddes of his feare, ah fole yᵗ I was quod he I trusted a woman with my hed, so was I not councelled of my fathere, whan he taughte me too truste the faythe of no woman, for that they were cruell deceytefull, chaũgeable, and full of dyuers passiõs, and I yll remēbryng the lesson put my lyfe in a womans handes. what yf anie man hadde knowne me when I was charged wythe wheate? what shame what slaunder hadde bothe I and myne hade for euer? The Emperoure wolde haue refused mee, and as lyghte and madde brayned, myght haue estemed me. What yf her husband had founde me in yᵉ closet? The cyuyll lawe is cruell too adulterers, but the furoure of the husband would haue had greater payne; the tone hadde ben but shorte deathe: the other, deathe wyth cruell tormentes. But set case that he hathe fauoured my lyfe, at yᵉ least he wold haue bounde me, and sent me shamed vnto the Emperoure. ye, thoughe I had escaped hys hãdes because hee hadde no weapon, and I had answered by my syde, yet hade he a man wythe hym, and weapnes honge at hande vpon the wall, and there manye seuauntes in the house, the noyse shoulde haue rysen and the dores shyt and I shoulde haue ben hãdled accordyng. Alas madde that I was, no wysdome, but chaunce hathe delyuered mee from this daunger. Sorowe for chaunce, and it was the readye wytte of her. O trusty woman. O wyse louer. O noble and excelente loue, why should I not trust vnto thee? why should I not truste thy faythe, yf I hadde a thousande lyues, durst truste with them all, thou arte faythfull and wyse, and wysely thou can loue, and healpe thy louer, who could so sone haue the waye too auoyde them that soughte mee, as thou hadde? thou hast saued my lyfe, and I vowe it vnto thee, the lyfe that I lyue is not myne, but thyne, and it shall not be greuous vnto mee, for thee to lease that by thee I haue, thou haste the ryght of my lyfe and commaundement on my deathe. O fayre breste. O pleasaunte tongue, O swete eyen, O freshe wittes,

O goodly lymmes and well furnyshed, whan shall I see you againe, whan shall I byte the same coral lyppe, and here thee speke within my mouthe? shall I neuer handell agayne those rounde brestes? O Achates, it is but lytle that thou haste seene in any woman in comparyson too this, the more nearer she is the more fayrer she is, Lydia the fayre wyfe of Candalus the Kynge was no fayrer: I wondere not yf hee woulde shewe her naked vnto Satius for to do him the greater pleasure; for one my faythe, yf I myghte, so woulde I shew thee this Lady, for els may I not declare vnto thee her beuty nor thou perceiue what ioye I had, but reioyce w^t me. I beseche thee that my pleasure was greater than canne be expressed wythe wordes. Thus talked Eurialus with Achates, and Lucres with her selfe sayde as muche, but soo muche lesse was her gladnesse that shee myghte truste none too shewe it vnto, and vnto Zosias shee durste not for shame tell all.

In the mean tyme a knight called Pacorus, of a noble House folowinge the Emperour, began to loue Lucres, and because hee was fayre and goodly, thoughte to be beloued, and onlye rekened the chastitye of the woman to let him, She as ye custō of Italy is behelde euery body withe a lourynge countenaūce, whether it were by disceit or crafte, least the true loue shuld appere. Pacorus rageth and cane not be in rest tyll he haue felte her minde. The matrones of Shene went ofte to visyte ye chapell of our lady of Bethlem. Hyther was Lucres come with two Maydens and an olde wyfe. Pacorus folowed her wyth a vyolet with goldē leaues in his hande in the stalke wherof he hadde hydde a letter of Loue, written in fine letters, and haue no maruayle thereof. For Cicero sayeth there was shewed him the hole History of Troye, so fynelye written, that it myghte all haue ben closed in a nout shel. Pacorus offereth the violette too Lucres, recommending him vnto her, and she refuseth it. He desyreth her instantlie to take it, Take the floure madame quod y⁰ olde wyfe, what feare you? there is no pearell, it is but a small thynge: wherein perauenture ye maye doo the gentelman pleasure. She folowed here councell, and tooke the floure, and whanne she hadde gonne a lyttle waye, she tooke it vnto the toone of her maydens, and shortelye after they mette wythe two scholers, which I wot not how lyghtly obtayned the flour of the maide, and openynge the stalke, founde the pleasaunt letter. Nowe after the matronnes of Scene had founde the louers, that the Emperoure broughte, and after the Courte was come thyther, theese folke were mocked and deceyued, and lyttle estemed, for the clatteringe of harneys delyted more theese women then eloquence of lernynge. Here vppon grewe greate enuye, and the longe gownes soughte alwayes howe to lette the courtiers. Than whan the crafte of the vyolet was knowne, strayghte was Menelaus gonne vnto, and desyred too red the letter, beyng verye angrye goeth home, blameth hys wyfe, and fylleth all the house wythe noyse. And shee to the contrarye denyeth that there is one faute in her, and tellynge the hole tale, bryngethe the olde wyfe for wytnesse. The Emperour is gone to, complaint is made, Pacorus is called for and he confessethe the faute, asketh forgeuenes and sweareth neuer more too vexe Lucres, but ryghte well knewe hee that Jupiter rather laughethe then takethe angerlye the periurynge of louers, and soo the more that he was let y⁰ more hee foloweth the vayne flame.

The winter is come and the Northe wyndes had broughte downe snows, y⁰ towne falth on plaing, the wiues cast snow balles into the stretes, and the yonge men oute of the stretes into theyr wyndowes. here hade Pacorus gottē occasiō, and had enclosed ī waxe an other leter, and putteth it in a snowe ball, and castynge it vnto Lucres wyndowe. Whoo wyll not saye that fortune ruleth all thynge? one happy hour is more worth to thee, thā if Mars shulde recomende thee in his letter to Uenus. Some saye that fortune hathe noo powere in wyse menne, I graunte too suche wyse menne that onlye delyght in vertue; and sufferynge pouertye, syckenesse, and presonne can thincke theym selfe blessed, which one yet I neuer sawe, nor neuer thyncke there was. The commone lyfe of menne neadeth fortunes fauoure. She whome she wyll she auaunceth, and whō shee lysteth ouerthroweth. Whoo hindered Pacorus but forteoune; was it not wysely handeled, in a violetes stalke to hide his letters and nowe agayne too sende hys letter clouced in snowe, woulde anye man saye it myghte be craftyer, so that yf fortune had holpe he had be iudged crafty, and excellently wyse, but contrary chaunce brought the ball that fell oute of her hande to the fyre, soo that the snowe ones wasted, and the waxe melted, ye letters appeared, which bothe an olde womanne y^t warned her, and Menelaus beynge by, dyde reade, and there be ganne a newe noyse, whiche Pacorus dydde not tarye too excuse, but wente hys waye. This noyse hoalped Eurialus, so that it is true y^t hath bene sayde: it is harde defendynge that is diuersly assauted.

The louers awaited for the secōd maryage and there was a lyttle strayte lane betwyxte Lucres house and her neyghboures, by the whiche settynge his fete vpon eche wall, hee had not ouer harde clymynge too Lucres wyndowe, but this myght only be by nyghte. Nowe must Menelaus go into ye countrey and there must he lye all nyghte, whiche daye was wayted for of those two louers, as it hade bene a Jubyle. The good manne is gone, and Eurialus, chaungynge hys clothes, is come into the lane, there hadde Menelaus a stable, wherein by the teaching of Zosias all the euenynge hee laye hydde in the haye, and loo where Dromo came, y^t was a seruaunte of Menelaus, and hadde rule of hys horses, to fyll the rackes, and harde by Eurialus syde dyd pulle out hay, and had taken more, and strykē in him with the forke, had not Zosias helped, who whan hee sawe the daungere, brothere quod he, geue me thys worke. I shall geue hay to the horses, thou in the meane tyme looke that oure supper be redy, we must be mery whyle our maysters is furthe, our maistres is better felowe, she is merye and lyberall, he is angrye, full of noyse, couetous, and harde; wee are neuer well whē he is at home; se I praye thee what lanke belyes we haue, hee is hungry hym selfe too sterue us to hunger, hee wyll not suffer one moyste peece of browne bread to be loste, but the fragmentes of one daye hee keapethe fyue dayes after, and the gobbets of salte fysh and salte eles of one supper he kepeth vnto another, and marketh the cut chese, leaste anye of it shulde be stolen. The fole y^t bi suche wretchednes soketh hys ryches for nothynge is more folysh thā to leue poore for to dye rychli. howe muche are we better w^t our maistres; y^t feedeth vs not onely with vele and kydde, but with hennes and byrdes, and plenty of wyne. Go Dromo and make the kytchē smoke. Mary quod Dromo, that shall be my charge, and soner shall I laye the tables thanne rub the horse. I broughte my maister into the countre to daye that the Deuyll breke hys necke, and neuer speake hee woorde vnto me butte badde me whan I brought home my horses, to tel my maistres that hee woulde not come home too nyghte; but by God quod he, I prayse the Zosias y^t at the last hast founde faute at my maysters condycions. I had forsaken my mayster, yf my maystres had not geuē me my morowe meles as she hath, lette vs not sleape to nyght Zosia, but lette vs eate and dryncke tyll it bee daye, my mayster shall not wynne so muche thys moneth, as we shall waste at one supper. gladlye dyd Eurialus here this, and marked the maners of seruants and thoughte he was serued a lyke, and whan Dromo was gonne Eurialus arose, and sayd, O happy nyght that throughe thy healpe Zosia I shall haue that haste brought me hether, and wyselye taken heede that I was not discouered, and thou shalt not see that I shal be vnkynde. The houre was come, and the glad Eurialus, that had passed two daungers, clame vppe the wall, and at the wyndowe wente in where al thing was ready and Lucres by the fire. She whan she sawe her louer, clasped him in her armes, ther was embracynge and kyssyng, and with full sayle they folowe theyr lusts, and weried Uenus, nowe with Ceres, and nowe wyth Bachus, was refreshed.

Alas, howe longe busynes and howe shoorte be the pleasures; skant hadde Eurialus one gladde houre lo where Zosias brought woorde that Menelaus was comme and marred all the playe. Eurialus maketh hym readye to departe.

¶ Lucres when she hadde hidden the banket meteth her husbande welcommynge hym home. Welcome quod she my husbande, by mi trouthe quod shee, I wened that thou haddest bene loste in husbandrye, what haste thou done in the countrye thus longe? why tariest thou nat at whome? thou makeste mee sadde with thyne absence, I feare leaste thou haue some other that thou louest, these husbandes be so false to theyr wiues; yf thou wylte that I shall not mystruste thee, neuer slepe oute of my companye. For I can slepe no nyghte w'oute thee, but lette vs suppe here and go to bedd. They were than in the hall, where they vsed to dyne and she sought for to haue kept him there tyl Eurialus had space for to go his waye, for it required somme leasure, but Menelaus had supped forthe, and hasted toward his chamber, Now on my fayth and trouth quod Lucres, y" arte vnkinde, why diddest thou not rather sup with me, because thou was from hence, I haue eaten noo meate to daye, and there were here men of the country that brought in maruelous good wynne, as they sayd, and yet I tasted not of it, but nowe that thou arte come lette vs goo into the celler I beseche thee, and tast yf the wyne be as they say, and so hauynge the lāterne in her one hande, pullynge her husbande w^t the other hāde, wente into the celler, and so longe perced thys vessell and that, and supped with her husbande, tyll she thoughte Eurialus was gonne, And so at the laste wente with her husbande to the euell pleasaunte bed.

¶ Eurialus in the styll of yᵉ night wente home. And on the morowe eyther for that it were necessarye to take hede or for some yll suspecte: Menelaus walled vppe the wyndowe: I thynke as our Cytezens be suspectuous and full of cōiectoures: so dyd hee feare the cōmodyte of the place, and woulde eschewe the occasyon, for thoughe he knewe noughte, yet wyste hee welle that she was muche desyred and daylie prouoked by greate requestes, and iudged a womans thought vnstable, which hath as many myndes as trees hath leues, and that theyr kynde alwaye is desyrous of new thynges, and seldom loue thei theyr husbandes, whom thei haue obteined. Therfore did he folowe the common opynyon of maried men: too auoyde myshape thoughe it come with good lucke, so was theyr meatinge lette, and theyr sendynge of Letters also stopped, for the Tauerner that dwelte behynde Lucres house, where as Eurialus was wounte to speke with here, and geue here letters: at Menelaus perswasion was putte out by the Aldermen, only remayned the behouldynge of theyr eyne, and wyth beckes the louers saluted eche other, and skante myght they vse this vttermoeste poynte of loue, theyr sorowes were greate, and theyr tormentes lyke yᵉ death, for the could neyther forgete, nor use their loue. Whyle Eurialus doothe study dyligentely what auyse hee myghte take in this mater, he remembred Lucres councell whiche she wrot vnto him of Menelaus cousyne Pandalus, and dyd as these cunnyng Physiciās, whose manners is, in daūgerous sycknes to geue indyfferente medecyns and in extreme to vse the last medecins, rather than leue the dysease incurable. He determyned to goo vnto Pandalus, and folowe that waye that afore he hadde forsaken, and when he had sente for him, called hym into a secrete place. Syte downe quod he my frende, I must tell thee a great thyng that requireth suche thynges as be in thee, that is dyligent, fayth, and secretnesse. I woulde erre nowe haue shewed it thee, but I knewe thee not, nowe I doo knowe thee, and, because thou arte an honest faythfull man, I loue thee, and entrete thee, soo that I knewe nothynge els, it is inoughe that thy neygheboures prayse thee, and my fellows to, wythe whome thou haste entred frendshyppe, and who and of what sorte thou arte they haue tould mee, of whome I haue learned that thou desyreste my frendeshyppe, whiche I promyse nowe vnto thee, for thou arte as well worthye myne as I am thyne.

Nowe for bycause amonge frendes a thynge is done in fewe wordes, what I woulde, I wyl shew thee. Thou knowest how the kynde of man is prone unto loue, whether it be vertue or vyce, reygneth euery where, nor no hart there is of fleshe that some tyme hathe not felte the prickes of loue. Thou knoweste that neyther the wyse Salomone nor the stronge Samson hath eschaped from this passyon. Furthermore the nature of a kyndeled harte and of a folyshe loue is this, the more it is lette, the more I bourne. Wyth nothinge soner is this dysease healed, than with obtayninge of the loued. manye there hath bene, both in oure tyme and in oure elder, to whome theyr let hath bene cause of cruel deathe, and agayne many after ye thīg obtained, haue left to rag. Nothynge is better when loue is crepte into the bones than too geeue place to the rage, for who soo stryueth agaynste the tempest, ofte tymes suffereth wracke and who dryueth with the storme escapeth.

This I tel y^e for that thou shalte knowe mee loue, and what for my sake thou muste doe, and then what profytte thou shalte haue thereby. I wyll shewe thee all, for nowe I reaken thee as one part of my harte. I loue Lucres, and truly Pandalus it is not by my faut but by ye gouernaunce of fortune: it whose hādes is the hole worlde, that we inhabyte. The customes of the countrey were vnknowne to mee, I thoughte your women hadde felte in theyr hartes that they sheweth with theyr eyene, and that hath deceyued me, for I thought Lucres hadde loued me, because she beheld me pleasantlye, and I agayne begane too loue her, for I thought suche a lady was not vnmeete to bee beloued for loue, and yet dyd I not know the, nor none of thy kynne. I loued and wened to haue bene loued; who is soo stonye harde (beyng loued) that doth not loue? (But after I sawe I was deceiued.) least my loue shuld be vayne, with all maner of wayes I assayed too kyndell her wythe lyke and lyke fyre, for I bourned and piteously wasted, and shame and trouble of my mynde daye and nyghte dyd maruelouslye tormente me, and I was soo tangled that wyth no wayes I coulde escape, and at the laste I contynued so long, that the loue of vs both lyke pearishe, nor we se noo remedy too oure lyues, but onelye thy healpe. Her husbande keepeth her in his chāber. The waker dragon dyd neuer keepe so well the goldē fleece, nor Cerberus the entre of hel, as Lucres is kepte. I knowe your kynrede, and also I knowe that ye are noble and ryche, and among the beste of thys towne beeloued, but who can withstand destenye? halas Pandalus it was not by my choyse, but by chaunce, and thus standeth this matter, it is as yet secrete, but withoute it be wel guyded, it is lyke, as God forbyd, to brede a greate myschef. I peraduenture myghte apeace my selfe yf I wente from hence, whiche thoughe it were greuous vnto me, I woulde do for your familyes, yf I thought that shoulde healpe, but well I know her rage, eyther she woulde folowe me, or els yf she were constrayned to tarye, woulde kyll her selfe, whiche woulde be vnto youre house a perpetuall dyshonoure.

That I sente for you, is for youre cause to wythstande these myscheues, nor there is none other waye but that thou wylt be gouernour of oure loue, that the dyssembled fyre maye bee secreate. I recommende, I geeue, and I vowe mee holy vnto thee, be diligent in this furoure, leaste whyle it bee lette, it flame the more. Do so much that wee maye mete together, and soo shall the heate boe aslaked, and made more sufferable; thou knowest the wayes of the house, thou knoweste when the good manne is absente, thou knowest howe to brynge me in, but Menelaus brother muste bee hadde oute of the waye, whiche wayteth euer dylygently for these matters, and kepeth Lucres in steade of her brother, and marketh dylygently her wordes, her lookes, her countenaunce, her spittynges, her coughes, her laughes, and eche thynge he consydereth, hem muste I deceyue, and it cannot bee wythoute thee. Healp therfore I beseche the, and whan her husbande Menelaus is frome home, aduertise me, and his brother that taryeth brynge theym out of the waye y' he neyther take hede to her, nor set none other kepers ouer her, which, if thou wilt vndertake, and healpe mee as my trust is in thee, all is safe, for thou mayste pryuelye, whyle the other be faste in sleape, lette me in, and ease oure furyous loue. What profyte shall ensue of this? I thynke thou vnderstādest by the discrecyō. For fyrste thou shalte saue the honoure of the house, and hyde the loue that in no wyse can be publyshed wythoute your shame. Secondly thou shalt saue thy cosē in lawes lyfe, and also too Menelaus, saue a wyfe, too whome it shall not bee so hurtefull that shee were myne for one nyght (no man knowynge of it) as yf hee shoulde lese her, all the worlde wonderyng whan she shoulde folowe me. Dyuers women folowed their louers, what yf she determined to folowe mee? what dyshonoure shoulde it be to your kynne! what mocke among people! what shame as well to al the towne as to you! some wolde peraduenture say, put her to deth rather than she shoulde doe thus, but woo be vnto hym that syleth hym with bludsheddynge, and remedieth one faute by a greater.

Myscheuousnes be not too be encreased but too be lessed. of two good thynges, wee knowe y' beste is to bee chosen, and of a good and of an ylle, the good, and of two ylles the least. Euerye waye is daungerous, but thys y^t I shewe the is leaste peryllous, by which y^u shalt not only helpe thine own bloud, but also me that am almoost oute of my wytte too see Lucres suffre as she doth for me: who I would rather dyd hate me, thā I woulde entreate thee; but thus it is and at thys poynte, and wythe oute thy crafte, thy wytte and thy dyligence ye shyppe be guyded ther remayneth noo hope of healthe. Helpe therefore bothe her and me, and saue thy house from shame, And thyncke not that I wyll bee vnkynde, thou knowest I maye doe wythe the Emperoure, and what thou wylte, I wyll gette thee graūted, and thys I promyse thee on my faythe thou shalt bee an Earle by patente, and all thy postoritye shall inioye the same tytle. I commyt vnto thee both Lucres, we, oure loue and fame, the honoure of thy kynne, I truste vnto thy fayth, thou art the arbyter, and all these be in thyne handes : Take hede nowe what dost, for lyke as thou mayst saue, so maist thou spil.

¶ Pandalus when he heard this smyled, and after a lytle pause sayde (Al this haue I knowne quod he Eurialus, and wolde God it had not happened, but nowe, as thou sayest, it is at that poynte that I must nedes doo as thou byddeste mee, excepte I wold shame all our kyn and rayse a greate slaunder : The woman īdede brenneth, and hath no power ouer her selfe, and w'out I healpe, she wyl sle her self w' some knyfe, or breke her necke oute of some wyndowe, neyther careth she for honoure nor for her selfe; she hath toulde me her desyre, I haue blamed her, I haue busyed me too quence the flame, and all in vayne, she careth for nought but for thee, thou arte alwaies in her mynde, that she wysheth, thee she desyreth, and thee onlye shee thynketh vpon, often tymes callynge mee by thy name. Soo is the womanne chaunged by loue, that she semeth not the same.

Halas what pytye and what sorowe, there was none in all the towne more chaste or more wyser then Lucres. It is a maruelous thyng yf nature haue geuen loue suche lawe ouer thee myndes of menne. Thys dyssease muste bee healped and with none other cure than thou haste shewed, I wyll goo aboute thys busynes, and whanne tyme is, I shall warne thee, nor seeke no rewarde of thee. It is not the offyce of an honeste manne to aske thanke where none is deserued. I do it to auoyde the fame of oure house, and yf thou take anye benefyte thereby, I am not therefore to be rewarde. Yet quod Eurialus for all that I thancke thee, and as I sayde, I promyse thee to cause thee to be made Erle and refuse not hardly thys honoure. I refuse it not quod Pandalus, but I woulde not it shoulde come by this meanes. Yf it come lette it come, I wyll nothynge dooe by couenaunte, yf I myghte haue done it by vnknowne to thee, that thou myghte haue bene with Lucres, I woulde gladly haue done it. Farewell, and thou also quod Eurialus, nowe that thou haste geuen me comforte, make fayne, fynde, or do by some meanes, that we maye be together. Thou shalt prayse me quod Pãdalus, and hee departed full glade that he hadde entred in Eurialus grace. Hopĩg to be an Earle, whereof hee was more desyrous, in as muche as he shewed leaste, for there bee manye men, so woman lyke, that whan they saye moste nay, they woulde fayneste. He hathe gotten by furtheraunce of loue the name of an Earle'and hys posteriars shall shewe for theyr noblenes a gylted bull.

Not longe after there was a fray in the coũtry among Menelaus husbandmen, and dyuers of them that hadde dronke ouer muche were slayne, wherfore Menelaus must go forth to set good order in these matters, to whome Lucres sayde, husbande thou art heaue and weake, and thy horse goeth harde, borowe therefore some ambelynge horse. And whan he asked where myghte borowe any, Mary quod Pandalus Eurialus hadde very good one, and sure he wyll gladly lende hym thee, yf thou wylte I shall aske hym.

Doe quod Menelaus, and Eurialus assone graũted as he was desyred, takynge it for a good tooken, and to him selfe saide, yf thou leape vppon my horse, I shall doe the same vnto thy wyfe. Nowe the couenaunte was that at fyue of ye clocke Eurialus shuld wayte in the streate, And shoulde hoope well yf he harden Pandalus sing. Menelaus was gone, and thee cloudy nyghte had couered the heuen. Lucres taried her time in her chambre, and Eurialus was afor the doore, and taryed y⁰ token, but he neyther harde hym synge nor spit. The houre was paste, Achates meued him too departe. It was hard too departe, and ymagyned nowe one cause nowe another. Pandalus sange not because Menelaus brother was lefte there, that soughte eche corner for feare of deceytes, and waked all the whyle, To whome Pandalus sayde, shall we not goo too bedde thys nyght and I am wonderous slepy, I wōder of thee that arte a yonge man, and lyke one olde manne, too whome drynes taketh awaye sleape, thou neuer dooste sleape, but before day when other men do ryse. Lètte vs goo to bedde, to what purpose do we watche : Lette vs go quod Agemennon, yf thou wylte, but lett vs looke fyrst to the dores yf they be well shutte for doute of theues And whan he was came to the dore, he putte to it, nowe one locke, nowe another, and bolted it.

There was a great barre of yron that scāte two coulde lyfte where wyth the dore was neuer shutte, whych whan Agamennon coulde not put too, desyred healpe. Thou shuttest the dore quod Pandalus as yf the house should be beseged, are we not in a sure city ? wee are at liberty in this towne, and quietnes is come to vs all. The Florentynes oure enemyes wᵗ whome we haue warre be farre hence. If thou dred enemyes this house can not healpe vs. I wyll this nyght lyfte noo burdons, my shoulders ake, and I am sore brused within. I am not meete for the burden, therefore lyfte thou thy selfe, or let it alone, Well then quod Agamennon it is ynoughe, and wente to bed, Then quod Eurialus, I wyll tarye here thys houre too se peraduēnture yf anye body doo appere. Achates that was with Eurialus was wery of soo longe tarying, and preuely cursed Eurialus whiche had kepte him so longe frō sleape. yet they taryed not longe after, but they sawe Lucres through a creues, carying a light in her hande. Towarde whō Eurialus w t and sayd God spede quod he my dere harte Lucres, and shee beyng a feard, woulde haue gone her waye, but thā remēbringe her selfe, What man arte yᵘ quod shee

x

yͭ callest mee? I thyne Eurialus am here quod he, opē the dore my delite, I haue taryed here halfe this nyghte. Lucres at the laste knewe his voyce, but because shee feared deceyte, she durste not opē tyll she knewe some token that it was he, and so with greate laboure she remoued yᵉ lockes, but because there were manye fastenynges too the dore that a womãs strēgth could not vndo, shee opened it but halfe a foote wyde. Good ynough quod Eurialus, and stretchyng hym selfe at last gate in and taketh her in his armes. Achates watched w'oute. Lucres, eyther for feare or for Joy swowned in Eurialus armes, and her strenght faylige wyth pale face semed all readye deade, but that her pulce and hete remayned. Eurialus wyth the sodeyne chaunce affeared, wyste not what to do, yf I go hence thought he, yᵉ faute of her death shal be in me to leaue a womanne in suche daūger, yf I tarye, Agamennon or some of the house shall come, and thā I am vndone. Alas vnhappy loue yͭ haste in the more gal than hony, yᵉ bytter worme wode is no more soure than thou arte, what daungers haste thou al redye put me in, wͭ howe manye dethes haste thou thretened my hed? and haste thou lefte me nowe too haue a woman dye in myne armes? whye haste yᵘ not rather slayne me? whye haste thou not torne me wͭ lyons. Alas howe muche had it bene yͭ I had dyed in her lappe, thā she in my bosome! Loue had ouercome the mā, and regarding not his own helth taryed with the womanne, and lyfting vppe her bodie al be moysted wythe teres, kyssed her, Alas Lucres quod he, wher art thou become? where bee thyne eares? whye answerest thou not? why herest thou not? open thyn eyes. I besoche the looke vpon me, smyle on mee as thou arte wonte; thy Eurialus is heare, he doth embrace thee, why dooste thou thus trouble me, I wonder, arte thou gone, or dooste thou slepe; where shall I seke the? yf thou wouldest dye, why dydest thou not warne me that I myght haue dyed with thee. If yᵘ wilt not heare me, my sword shal straight open my syde, and we shall booth dye at ones. Ah my lyfe, my darlynge, my delyte, and my only hoppe, and my hole healthe, shall I thus lese thee? open thyne eyne, lyfte vp thy head, thou art not yet ded, I fele thou arte warme, and thy breathe is yet in thee. Whye doste thou not speake to me? doste thou receyue me of this sort? doste y^u call me to suche pastyme? dooste thou gyue me suche a nyght? Rise I beseche the my dere hart, looke on thy Eurialus, I am here; and wyth that worde he stoude of, his teres flushed so vppon her face, that as wyth droppes of water ye woman awaked out of her slepe, and seynge her louer, Alas quod she Eurialus, where haue I ben? why dydest thou not suffer me to dye? happlie had I dyed in thy armes, and would god I myght so dye eare thou should depart ye towne. Thus talckynge together, they wente into the chamber, where they hadde suche a nyghte as we iudge the two louers Paris and Helena had after he had taken her away, and it was vnto thē so pleasaunte, that they thoughte Mars and Uenus hadde neuer none suche. Thou arte quod Lucres my Ganimedes, my Ypolitus, my Diomedes. Thou arte quod Eurialus my Polexeno, my emly, ye and Uenus her selfe; and her mouth and now her eyene and now her chekes he kysseth, and sometyme casting doune the clothes, he sawe suche beautye as he neuer afore saw. I haue found more quod he than I wened, suche a one sawe Acteon of Diana, whanne she bathed her in the foūtayne. What is more pleasaunter or more fayrer than these limmes? nowe haue I bought them wyth pearyll, but what thinge shuld I not haue suffred for thee? O fayre necke, and plesaūt brestes, is it you y^t I touche, is it you that I haue? are ye in my handes? O round lymmes, O swete body, haue I thee in my armes? Nowe where doth pleasāt in the freshnesse of my ioye, that no displeasure myghte here after hurte it. Do I holde thee or do I dreme? O pleasaunte kysses, Oh dere embrachynges, O swete bytinges, no man lyuenge is more happe than I, or more blessed.

But alas howe swyfte bee these houres! Thou spetefull nyghte, why goest yᵘ awaye? abyde Apollo and tarye vnder the earth. Why dost thou so sone put thy horse into the chayret? lete them repast; geue me this nyght as thou dyddest to Alcmena. Whi doest thou Aurora leue so sone the bed of Titan. Yf thou were as pleasaunte vnto hym as Lucres is to me, he wold not suffer thee to aryse so earlye. Neuer sawe I so shorte a nyghte, yet haue I bene in Britayne and in Denmarke: thus saide Eurialus, and Lucres sayde noo lesse, nor suffered not one kysse not one woorde too passe vnrecompēced. He strained and she strained, and whā they had done they were not wearye, but as Athens rose from the grounde strōger, soo after battell were they more desyrous of warre. The nyghte ended whan Aurora tooke from the Ocean her dewe heere. He departed and longe after myghte not retourne, by thee dayelye watche that was put vnto her.

Bet loue ouercame all thynge, and at laste they founde waie for their mytynge, which long whyle they vsed.

In the meane tyme the Emperoure, that all redy was reconcyled to Eugenius, determyne to goo to Rome. This dyd Lucres perceyue, for what is that that loue knoweth not? or who can deceiue a louer? one therefore Lucres wrote thus vnto Eurialus.

If my minde could be wroth toward the, I wold now be angrye with thee, for that thou haste dyssembled thy departynge, but it loueth thee better then me, and maye for no cause be meaued againste thee. Alasse my hert, whi haste thou not told me of the Emperoures departure? hee makethe hym redye toward hys iourney and I knowe yᵘ shalte not tary behind. Alas what shall bee come of mee, what shal I do pore womā, wher shal I reste? yf thou doo forsake me, my lyfe lasteth not two dayes. For theese letters therefore moysted with my teares, and for thye ryghte hande, and thy promysed fayth, yf euer I haue deserued ani thyng of thee, or yf euer thou hast had anye delyte by me, haue pyty on thy vnhappy louer. My desire is not that thou shuldist tary but that thou shouldest take me with thee. I wel make as I would go in the euenyng to Bethlē, and take but one olde womā with me, Let two or thre of thy seruauntes bee ther, and by force take me awaye. It is noo greate payne too take one awaye that woulde be gone, nor thynke it noo shame, for Parys the sonne of a kinge dyd lyke wyse, and yᵘ shalte doe no wronge vnto my husbande, for hee shall algates lease mee, for yf it be not by thy takyng, it shal be by death. But I am sure thou wylte not bee so cruell to leaue mee behynde too dye, that euer hath made more of thee than of my lyfe. Farewel mi onlye trust.

To whome Eurialus aunswered after this facion.

Hetherto haue I hydde from thee my Lucres my departynge, because thou shouldest not tourmēte thee ouermuch afore the tyme. I knowe thy condicions, and vnder what manner thou soroweste, but yᵉ Emperoure departeth not so that he shall not retourne, and whan we shall retourne from Rome, this is in oure waye to our contrey, and yf so bee yᵉ Emperoure wyll goo any other waye, yf I leue thou shalte se me retourne. Let god neuer suffer mee to come into my countreye, But make me wander lyke Ulyses, yf I come not hether. So comfort thy selfe therfore my dere hert and be of good cheare, bee not sade, but rather lyue mercly. Thou sayest thi takynge awaye shoulde bee thee greatest pleasure that coulde bee to me ; it is trouthe, and greater delyte I coulde not haue, thā thee alwais at mi desire : But I must rather take heede to my honoure than to my lust, for the fayth that thou berest vnto me, byndeth me to geue thee such fayth full counseyle as shulde bee mete for thee. Thou knoweste thou art maryed into a noble famylye, and haste yͬ name of a ryght beautyfull and chaste Lady, and it is not onlye in Italye, but as well in Teutonya, Panonia, Bohemia, and all the worthye partyes, so that yf I take thee awaye (besyd my shame yᵗ for thy sake I set little by), what dyshonoure shuldeste thou do to all thy frendes! what sorow shulde thy mother take! what shulde be then spoken of the? what rumeure shoulde all the worlde heare of thee? Lo. Lucres, that was called more chast thē yͤ wyfe of Brutus and better thā Penelope, foloweth an adultherer not remembringe neyther her parentes nor countreye; it is not Lucres, but Ippia, or Medea, yᵗ folowed Jason. Halas what grefe shuld it be to me to here such thinges of the! oure loue is yet secret, there is noo man that dyspraiseth thee, Thy taking awaie shulde marre all, nor thou were not so praysed as thou shuldest then be blamed. But besides our honour howe were it possible that we shuld use our loue? I serue the Emperoure, he hath made me riche and of great power, and I cannot departe frō hym wythout the losse of my state, so that yf I shulde leaue hym, I coulde not conuenientlye entertaine thee, ye I shulde contynuallye folowe the courte. We haue no reast, euerye day we chaunge places. The Emperoure hath taryed no where so longe as he hathe done here, and that because of warre, soo that yf I shoulde carye thee about wyth me, and haue thee in my Tent as a folower of the feelde, what reprefe and shame shulde it be both to the and me! For these causes I beseche yᵗ my Lucres put awaye this mynde and remember thy honoure, and flatter not rather thy rage than thy selfe. Another louer peraduenture wolde other wyse counsel thee, and desyre thee to ronne thy waye, that he might abuse thee as longe as he mighte, nothynge regardyng what shuld be fal of it while he mighte satisfye hys appetite, but he were noo true louer that wolde regarde rather his owne lust than thy fame. I councell the my Lucres for the best, tary heare I beseche the and doubte not in my retourne: what so euer the Emperour hath to do here, I wyll sue to haue it cōmytted vnto me y^t Imaye accōpanye with thee withoute daunger. Farewell, liue and loue me, and thinke my fyre no lesse than thine owne, and moost contrary to my minde I departe. Farewell agayne the delyte and fode of my lyfe.

¶ Wyth these letters the woman somewhat had appesed her selfe, and aunswered that shee woulde folowe his councell.

Shortly after Eurialus wente to Rome withe the Emperoure, where he had not bene longe but he was sicke of an hote ague. The pore vnhappy man when he was burnyng in loue, began also to burne in sycknes, and when loue had wasted his strength by doloure and of ye disease, litle remaineth of his lyfe, and that spirit was rather entertained with Physiciōs thā taried of it selfe. The Emperour visyted hym dayly, confortīg hym as his sonne, and commaunded that he shoulde haue all cure of medecynes that myghte bee, but none was of more effecte for hys remedye then a letter from Lucres, whereby hee vnderstode her helth, which somewhat mynysheth hys sycknes, and made him recouer hys fete, so that hee was at the coronacion of the Emperoure, and there was made knyght. After thys, whā the Emperoure wente too Perusia, hee taryed at Rome, and fro thence wente too Scene, all thoughe hee were but yet weke and verye grene of hys sycknes, but he myghte onelye behoulde Lucres and not speake to her. Many letters wente betwixt them, and agayne there was practysynge for her goynge away. Thre dayes did Eurialus tarye there, and whē he sawe no maner of wayes to come to her, y^t as thē was takē from hym, hee dyd aduertise hys lady of his departynge, but neuer had they suche plesure in theyr cōuersacyon as they had dyspleasur in theyre departinge. Lucres was in her wyndowe when Eurialus rid through the strete, and wyth theyr moyste eyen the one beheld the other. He wept and she wept, and bothe were destrayned with greuous doloures, as they that felte theyr hartes tourne of theyr places. If anye mā doth not know the dolour of death let him cōsider the departynge of two louers, whiche hath more heuynes and more paynefull tormēt. The soule suffreth in death, for that it parte frō the beloued bodye, and the bodye (the soule ones departed) suffreth not, but whanne two mindes bee ioyned together, soo much is the diuision more full in so muche as the delyte of eyther of them is more sencyble.

And surelye heare was not two myndes, but surelye, as wenethe Aristophanes, one soule in two bodies so departed, not one minde from another, but one loue and one mynd was in two deuyded, and the harte suffred particion. Parte of the minde wente and part remayned and all the sences were disperpled and playned too departe frō theyr owne selfe. Nor one drope of bloude remained in the louers faces, but only teares and bewaylinges, and verye death apered in theyr vesages. Who maye wryte or declare, to thynk the grefes of those mindes, but he y^t hath ones in hys lyfe bene like wyse made? Laodomya, whan Prothesilaus wēt to ye siege of Troy, snowned, and whan she knewe of his deathe dyed. Dido, after the predestinate departynge of Eneas, slewe herselfe, And Percia woldc not lyue after Brutus deathe. But thys our Lucres, after Eurialus was out of her syght, fallinge too the earthe, was taken vp by her maidens, and layde in her beade, and when she came to her selfe, al purple and golden clothes and glad apparel she layde a parte, and were dyspleasaunte tawnye and neuer after was harde synge or seene laughe, nor by no sportes nor ioye, nor myrth, myghte neuer bee reconforted, in whiche condycion when she had a lytle whyle continued, she fel into sycknes, and, because her hearte was absente, the mynde woulde receyue no consolacyon, and at the laste betwyxte the armes of her muche wepynge mother (vsynge vayne cōfortable woordes) she gaue vpe the weryd gooste, dysdaynynge the sorowfull lyfe.

Eurialus, after he had passed the syght of those eyn y‘ shuld neuer agayne see hym, neuer speke to anye bodye in hys iourney, but caryed onlye Lucres in his mynde, and thoughte busylye yf he myghte retourne, and at last came vnto the Emperoure at Perusia, and wente wyth hym too Ferrar, to Mantua, to Trydente, to Constantia, and to Basyle, and so into Hungery, and to Bohemy. But lyke as he folowed the Emperoure so dyd Lucres folow hym in hys sleepe and suffred hym noo nyghtes rest, whō whē he knewe hys true louer to be deed meaued by extreme doloure clothed him in mournynge apparell, and vtterly excluded all cōforte, and yet though the Emperoure gaue hym in mariage a ryghte noble and excellente Ladye, yet he neuer
enioyed after, but in
conclusyon piti-
fully wasted
his painful
lyfe.

***

¶ Imprynted at London in
Louthbury by me Wyl-
lyam Copland.

***

THE NORTHREN MOTHERS BLESSING.

The way of Thrift.

VVritten nine yeares *before the death of G.* Chaucer.

LONDON,
Printed by Robert Robinson for
Robert Dexter. 1597.

The Northren Mothers Blessing.

God wold that euery wife that wonnyth in this land
Wold teach her doughter as ye shal vnderstand,
As a good wife did of the North countré
How her doughter should lere a good wife to bee:
    For lack of the moders teaching
    Makes the doughter of euill liuing,
        My leue dere child.

My doughter gif thou be a wife, wisely thou werke,
Looke euer thou loue God and the holy Kirke,
Go to Kirke when thou may, and let for no rayne,
And then shall thou fare the bet, when thou God has
    Ful well may they thriue   (sayn :
    That seruen God in their liue,
        My leue dere child.

Gladly giue thou thy tithes and thine offrings both
To the poore at thy gate, be thou neuer loath ;
Gif hem of thy good, and be not ouer hard ;
Seldom is that house poore there God is steward :
    For that is best I spende,
    That for Gods loue I lend.
        My leeue deere childe.

The Northren Mothers Blessing.

When thou sits in the Kirke thy Bedes shalt thou bid,
Therein make no iangling with friend ne sib,
Laugh not to scorne nodir old ne yong,
Be of good bering and haue a good tongue :
    For after thy bering,
    So shall thy name spring,
      My leeue dere child.

Gif any man with worship desire to wed thee,
Wisely him answere, scorne him not what he be,
And tell it to thy friends and hide thou it nought,
Sit not by him nor städ not that sin mow be wrought :
    For gif a slaunder be once raysed,
    It is not so sone stilled,
      My leeue dere child.

What man that shall wed the fore God with a ring,
Looke thou loue him best of any earthly thing,
And meekly him answere and not too snatching;
So may thou slake his yre and be his darling :
    Faire Words slaken yre,
    Suffer and haue thy desire,
      My leue dere child.

Sweete of spech be thou and of milde moode,
True in word and dede, so bids our Lord God,
And keepe the euer doughter fro velony and shame
That men for thy doing speake the no blame :
    Good life ends wele,
    Be true euer as the stele,
      My leue dere child.

The Northren Mothers Blessing.

Be of fayre sembland and of good manere,
Change not thy coūtnaunce for ought thou can here,
Ne fare not as a giglot what euer thee betyde,
Laugh not too loud ne gape not too wide :
    Maydens should laugh softlye
    That men here not they bee,
        My leue dere child.

When thou goes by the gate go not too fast,
Ne bridle not with thy head, ne thy shoulders cast,
Be not of many words ne sweare not to gret,
All euill vices my doughter thou foryet :
    For gif thou haue an euill name,
    It will turne the to grame.
        My leue dere child.

Goe not oft to the towne as it were a gaze
Fro one house to odir for to seeke the maze,
Ne go not to market thy barrell to fill,
Ne vse not the Tauern thy worship to spill.
    For who the Tauerne vsis
    His thrift he refusis,
        My leue dere child.

Gif thou be in place where good drinke is on loft,
Wheder that thou serue or thou sit softe,
Mesurely take thou, and get the no blame ;
Gif thou be drunken it turnes the to shame.
    Who so loues measure and skill,
    He shall ofte haue his will,
        My leeue dere child.

Go not to the wrastling, ne shoting the cock,
As it were a strumpet or a giglot :
Be at home doughter and thy things tend,
For thine owne profit at the latter end :
    Mery is owne thing to see,
    My dere doughter I tell it thee,
        My leue dere child.

Acquaint the not with euery man goes by the strete,
When folks thee bespeaken curtesly hem grete,
Let hem not by the wey, nor by hem doe not stond,
That they with velony make not thine hert bond :
    For all men are not tristy,
    Gif they speake to thee gayly,
        My leue dere child.

Of lefe men doughter gift thou none take,
But thou wote wele how sone it forsake :
Men with their gifts wemen oregone
Gif they of herts be herd as stone :
    Bounden is he or shee
    That gifts takis securely,
        My leue dere child.

In odur mens housen make thee no mastrye,
Ne blame thou nothing thou sees with thine eye,
Doughter I the prey bere thee so wele
That all men may sey thou art true as steele :
    For wise men and old
    Sayne good name is worth gold,
        My leue &c.

Be thou no chider ne of wordis bold,
To missay thy neighburs neder young ne old,
Be thou not too proud ne too enuious
For thing that may betyde in odir mens house :
 For an enuious hert
 Procures mickle smert,
  My leue &c.

Gif thy neighburs haue riche instore or tyre
Therefore make thou no strife ne bren not as fire,
But thanke God of goods he has thee yeuen,
And so shalt thou doughter good life liuen.
 For oft at ease he is
 That loues peace I wis,
  My leue &c.

Huswifely shall thou go on the werk-day,
Pride, rest, and idlenes put hem cleane away,
And after on the holyday well clad shalt thou be
The haliday to worship, God will loue the,
 More for worship of our lord
 Than for pride of the world.
  My leue &c.

Mekill shame doughter shall that wife tyde
That maken poore their husbond with their great pride :
Therefore doughter be huswife good,
After the wren has vaines men may let blood.
 For their thrift wexis thin
 That spend more than they win,
  My leue dere child.

Wisely looke thy houshold thy meynye,
To bitter ne to boner with hem ne bee,
And looke what neede is best to be done
And thereto set thy meiney sone :
　　Before done deede
　　Another may speede
　　　My leue &c.

Looke to thy meyny and let them not be ydell,
Thy husband out, looke who does much or litell,
And he that does well quite him his meede
And gif he doe amisse amend thou him bidde,
And gif the work be great and the time strait
Set to thy hond, and make a huswifes brayd,
　　For they will do better gif thou by them stond,
　　The worke is soner done there as is many hond
　　　My leue &c.

And looke what thy men doon, & about him wĕd,
At euery deede done be at the tone end,
And gif thou finde any fault soone it amend,
Eft will they doe the better and thou be nere hand.
　　Mikell him behoues to doe
　　A good house that will looke to.
　　　My leue &c.

Looke all thing be well when they worke leauen,
And take thy keyes to the when it is euen,
Looke all thing be well, and let for no shame
And gif thou so do, thou gets thee the lasse blame :
　　Trust no man bett than thy selfe
　　Whilest thou art in thy helth :
　　　My leue &c.

The Northren Mothers Blessing. 169

Borrow not too gladly, ne take not to trest
But the more neede it make or the more breste
Make the not rich of oder mens thing
The bolder to spend the worse thriuing
    For at the ending
      Home will the borrowed thing,
        My leue &c.

Giue thy meiney their hire at the terme-day
Wheder they abiden or els gone away,
Be wise euer doughter of their doing
That thy friende may haue ioy of thy prouing
    Loose not the loue of thy frind,
      For a litle that thou mighst spend,
        My leue &c.

Now haue I taught the doughter, so did my moder mee
And therfore do therafter gif thou think to the,
Look or thou wed any mā, that he haue a good name,
True of hand and tongue without any blame:
    For better it is a childe to be vnborne,
      Than for vnteaching to be forlorne,
        My leue &c.

Sit not at euen too long at gaze with the cup
For to wassell and drinke all vppe,
So to bed betimes, at morne rise beliue
And so may thou better learne to thriue:
    He that woll a good house keepe
      Must ofte-times breake a sleepe,
        My leue &c.

Gif it betide doughter thy friend fro the fall
And god send the children that for bread will call,
And thou haue mickle neede, helpe litle or none,
Thou must then care and spare hard as the stone :
  For euill that may betide,
   A man before should dread,
    My leue &c.

Of all thing doughter looke thou thinke,
Gif men wold for worship set thee on the benk,
Be not too statly doughter noder young ne old,
For some folk are now pore that somtime ware gold :
  Many folk for pride
   After weren a naked side,
    My leue &c.

Gif thou be a rich wife be not ouer hard,
Welcome thy neigbours that come the toward,
Giue hem meat and drink, the more is thy meed
Each bodie to his state shold giue the pore at need :
  For thing that may thee betide,
   Loue well thy neighbour thee beside,
    My leue &c.

Take heed to thy children which thou hast born
And wait wel to thy doughters that they be not forlorne,
And put hem betime to their mariage
And giue them of thy good when they be of age.
  For maydens bene louely,
   But they bin vntrusty,
    My leue &c.

The Northren Mothers Blessing.

Gif thou loue thy children hold thou hem lowe
And gif any of hem misdo banne hem not ne blow,
But take a good smart rod and beat hem arowe
Till they cry mercy and their gilts bee know.
 For gif thou loue thy children wele
 Spare not the yard neuer a deale,
  My leue &c.

Now looke thou do doughter as I haue taught thee
And thou shalt haue my blessing the better may thou the,
And euery maiden that good wife wold bee
Do as I haue taught you for saint charity :
 And all that so will do God giue hem his blessing
 And send hem all heauen at her last ending.

AMEN.

Explicit.

The Way to Thrift.

Lord God what is this worldes wele,
Riches, reuell and great aray?
Nothing to spare, and all day to spill,
Full sone it wastes and weares awey.
When plenty may no lenger paye
What wight with him wold then abide?
A carefull man both night and day
With heauie hart his head must hide,
And all is for default of grace,
That God grutches ayenst our gouernaunce
When measure may not medle in place.
What is it to a man more grieuance,
Than sodenly fro manhood for to fall
In pride his simple purueyance
There pouertie is steward in hall:
But hee that can in some season
Gedder and keepe or that hee grynde
In winter tyme by way of reason
Hee shall not be farre behinde.
For ther as measure is in mynde
Good rule may not long faile,
Yet beware to bee ouer kinde
For skoring in the comiter tayle;
But wele and worship with welfare
Mickle wastes with little winne
Full soone brings a housholder bare,

With large spending both out and in,
Then bee aduised or thou beginne
That thou haue none need to plaine,
Think what a state theu standest in
For Pouerty is a priuie payn,
And if thou haue hope of help and trist
Of lords aud ladies with her pleasance
And yet beware of Had I wist
For old enuy makes new distaunce
In pride and pouerty is great penaunce
And yet is danger most disease.
Here is a cumberrouse acquaintance
When noder of hem oder please,
Fer Had I wist comes euer too late
When there lackes both lock and key,
What nede is then to spare the yat
When nothing is leaued in the way
With a pennylesse purse for to pay.
How can he then his people please,
Many a man had a leue dye,
As long to liue in such disease.
A bare beard may soon be shauen
There as is none heyre about
It faireth as a man that mickle wold hauen
And is not else but pore and proud,
But euer ready in ilke rout
And lay to wed both pot and panne.
When the fire clean is blowne out
Where shall wee go dyne than?
What need is it to delue deep,
There as is no seed to sowe?
The pot is easy for to keep

When all the fat is ouerblowe,
Noder for the kyte ne for the crow
Incumber not thine owne nest.
Too mickle bend will breake thy bow
When thy game is alder best,
Ensample men may see all day.
Yet keep I no man to defend.
The houshold and great aray
Is Lords life and Ladies game,
When gladshippe grows into grame
And for need must begge and borrwo
First comes pride and after shame,
And from solace turnes to suddain sorrow.

FINIS.

THE
Mirror of Martyrs,
OR
The life and death of
that thrice valiant Capitaine, and most godly Martyre
Sir *Iohn Old-castle* knight
Lord Cobham.

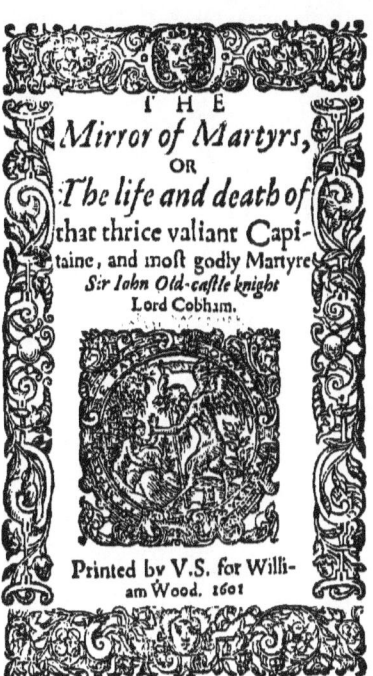

Printed by V.S. for William Wood. 1601

To the liuely image of all morall Virtues, and
true perfection of heauen-borne Arts,
William Couell Bachelor of Diuinitie,
all successe agreeable to the auncient worth
of his ancestors.

This Poem (Right Wor:) which I present to your learned view, some two yeares agoe was made fit for the Print; that so long keeping the corner of my studie, wherein I vse to put waste paper: This first trew Oldcastle, thought himselfe iniurde, because he might not bee suffered to sustaine the second Martyrdome of the Presse: In somuch that I was contented he should stand bare-headed to these churlish times, and endure the censure of his vtmost enemies, onely to make his Death more glorious. Howsoeuer, now he passeth vnder your protection; and though my pensill be too weake, either for his or your picture, accept of the same, because it comes from zeale.

The admirer of your vertues,

Io Weeuer.

To the Authors most honored friend,
Richard Dalton of Pilling,
enricht with all gifts of Nature, and graced
with the chiefe ornaments of
true Gentilitie.

How ioyfully the Authors Poem goes,
To thee, whose wit, whose vertues he admires,
With what a willing soule hee daily shows,
That loue, the which thy loue of him requires,
 Whose name he honors, and whose machlesse worth,
 He can imagine better than set forth.

His minde farre more is, than his feeble might,
Yet hath he wouen of this home-spunne thred,
So fine a webbe, so richly scourde and dight,
(Minerua like) beyond the wisest head :
 The which to praise, were onely to this end,
 To marre the loome, and not the cloth to mend.

The Life and death of Sir Io: Oldcastle knight, Lord Cobham.

Faire Lucifer, the messenger of light,
Vpon the bosome of the star-deckt skie,
Begins to chase the rauen-fethered night:
That stops the passage of his percing eie:
   And heauing vp the brim of his bright beuer,
   Would make that day, which day was counted neuer.

But Mercurie, be thou the morning Star,
Beare my embassage from Elysium,
Shew to my countrie hence remoued far,
From these pauilions I can neuer come:
   Staind vice ascends from out th'infernall deepes,
   But in the heauens vnspotted vertue keepes.

Deliuer but in swasiue eloquence,
Both of my life and death the veritie,
Set vp a *Si quis*, giue intelligence,
That such a day shall be my Tragedie:
   If thousands flocke to heare a Poets pen,
   To heare a god, how many millions then?

The many-headed multitude were drawne
By Brutus speach, that Cæsar was ambitious,
When eloquent Mark Antonie had showne
His vertues, who but Brutus then was vicious?
   Mans memory, with new, forgets the old,
   One tale is good vntill another's told.

Sing thou my dirgies like a dying Swan,
Whose painfull death requires a playning dittie:
That my complaint may pierce the hart of man,
Plaine be thy song, sweete, pleasing, full of pittie:
   And more, to moue the multitude to ruth,
   Let my apparell be the naked truth.

Truth bring I nak't, for other weedes she scorneth,
Saue that her smocke in flames of coulored silke
Is strangelie wrought, her beawtie it adorneth,
As through the same it peares more white then milke:
   In open view she comes, faire, comelie, meeke,
   For, Truth the hidden corners doth not seeke.

My father Reignold Cobham (whom so many
Haue crown'd with euer-greene victorious baies),
For valorous worth before him plac'd not any;
O but I must be parciall in his praise.
   T'emblazon forth her owne truth, Truth's denide,
   Herein the Truth, for Truth, is counted pride.

Within the Spring-tide of my flowring youth
He stept into the winter of his age :
Made meanes (Mercurius thus begins the Truth,)
That I was made Sir Thomas Mowbraies page :
  A meanes to die, who meanes to liue so long,
  Aged in ill, in goodnesse euer yong.

There did I spend my purple-coloured May,
Bathing in blisse, and courtlie blandishment ;
Vntill the sentence on Saint Lamberts day
Pronounced was of Mowbraies banishment ;
  Of Englands woe, of Richards lowe deposing.
  Of Herfords honour, of my seruice losing.

He might haue seen how Fate that day fore-pointed,
That gloomie day wherein the heauens did mone :
She would haue Herford Englands king annointed,
To rend the wreath of Diamonds from his Throne :
  But Majesty, whose lustre is so bright,
  Destroies the sense, and dazleth the sight.

Fate the foule of-spring of black Erebus,
Th'inhabitresse of foamie Phlegeton :
Ill fortunes day star, good lucks Hesperus,
Pale Deaths fore-teller, grim Porphyrion.
  Ioues scribe in brasse with pens of dragons wings,
  The chiefe commaundresse both of gods and kings.

Earths Genius, mans inauspicious starre,
A triple power, the knowledge of things past,
To come, and present, Trumpeter to warre,
Ill at the first, injurious at the last;
   A crosse wherewith we all must rest contented,
   Fate tho fore-seene can seldome bee preuented.

Then whil'st the Aprill of my yong yeares lasted,
(Aged in nothing onely but my name:)
Her forward budding in the prime I blasted,
With wind of pride, and hoarie frost of shame;
   With riotous Loue, whose highest point's a pleasure,
   With paine before, repentance at more leasure.

And like a Trau'ler which his way hath lost,
In th' vnknowne woods, when vp and downe he rangeth,
On euery side with blind Meander's crost,
And this for that, that for another changeth:
   Within the sharp-set thickets long thus tost,
   At length finds this that he himselfe hath lost.

So in my youth I was a Traueler,
Within this world a wildernesse of woe,
No Palmers then could tell a Passenger
Which way from danger safely he might goe:
   Led once astray in youth, who euer found
   His first trode path, where pleasures do abound.

Thus lost within the Laborinth of sin,
Wandring the woods in Egypts gloomie Night,
Tying no threed from whence I first came in,
No Sun to shine, no star to giue me light:
   Echidnaes ofspring, hell-borne serpents knew me,
   And at their pleasures to strange pleasures drew me.

Some way I left before I had begun it,
And some was knottie, othersome would bryre me:
This marrish ground, and yet I could not shun it,
This steepe and sandie sooner it would tyre me;
   This way to follow vertue would procure me,
   To this my youthful head-strong yeares did lure me.

And youth excusd the errours in my nature,
Whose greenenes tooke vpon him all the fault:
Perswading me, such power was in no creature,
Once to resist vice when it gaue assault:
   Perswasion's vaine, for one to vices bent,
   The minde agrees, as Nature doth consent.

Audacious Youth, impatient being moued,
A witlesse substance in a seeming show;
Scorner of age, of age yet best beloued;
By Phaeton the world's ouerthrow,
   A sleepe, a dreame, a brauling lunacie,
   A selfe-conceit short-killing plurasie.

Before this Youth in mirthfull sports was lauisht,
No meane Cumrades, no base associates,
In company with my perfections rauisht,
Swore me for one of their confederates,
    For valour, wit, and court-ship few came nie me,
    In all which, Richard, Henries both did trie me.

But valour, court-ship, wit, and all good parts,
Make without maners but a glittring show :
Nature is onely beautified with arts :
Wit oftentimes is her owne ouerthrow.
    This court-ship, valour, wit, al are disgraced,
    Within the minde when vertue is not placed.

For strange attempts, for Mars-like chiualrie,
Among my fellowes yet I beare the bell,
In hastie wroth, and heedlesse hazardrie,
I counted vertue alwaies to excell,
    And deem'd it better perish in the field,
    Then for base feare my weapons vp to yeeld.

Feare the minds fall with lasting infamie,
In expectation of some future ill :
Twixt Mars and Venus got in luxurie,
A cold congealed ice, a bloudlesse chill,
    An Ecstasis, a breeder of gray haires,
    An abject spirit, scorne to youthfull yeares.

Yet the world poys'ned with a swaggering humour,
Of some shape-altring Succubus begot;
A wynd-swolne monster, many headed Rumour:
Vices preseruer, vertues festred rot;
   Prides male-content, minds putrified wound,
   A liqour moist distilled from the ground.

This ayres innate and chiefest qualitie,
This Ship-mans hose; this heat-extinguisher,
This gallants wisdome, wise-mens gullerie,
This paynted wethercocke, Arts diminisher.
   With cowardize beginneth to empeach me,
   Because in worth not able for to reach me.

We daft the world with time ourselues beguiled,
Dreaming on nought saue on eternitie,
And good Successe from highest heauens smiled
On our attempts and mirthfull jollitie:
   For that seemes good which present pleasures brings,
   Tho't bee the roote, from whence all euil springs.

Successe, the friend of famous Conquerours,
Faire Fortunes handmaid, daughter of pure blood,
The worlds darling, wish of Emperours,
Desyres great Goddesse, fauorite of the good,
   From pale facde death or danger euer blest me,
   And with the robe of honour doth inuest me.

And seeking how she might the more inhaunce me,
Though lewd my hauiour was, vnsound my carriage,
With roialtie and high discent t'aduance me,
Shee join'd me with a Ladie faire in mariage ;
   By whose high honour I first won the name
   And Seignorie of Cobhams endlesse fame.

Long I injoi'd this weary wing of Fame,
My beauteous wife, my Margarite of worth,
Whose Nature was more precious then her name,
All titles were but staines to set her forth ;
   For stature, bewtie, vertue, wit, and blood,
   More comelie none, faire, sober, matchlesse, good.

But bewtie, stature, vertue, wit, nor blood,
Nor yet the ripenesse of a flowring age,
Faire, comelie, sober, matchlesse, lustie, good,
Can aught at all delay deaths murdrous rage,
   For all these gifts from Margarite ycome,
   And buried lie with Margarite in her tombe.

Hymen put on his saffron-coloured cote,
And now vice had no warrantize by yeares,
With that I gin my fellowes faults to note,
Sounding sweete councell in their Adders eares.
   But ill it seem d me them to blame : though I
   Censurd my selfe like mine owne enemy.

Delight saw this, and would not slip the season,
But in my soule shee made a strange diuision;
The sensuall parts shee armed all gainst Reason,
Defending goodnesse to be superstition;
   A fopperie, a fond Precisians toy,
   The which who loues, doth liue still void of ioy.

My wil, whose obiect was the chiefest good,
And vnderstanding facultie the truth,
This sharpe encounter cowardlie withstood,
So weakned with the pleasures of my youth.
   Tis hard to hate vice which we long haue loued,
   An habite got once, seldom is remoued.

The troupes disperst, now darknesse ends the fight,
And reason held his late-won victorie:
But inward Senses skirmish in the night,
The common sense, Remembrance, Phantasie,
   Whose warre, is warre, warre onely to increase,
   When Reasons warre, is warre to liue in peace.

Faire was the field where first we met, and spatious,
Enuironed with odoriferous meads,
Ioyn'd to a Citie, to the sight most gratious,
Where stately Trees, with wood-bine pleighted heads,
   Of Mandrake, Poppie, euer greene did flourish,
   With hearbs whose iuice the drowsy sense wold nourish.

Here none saue night-byrds houer with their wings,
The fatall scritch-owles, feast profaning Bats ;
From two faire founts the Riuer Lethe springs :
And on the clearest Minerall she pats ;
　Whose stealing streames along the channell fals,
　Like Euphrates, at first, twixt Edens wals.

This crawling runner, hony-bubbling fountaine,
Whil'st thousands slept in Nights securitie ;
Descending from the Diamond-rockie mountaine,
Like the mellifluent brooke of Castilie ;
　Turning the sand, and playing with the stones,
　Would alway answere both their sighes and grones.

The Citie with two entrances is graced,
Whose workmanship the matter seemes to scorne ;
The first, wherein expreslie dreames are placed,
With curious Art is builded all of horne ;
　The other made of polisht Iuorie,
　Where dreames vnvail'd, and ouershaddowed be.

A sumptuous Temple all of burnisht gold,
Within the wals erected vnto night,
Which Phantasies in greatest reucrence hold ;
Another Chappell Alethia hight,
　With diuers formes, to diuers shapes, some tall,
　Some vglie, winged, wither'd, grosse, some small.

With scaling ladders on the walls I venter,
(In which fierce entrance well I might haue perisht,)
Whose Pallaces no sooner could I enter,
But pleasant sights, my soule and senses cherisht :
   From ghastly feare faire Icolon me keepes,
   And lullabies my thoughts with carelesse sleepes.

Sweete Sleepe, distresse and sorrowes soueraigne cure,
Worthie entitled Nox sonne Morpheus,
Send downe from Heauen vnto Pallinure,
Mans king and Gods endeard by Orpheus,
   Within the circuit of this pallace knew me,
   And pleasures past, with what would come, did shew me.

For the Idæa of a thing in sleepe,
May be imprinted in the Phantasie,
With shape-transforming visions so deepe,
That it deludes the senses outwardly,
   And so in forme and in estate appeere
   Within the mind as if he waking were.

Thus neere Iberiaes foremost fertile coast,
I entred in Gades two-leau'd brasen dore,
Where I espide of Demi-gods an hoast,
Landing vpon the sea-Atlanticke shore,
   In yeeres none yong, with yeeres not any olde,
   None parcht with heate, none withered with colde.

These Deities liu'd in so rare a ground,
Which thrice a yeere her fruitfulnes did show,
Yet plow nor planting did her forehead wound,
No other winde but Zephyrus did blow,
  No showres, no raine, for fruits will neuer perish,
  Which the danke moisture of the ayre doth cherish.

Downe in a dale enameled with roses,
Ten thousand Adones standing on a raw,
And by a crannie which a garden closes,
So many Virgins and wood Nymphs I saw,
  With brests halfe hid, with loose dishevil'd haire,
  To catch the baulme-sweete breathing of the aire.

Which gamesomlie into their bosomes got,
Whisks vp and downe, twines, curls vp their tresses,
And enterlaces with a Trew-loues knot ;
And last ; diuides each haire, each plight vndresses ;
  Playes fast and loose, as fearing least his sport
  Should end too soone, his pleasure be too short.

Thrice twenty thousand Cupids in their eies,
Bathing them selues ; so many Graces set
Vpon the bancks their browes ; each (naked) hies :
The first place in this paradize to get.
  Tell me the man these visions would not moue,
  For Sight breedes wonder, wonder bringeth Loue.

One thought of hate, ten thoughts of loue reuiueth,
Whilst beauty charmes the vertue of the senses,
Great powers small aide gainst loues encounter giueth :
Wit's but a warrant for these sweete offences :
    What hope hath reason now to quench loues fire,
    When hate breedes loue, wit kindleth loues desire ?

Mine inward sense thus argu'd with my reason,
Told her these saints, this heauenly place enioying :
Spent all their life in mirth, their baiting season
Slept in delights ; and past in amorous toying :
    Gainst heauen herselfe who would not be rebelling,
    To liue, where loue, youth, beutie haue their dwelling.

With that I stretcht my lims along the bed,
Hauing no power to ope my gowlie eyes ;
Thrice ore the caddow I mine armes out spred :
Thrice did I fall, before I once could rise :
    Leaning vpon mine elbow for a rest,
    Nodding, I knockt my chin against my brest.

Then sigh'd, slipt downe, and twixt the sheete and
I nuzled in, joyn'd knees and chin together : [pillow
I dream'd I wore a garland of greene willow.
But snuffling low, I prickt me with a fether ;
    So wakt, the bolster for my backe I chose,
    And yawning thrice, I rub'd mine eyes and rose.

At length, well wakened from the pleasing slumber:
(O that such slumbers euer should awake!)
As I began my follies past to number,
Despaire gainst comfort gins a head to make.
  Yet in remembrance of my youthfull yeares,
  Innumerable sins, I spent innumerable teares.

Like to a needle plac'd in equall distance,
Betwixt a Load-stone and an Adamant,
By either drawne, to neither makes resistance:
But stands immote as she their force did dant.
  So do I stand in great perplexitie,
  And onely certaine in vncertaintie.

I'm in a wood, greene may it euer grow,
Yet o're my head a threatening Rocke still hingeth;
The Rocke despaire, the wood doth comfort show,
The rocke my soule, which worme of conscience stingeth.
  Twixt wood and rocke, I stand on six and seauen,
  Yet makes the wood my through-fare into heauen.

So (but I list not of my valour boast,
Tis no ambition though, to boast of good:)
Reason outbrau'd this heauen-aspiring hoast,
And left them wallowing in their loathsome blood,
  Whilst many fled, which made the more affraide,
  Thus I mine ensignes in the aire displaide.

But Rochester shall Eccho forth my praise,
If Rochester remaine not most vngratefull,
A sin in fashion for these humerous daies:
To whom wee owe, to them we are most hatefull:
  O that it were in fashion; I am sure
  Nine daies (like wonders) fashions but endure.

I must vpbraide her else, not praises giuing,
How first my fauours patronag'd her pride:
But in too much remembrance of the liuing,
In darke obliuion dead mens praise wee hide.
  A begger from the dunghill once extold,
  Forgets himselfe, whom what he was of old.

When first her grauell-purified riuer,
No bridge vpon her bote-lod'n bosome bore,
Some high renowne I striued for to giue her,
And made a bridge her swiftest currant o're.
  Sir Robert Knowles was in the same an actor:
  But Cobham was the chiefest benefactor.

And Walter Merton, Merton Colledge founder,
(Why doth mischance neere charitie thus dwell?)
With lime and sand gainst tempest-beating bound her,
Who from her top by great misfortune fell,
  Riding along the workemen for to see:
  Fortune is alwaies vertues enemie.

Kinde Rochester it seemes hath yet respected,
His name should liue in ages for to come,
In whose memoriall lately is erected
An Epitaph upon a Marble tombe :
   But one good turne another still doth craue :
   For this ; they found a goblet in his graue.

Warham, th'archbishop once of Canterbery,
The Iron barres vpon the bridge bestow'd :
Warner the copings did reedifie,
And many since their liberall minds haue show'd,
   Whose deedes in life (if deedes can heauen merit)
   Made them in death all heauenly joyes inherit.

Thus Medway by this faire stone bridge adorned,
Made Thamesis enamor'd of her beauty :
All other riuers England had he scorned,
Yeelding to her kinde loue-deseruing duty,   [ings,
   In smiles, embracements, gratious lookes and greet-
   In amorous kisses, murmures, night-set meetings.

But how he courted, how himselfe hee carri'd,
And how the fauour of this Nimph he wonne,
And with what pompe Thames was to Medway marri'd,
Sweete Spenser shewes (O griefe that Spenser's gone !)
   With whose life heauens a while enricht vs more,
   That by his death wee might be euer pore.

With swifter currant Medway to this day
From Maidstone runs, in hope the bridge to kisse,
One streame another chasing fast away,
That thousands hasting of their purpose misse :
  And downe the gullet all in anger glide,
  Yet turne in whirle-pooles round, to vew her side.

One streame stands kissing with a naked piller,
Whose force rebutts the streame which runneth after,
And backe retires, with glauncing lookes to fill her
Long-wisht desire ; and smiles, and falls to laughter,
  Last (in her language) when she slides away,
  She seemes to thanke mee for her marriage day.

With thanks the gods, with thankes good men are pleased,
And thankes she giues him that this bridge first founded :
Because this rest her wearie streame hath eased,
And now with oares her sides are neuer wounded,
  But thankefull she, vnthankefull all the towne,
  The cause (no doubt) was once the bridge fell downe.

Ioues issue borne of faire Eurynomes,
Mirth's naked mothers, snow-white Charites :
Daughters of th'Ocean, riuers Presides,
The pride of Desarts, sweete mouth'd Naides,
  These Nimphs of Ashdon forrest neuer haunted
  Medways flour'd banks whilst this fair bridge she wāted.

For goddesses could not abide the sauour
Of millions ouerwhelmed in her brooke :
These deyties now take it for a fauour,
Their beautie in her glassie streames to looke,
   All do rejoyce; and are most thankefull; man,
   Which should be thankefull, most vnthankefull than.

Let marriners which shute his arches through
Describe aright his length, his bredth, his beautie;
Riding in's sight, they vaile their bonnet low,
And strike their top-saile in submissiue dutie :
   Hee'l not be brau'd; no vessell since the marriage
   Will he receiue, but of a lowly carriage.

Some higher ship, whose sailes are swolne with pride,
Whose bloudy flaggs like fierie streamers hing,
At Chattam lies, and from her hollow side,
With double charge sendes forth a culuering,
   Which rends the shore, and makes the towne to shake,
   The bridge her breath, herselfe in snuffe doth take.

The fierie smoake this Engine vomits out,
To him transported by the aire and wind,
Hee straight recciues; and prisons in throughout
His hollow vaults, his creuices, and rindes,
   So th'aire redoubling in his arches slips
   A mocking eccho to these prowder ships.

This bridge reuiues my dying memorie,
Ouer the which I passe into the towne,
To view the sacred church of Trinitie:
Built by Sir Robert Knowles: and (though vnknowne)
  That Chauntrey joyning to the same I founded,
  Where Harmonie for euer should be sounded.

Sweete Harmonie suppos'd of Pithagoreans,
To be the spheares and heauenly bodies motion,
Of Platonists, Amphibolites, and Iouians,
A Simmetrie within the soules sharp notion:
  Heauens handmaide, one of the liberall arts,
  A concord, all of disagreeing parts.

Soule-drowning pleasure rauisher of sense,
Elisiums Anthem, court-enchanting spell,
Our nouice lady-woing eloquence,
The fetcher of Euridice from hell,
  The cowards courage to vphold his armes,
  The valiant mans encountring fresh alarmes.

The ioy to griefe-accloyd calamitie,
Thebes singing Syren to display her banners,
Prisoners comfort in cold miserie,
Cares cosoner, reformer of the manners;
  In sorrow, smart, exilement, hunger, anguish,
  An helper, least we faint, despaire, or languish.

Wench-wanton Ioue, and faire Electraes daughter,
Of seauen starres, the seauenth not appearing,
Empresse of solace, greatest Queene of laughter,
Venus white doue, and Mars his onely dearing,
  Why am I thus in thy remembrance rotten,
  And in thy sweete saint-pleasing songs forgotten?

Had some feirce Lionesse by the Libian fountaines,
Or blacke-mouth'd barking Scilla brought thee forth,
On flintie Etnaes sulphur-flaming mountaines:
By Tygres nurs'd in th'ice congealed north,
  Thou couldst not be more frozen harted hatefull,
  Injurious more, lesse louing, more vngratefull.

Neptune obtayning but his Amphitrite,
By the Dolphins meanes in heauens azure frame;
In the remembrance of this benefite:
Ten stars compacted by the Dolphins name;
  Nor Gods, nor men, but Clownes, illiterate, rude,
  Would thus be poisned with ingratitude.

O but I heare thy notes Angelicall,
On Orpheus siluer-sounding Harp excuse thee,
Whose strayned ditties most melodicall
Tell me, the world in dotage doth abuse me:
  The world is old, and I more old in name,
  Old age, by youth's preseru'd, not by the same.

The time's in dotage, and the world in yeares,
This organ-aged litle world man,
Which cradle-witted infant-waxen peares,
Gray coated, fond, pale, hoarie, feeble, wan,
  Bald, drie, diseased, rheumaticke, and cold:
  Therefore the world is earthlie doting old.

He that lyes well, does well this ill age fit,
Hee's a bare foole which speakes the naked Truth;
The one wise follie, th'other foolish wit:
This stripling world is alwaies thus in youth:
  Such wisdome's doting, doting's frostie cold:
  Therefore the world is foolish doting old.

Old age within her hart a Fox doth hold,
A Kyte in hand; a Bee within her brest;
Fox false, deceaues, Kyte greedie, catch thee wold,
Bee angrie, stings, beleev'd, come neare, deprest;
  These signes all shew within this world I could,
  Therefore the world is crooked dooting old.

Shee builds highe roofes with ruines of the Church,
Sels lyes for nothing, Nothing for too much;
Faith for three farthings, t'haue thee in the lurch:
Shee's meale mouth'd, simple, scarse abiding tuch.
  First shee is greedie, next, her craft behold:
  Therefore the world is wylie doting old.

When for a looke shee will be in the lawe,
To take the wall, is by the wall to dye,
At a great word she will her poynard draw,
Looke for the pincke if once thou giue the lye.
  Is she not angry, hot, audacious bold ?
  Therefore the world is testie doting old.

Tis greedie, first, which vsurers will nourish,
Tis craftie, Lawers lie not to the truth,
Tis angry, Fencers euery where do flourish,
Craft, anger, vsury, neuer seene in youth :
  In crabbed age these vices we behold,
  Doubtlesse the world is wonderous doting old.

But all the world in question is not cald,
For art can varnish o're decayed nature,
Old men haue haire, and many yong men bald,
Yet periwigs and painting helpe their feature,
  In nature weake, in art the world's strong,
  The world in age againe thus waxeth yong.

When great Apollo shewes his threefold might,
And by his issue dayly's made the yonger,
Keeping his vertue, influence, and light,
May not man thinke thereby to liue the longer ?
  No, he's a father, though his chin be bare,
  But man's a monster if he want his haire.

Time was of old, when all of vs were yong,
Then we learn'd much, for litle were we knowing,
When riper yeares and manhoode made vs strong,
Then we knew much, and more still would be showing,
    Age knowes all well, do nothing well it would,
    In vertue yong the world, in knowledge old.

Our fixed stars, a pur-blind old man's eyes,
The aire's a gnastie old mans breath ill smelling,
Water a rhume in dropsie when he lyes,
Valleyes rough wrinckles, mountaines gowtie swelling;
    The earth a sleepy old man's long-kept dregs,
    Men now a feeble old mans windie egs.

Let vs but looke into the giants age,
Danske Corioneus English Albion,
Or Titans broode which gainst the heauens did rage,
Fierce Lentesmophius, Effra, Gration,
    These were the worlds first youthfull progenie,
    To these our men are an Epitomie.

Whose dig'd vp reliques, if we but behold,
Do we not wonder at their ribs or teeth?
Like props and and milstones so our issue old
Will wonder at our greatnesse which she seeth,
    Now are we dwarfs, they will be pismires then,
    This is the fumbling of our aged men.

Nor thou faire frame with azure lines thicke quoted,
Bright heauen thy swift orbicular round motion,
(As Linceus-eyde Astronomers haue noted :)
From East to West keepes not thy reuolution,
   Seauen stars their seates haue left, and lost some light:
   The world is old when heauen is dimme of sight.

Ioue's gone to Libra from his amorous maide,
And Mercurie thou'rt fled to Scorpio, then
From Scorpio Saturne to the Shooters straide,
Mars loaths the crab, lies in the lion's den :
   How can the course of this our world go euen :
   When all this ods and jarring is in heauen ?

Pure, thin, and pleasing, was the aires first breath,
Now thick, grosse, noysome tis whereon we feede,
A vile contagious mist which can vnneath
But pestilence or worse diseases breede :
   If sicknes thus infect her from the skies,
   Then the world's old, and on her death-bed lies.

The water famous by a Nimphs faire name,
Of some foue-leprous body now's the lees :
The sea a sinke, and riuers to the same
Are rotten pipes, so fountaines in degrees,
   The world o'reworne, vnwholesome, for new birth
   Shee must returne needes to her grandame earth.

Our grandame earth, whose for-head is o're thwarted,
With high-wayes bald, whose backe huge buildings
    sway,
Whose bellie's stuft with piles of men departed,
Boweld, puld out, and garbisht euery day,
  Heauen, earth, aire, water, man, the world and all,
  Are doting old and must to ruine fall.

Deceiptfull world, blood-thirsty, couetous,
Bleare-eyde, mishapt, vntoward, impious,
Three-legd, treble-tong'd, bifronted, traiterous,
Backe-broken, bald, enuie-swolne, obliuious,
  Aire, water, putrifide, heauen, earth, infectious,
  To gods, to men, and to thy selfe injurious.

Wax old and die, what? dost thou want a toombe?
Into thy Chaos backe againe returne:
And thus twise child perhappes thou maist becoome,
Wax old, a new the sooner to be borne,
  Meaue while encrease, thou maist decrease thereby,
  At length wax old, and last for euer die.

Die thou for euer with thy harmonie,
Extenuate no more worth's matchlesse deedes,
Rochester blot me out of memorie,
Let Cobham haue disdaine for worthie meedes:
  For slaue-born pesants are for worthies deemed
  And worthies worse then pesants are esteemed.

2 D 2

Ioues Pursiuant, nimble Mercurius,
The proloquutor of my worlds wonne glorie,
Swift as Medusaes flying Pegasus :
Heare now (O heare) the processe of my storie,
   Greiu'd at the world, in anger ouer-shot,
   My iust complaint I almost had forgot.

Looke when the sun most bride-groome like doth rise,
Soone as the morne vnbarres her christall gate :
So Bullingbrooke vnto the gazers eyes
Riseth in Richards royall chaire of state,
   Whose rising was the cause that millions fel,
   That we in peace and endlesse pleasure dwel.

Great Bolingbrooke this type of chiualrie,
In ayding false-faith-breaking Orleance,
Against the hote assault of Burgundie,
Whose ciuil warres neere driue him out of France,
   To higher honour willing me to call,
   Of al the forces made me generall.

Then ledde I warre mailde vp in sheetes of brasse,
Drawne in a Charriot with amaze and horror,
Whose fiery steedes Bellona sterne would lash,
To strike the Frenchmen in an vncouth terror ;
   Feare, clamour, wrath, warres followers but assembled,
   The French astonisht, turned backe and trembled.

Burgundie stonisht, which so prowdly vaunted,
Turn'd backe and trembled, turning warre to peace,
So much our souldiers sight his courage daunted,
So much the Frenchmen lou'd to liue at ease :
  How would these warriors then haue feard to fight,
  When with our looks whole myriads tooke their
    flight.

Marke what ensues (for marking it deserues,)
With this dayes honour Orleance not content,
But from his oath and neare alliance swerues ;
And a bold challenge to king Henry sent :
  But once forsworne and be forsworne for euer :
  A Traitor once will be a subiect neuer.

Henry (to calme the Sea of war) betraid,
Rebates the edge of choller with aduise :
Most mildlie answeres to the challenge made ;
So of himselfe the Conquerour did rise.
  Which conquest is a far more kinglie boast,
  Then for to brag the conquering of an hoast.

Proude Orleance marching with six thousand strong,
(For hate deepe rooted hardlie left in Frenchmen)
Beseig'd the towne of Vergie three moneths long :
Three hundred English onlie there entrencht then :
  Of which smal force, (in force great to withstand hers,)
  I and Sir Robert Antfield were commaunders.

Three months expyr'd, mind-loftie Orleance
Saw that his Souldiers courage gan recoile,
With that retyr'd his forces back to France,
Without all honour, victorie, or spoile.
   All Guien since for sauing of their Towne
   Long time gaue tribute vnto Englands Crowne.

With Thomas Percie Worcesters braue Earle,
Against the French againe I went to fight:
Percie of bold aduenterous knights the pearle:
Many to sword; but more we put to flight.
   In wars abroad, in ciuill broiles at home,
   Oldcastle still selected was for one.

Then high-resolued Hotspur, Scotlands terrour,
The child of Mars and magnanimitie;
The throne of fame, wars palme, & knighthoods mirrour,
Ioin'd with the Yorkists, made a mutinie.
   Thus ill to worse, and worse to worse did fall,
   Worst to rebellion, which was worse then all.

To raise all people sooner to commotion,
The Archbishop let the commons vnderstand
In guilfull Rhetoricke that it was deuotion,
Which caus'd them take these home-bred warrs in hand.
   This euer is a Rebels chiefe pretence,
   To vaile his treason o're with innocence.

Looke how a swarme of hony-gathering Bees,
(The Muses birds) leauing their luscious bowers,
Follow their king in order and degrees,
Vntill they find some arbour deckt with flowers:
   And then they murmur, hum, and all rejoice:
   Euen so the Commons yeelding, made a noice.

And followed Percie to these ciuill broiles,
Who made no doubt of Henries victorie:
Emboldened by Scotlands late-won spoiles,
Yet left him slaine behind at Shrewsbury:
   And all the Armie, ventrous, valorous, bold,
   Hote on the spur, now in the spur lie cold.

If this deserue a Conquerours praise,
For with a Conquest this may make comparison;
Engirt my temples with triumphant baies:
Gainst Percie then I led a garrison.
   Percie so cald; because he pierst the eie
   Of the Scots king, and set Northumbers free.

Prest then I was with Iohn of Lancaster,
Vertues Pyramides, fames imagerie.
We vanquished our foes at Doncaster
With wisedome, not with rash temeritie.
   Tis often seen, ill-pleasing accidents
   Proceed from rage and hare-braind hardiments.

No day which would not me to wars importune ;
No warres, but got palme-crowned victorie ;
No victorie, but brought her handmaide fortune ;
No fortune, but enlarg'd my dignitie.
  Daies, wars, victorie, fortune, and renowne,
  Cald me so high, to cast me lower downe.

On Sea the mild-aspecting heauens would guide me,
(Whereon who fares may not commaund his waies ;)
Cherubs on earth, and Seraphins would hide me
Vnder their brode gold-flaming winged raies,
  On Sea, on Land, the Heauens, and Angels all,
  First fauoured me, at last to make me fall.

Fall, ah ! no fall, but honour-climing staire :
Staire, ah no staire ; but prince-ascending Throne :
Throne, ah no throne ; but Ioues gold-scorning chaire :
Chaire, ah no chaire ; but Heauen her selfe alone :
  That no tong, mind, nor Art, can tell, think, measure,
  My crownd, soule-pleasing, sweet, joy, mirth, &
    plesure.

The radiant Eos, which so brightlie shone,
Whose lamps enlightned all this Hemisphare :
Henry the fourth vnto Elisium's gone ;
Of whose departure England gins to feare
  Her soddain fall ; and, iudg'd by outward signe,
  Henry the fifth would lose his fathers shine.

Looke how the Suns approach doth ouershade
The lesser stars from entercourse of sight;
But from the worlds quick-eie the Sun conuaide,
The Stars receiue from him their former light.
　Stars by the Sun; Sun in the stars be graced,
　In Sun, in Stars, heauens sun-bright glori's placed.

Henry the Fift euen thus did rise, whose shine
Of vertue dimm'd all kings before him quight;
He being barred from his glorious shrine,
Their memorie reuiu'd, and shone more bright:
　Thus they by him, and he in them was graced,
　In them, in him, faire Englands glorie placed.

Now one, by none, but one makes all illustrious,
One the first mouer of this firmament,
In ruling all her orbes and spheares industrious;
Sun, stars, all plannets are to her obedient;
　Like the first mouer as she now appeares,
　O that she might all England moue his yeares.

When Henry first injoi'd th'imperiall Crowne,
A blazing Comet in the West appeared;
At which strange vision, pointed streaming downe,
The common sort Art-ignorant much feared.
　A cause, or signe, some said twas, to portend,
　The kingdomes fall, or kings vntimely end.

Our sharper wits suppos'd thus Ouid wrasted
The fable of foole-hardie Phaeton,
When some huge Comet was dissolu'd and wasted,
Great heat, and drinesse following therevpon,
   For want of water so the world burned,
   But vpside downe the Suns carr neuer turned.

This all-affrighting Comet I haue heard
To be the plighted tresse of Meropes,
Or staring haires within the curled beard
Of Vulcans prentice swartie Steropes.
   Be what it will, this much I do define,
   Of kingdomes fall tis neither cause nor signe.

A Comet is an earth-agreeing vapour,
Drawne by the power attractiue of some star,
Fyr'd by the Suns beames, burneth like a tapour:
Seen in the supream region of the aire:
   Turning those beames, receiueth forme withall,
   Bearded, or trest, or stretching forth his taile.

Why should a mist-hung Star-exhaled Meteor
To kings or kingdomes be prestigious?
Whose cause is not aboue the power of Nature:
Why should it seeme to men prodigious?
   Vnlesse we would this Axiom reject,
   A naturall cause, a naturall effect.

In Europe many Comets haue we seen
Fore-running kings, nor kingdomes ouerthrow,
And kings with kingdomes vanquished haue been,
When neuer Comet in the Aire did show.
  To prophesie from Comets, or deuine,
  Tis foolerie, they neither cause nor signe.

If euer sheild-shapt Comet was portent
Of Criticke day, foule and pernitious :
Then to the Frenchmen, this assigne was sent,
Disaster, fatall, inauspitious :
  Whose bloudie tresses tilting did foreshow,
  At Agincourt their blooddie ouerthrow.

Or else it was (would it had neuer been,)
But the fore-runner of my Tragedie :
And heauens saw (oh had they neuer seen)
I should sollicite nimble Mercurie,
  To ingraue my words vpon the hardest mettle,
  Whose Characters in harts of steele may setle.

Which when heauens saw, (what doth not heauens see?)
With raine of teares she seemes my case to weepe,
Vsing all meanes, but all meanes would not bee,
From death insuing danger me to keepe.
  But hard it is for heauens to preuent,
  When destinies for death giue once consent.

My Destinies are set in parlament,
Aboue their heades a curious frame of stone :
Marble below, and during Adamant,
On each side flint, and softer object none,
   Saue that in chaires of hardest oake they sate,
   Insteede of wooll-packes neere the barred gate.

In scarlet vestments, winter-coloured tresses,
Iron their wands, of brasse their writing table,
Penns made of tinne ; for inke strong *aqua fortis*,
Their paper steele, their carpet Indian sable,
   Their countenance like Caiphas, mou'd to ruth ;
   For god, religion, valour, age, nor youth.

In Paules thus sate this vniuersall Sinode,
The cheife Archbishop Thomas Arundell,
More sterne then Minos, Eacus, or Herode,
Like Rhadamanth the grim-fac'd iudge of hell :
   In the first yeare of Henries happy raigne,
   Last of my ioy, and midle of my paine.

First the forsworne Inquisitours sent to them,
Of Wickleues (as they tearm'd them) villanies,
Out of whose bookes they did collect, to shoe them,
Two hundred sixtie and six heresies ;
   All stricken dumbe, they star'd as if their eies
   Should for an answere then intreate the skies.

To stop the worlds talkatiue wide mouth,
Wherefore they sate vpon this conuocation,
They hired men to blazon for a truth,
It was all for the churches reformation;
   Thus mischiefe will her vice in vertue smother,
   Blearing mens eyes with one deceit or other.

For first the sun dissolue might with his beames,
The icie bulke of waylesse Caucasus,
On whose snowie mantled top it neuer gleames,
Then these frost-bitten prelates sembled thus
   Would otherwise haue all their causes ended,
   But as before the Sinode they pretended.

Nay Mercurie, if with thy charming wand
Thou had'st descended from the Olimpique spheares,
To plead for pittie, at their feete to stand
With both thine eyelids full of swelling teares,
   This sense-beguiling action had but ended,
   My iudgement as before it was pretended.

Before these deepe-braind all-fore-seeing Doctours,
These reuerent fathers purgatorie teachers,
I was complain'd of by the generall proctours,
To be a great maintainer of good preachers.
   O times vntaught, men scorners of sound teaching,
   Louers of playes, and loathers of good preaching.

That Richard, Henries both I had enformed
Of the clergies great and manifold abuses:
That popish bulls and ceremonies scorned,
Roomes dignitie, her rites, and sacred vses,
 And that I wisht the popes dominion
 Might stretch no furr then Callis Ocean.

That I had caused Wickleues bookes be sent,
Faire writ, to Boheme, France, and Germanie,
Whereof two hundred openly were brent
By Prages Archbishops great authoritie,
 That I preferd vp Bills in Parliament,
 Wherto the King and Lords gaue all consent.

Of all the Cleargies villainous abusion,
Which I put vp in open Parlement,
Writ in a briefe-containing sharpe conclusion,
These verses were the summarie content,
 Whose soules with sin empoisning hate did anguish,
 That they ne're left me till they saw me languish.

Plangunt Anglorum Gentes crimen Sodomorum,
Paulus fert horum sunt idola causa malorum,
Surgunt ingrati Giezite symone nati,
Nomine prelati, hoc defensare parati,
 Qui reges estis, populis quicunque præestis,
 Qualiter hijs estis gladios prohibere potestis.

His owne translation.

Bewaile may England sinne of Sodomites,
For Idoles and they are ground of all their wo,
Of Symon Magus a sect of hypocrites,
Surnamed Prelates, are vp with them to go,
And to vphold them in all that they may do :
   You that be rulers peculiarly selected,
   How can you suffer such mischiefes vncorrected ?

Now least delay bred danger, they were prest
For to proclaime me for an heretike,
But one of more experience than the rest,
Such hazard rash proceedings did not like,
   Because I was in fauour with the King,
   Twas best (he thought) to haue his councelling

My life-surmising Bishops swolne in rage,
Ambitiously (high Prelates lowlines)
As if th'ad vow'd sin-pard'ning pilgrimage,
With tapers to Saint Peters holines,
   Went to the king, made great complaints and lies,
   Blemisht my name with grieuious blasphemies.

Which when he heard (kings then too much would
   heare them)
Then he desir'd (why should not kings cōmand ?)
In mild-perswading words and deedes to beare them
To mee the chiefest pillar of his land.
   Vnto the church to bring me without rigour,
   Respecting knighthood, prowesse, stocke, and vigour.

And promis'd them vpon his excellence,
(If in pursute they tooke deliberation,)
In smoother-edge-rebating eloquence
To conquer me by might of sweete perswasion :
   The clergie gone, Henry for Cobham sent,
   I came, and shew'd myselfe obedient.

Looke how some tender bleeding-harted father,
When's son hath vow'd a vertue-gaining voyage,
Flint-rock-relenting arguments will gather
All to diswade him from this pilgrimage,
   And prayes, intreates ; intreates, and prayers vaine,
   At length considers tis for vertues gaine.

Yet bout his necke he vseth kissing charmes,
And downe his bosome raines a shower of teares,
Hugges, culles, and clippes him in his aged armes :
This thing he doubts, another thing he feares,
   Takes leaue, turnes backe, returnes, intreates anew,
   Giues ouer, weepes, and last, bids him adew.

Euen so the king, to stay my voyage tended,
(My vowed voyage to the holy land,)
Ten thousand reasons both begunne and ended,
That gainst the Pope I should in no wise stand :
   Then vowes, prayes, treates ; vowes, treates, and
     praiers vaine,
   From prayers, treates, and vowes he doth refraine.

To whom I answerd in humilitie,
(Because I knew kings were the Lords anoynted)
To him I yeelded all supremacie,
As Gods sword-bearing minister appointed :
  My body, goods, my life, my loue, my land
  Were his to vse, distribute, or command.

Then in a sorrow-sighing extasie,
(Seeing my zealous burning true affection,)
Denying to the Pope supremacie,
Yeelding to him foote-treading low subjection :)
  Henry tooke leaue, turn'd backe, entreated new,
  Gaue ouer, wept, and last bade me adew.

If tyrants will, vsurpt authoritie
Must be obey'd, what reuerence me behoued
To giue this king, this tyrants enemie,
Feared for loue, and for his vertues loued,
  Whose honours ensigne o're the world had spred him,
  In warres, and peace, if church men had not led him.

And tyrants tended on with injurie,
With murders, rapes, lou'd only but for feare,
Whose sword and scepter gards iniquitie,
Ought t'haue their subiects reuerence to them beare,
  As we ourselues, so must the common wealth,
  Some sicknesse, sometimes suffer, sometimes health.

As some disease, or bed infecting bile,
Whose pricking ach, sharpe agonie, and stings,
Must be sustaind and suffred for a while,
Till time to his maturitie him brings,
  Not rashly then, but as the Surgeon will,
  Least suddain handling all the bodie spill.

Euen so a Tyrant (Realmes infectious bile,)
Must not be robd of his regalitie,
Till death him of his regiment beguile :
Or wise men for this griefe find remedie :
  Not rashly then, for altring of a State
  Breedes often outrage, bloodshed, and debate.

Euen as the head the bodie should commaund,
And all his parts, to peace or warfare lead :
So with a mightie Monarch doth it stand,
His subiects parts, and he himselfe the head :
  But if those parts do grudge and disobay,
  Head, bodie, Monarch, subiects, all decay.

A God, a King, are conuertible voices,
Then Kings like Gods should gouerne and beare sway :
What Gyants broode in vprore so rejoices,
That gainst the Gods his banners will display ?
  Though with his huge weight Pelion Ossa prest,
  And fought with Ioue, he neuer got the best.

How many blessed Patriarches suffred wrong
By cruell Tyrants sin-reuenging rod!
And haue endur'd such heauie bondage long,
Accounting it a torture sent from God.
  The Tyrant as a man may be rejected,
  His place and office yet must be respected.

What punishment for practizing belongs?
But punishment, nor practise will I name:
Men more doe follow most forbidden wrongs
When by forbidding they doe knowe the same.
  For Parricide the Romaines made no Law,
  Least such a sin the people so might knaw.

Now Arundel resorts vnto the King,
By Popish charmes inchaunting him thereto,
To send Cytations, fore them me to bring.
(What was it not but Clergie men could do?)
  The Sumner came to Cowling, but as one
  Afraid, turnd back his message left vndone.

The Kings doore-keeper (in the silent night,)
John Butler sent for was by Arundell:
For this heauen-martyring deede he doubtlesse might
In Cerberus place haue kept the doore of Hell.
  With great rewards, and warrantize from blame,
  He caus'd him cyte me in king Henries name.

2 F 2

This kiss-betraying Iudas writ I stood,
Who with a lie thus left me in the lurch :
But still the Bishop thirstie of my blood,
Caus'd writs be set on Rochesters great Church.
  In paine of curse commaunding me remember
  To appeare at Ledes th'eleuenth of September.

All were rent downe. He excommunicates
And cites afresh with curse and interdiction,
Compels the Lay power ; them he animates
T'assist him in Apostataes conuiction.
  In more reproach and vile contempt to haue me ;
  Such like opprobrious names the Bishop gaue me.

At last (thus tost) I writ my faiths confession,
Vnto the foure chiefe Articles answered :
Of Penance, Shrift, Saints, transubstantiation,
Which gainst me all by Arundell were laid.
  I come to Court and written with me bring,
  My Swans last funerall dirgee to the king.

Which to recieue Henry began to grudge :
(Marke but the power of Clergie men those daies)
Commaunding me deliuer it to my judge
(Here Arundell both sword and miter swaies)
  The Archbishop : But with a flat deniall,
  I did appeale vnto the Pope for triall,

But this denyde in presence of the king,
(Without vainglorious ostentation,)
I proffred an hundreth Knights to bring,
Esquiers as many, for my iust purgation.
   Not once depending on their safe protection,
   But to the King shew dutifull subjection.

Againe I offred in my faiths true quarrell,
By law of Armes to fight for life or death,
With Christ'n, Heathen, Turk, Iew, Infidell:
The king excepted, any that drew breath.
   They answered me, I was too valorous bold:
   Then in the Tower they laid me fast in hold.

Valour the sonne of mightie Ioue esteemed
Where blooddie Mauors borroweth his name,
Of old Philosophers onelie vertue deemed:
Learnings bright sheild, the register of Fame.
   Which to expresse the Grecians could afford,
   For Valour, Mauors, Vertue, but one word,

Death-scorning Arioth, why is not regarded
Thy Sun-resplendant kingdome conquering power?
Is Mars-amazing Turnaments rewarded
With Traitors meede impris'nment in the Tower?
   From bearing Armes valour hath me exempted;
   Why was my challenge else not then accepted?

Sir Robert Morley then the Towers Lieutenant,
Twice (to be briefe) did bring me to appeare;
In Plutoes court before this Rhadamant:
The Arguments of my strong faith to heare.
   Yet he no faith had, was it not a wonder,
   That he was faithlesse, all the Church Faith vnder?

In all mine answeares taking great aduise,
As a true faith professing Protestant,
Not superstitious, nor too fond precise,
Whose firme resolue no tyrannie can dant.
   So with mine answeares as it seemd amazed,
   My iudgement on the soddaine forth they blazed.

To heauens all seeing light vpon my knees,
(The sentence giuen) humblie did I fall,
With heau'd-vp hands pray'd for mine enemies,
In his great mercie to forgiue them all:
   Bound hand and foote back through the Sluce I'm led,
   The gazers eyes like sluces in his head.

Whilst there I lie in midnight-dark immur'd,
My friends emblazoned forth mine injurie:
Whereby the Priests great obloquie incur'd,
Both of the Commons, and Nobilitie,
   In pollicie, to haue this tempest staid,
   They to my Bils an abjuration made.

of Sir Iohn Oldcastle, knight.

A parlament was cald at Leicester,
(Because I had such fauour bout the citie,
They would not haue it kept at Westminster:)
This act establisht was; O more then pittie,
 That such strange acts should be establisht euer,
 Which man from wife, from goods and land doth seuer.

That whosoeuer in the mothers tong,
Should reade, heare, the sacred Scriptures scand:
For this so hainous heauen-offending wrong,
From him, his heires, should lose his goods and land;
 Gainst Heauens, and gainst the Kings great majestie,
 He should be hang'd for treason, burnt for heresie.

O murder-poisned ruthlesse Rhadamants,
Blood-thurstie Neroes, brainsicke Bacchides,
Earth swallowed Typhons, currish Coribants,
Beare-fostered Dracons, damn'd Busirides.
 Liue by your euill, know for euill done,
 Liues with the father, dyes not with the son.

Now to release my bodie from the Tower,
(How might the Tower include so old a castle,)
Case-altring bribes I vs'd not, strength, nor power;
But with my wit, out of her bonds I wrastle.
 The prentice bard of freedom thus aduentures
 To break his bonds and cancell his indentures.

Riches in thraldome no contentment bring,
All lordship's lost when libertie is gone,
What vaileth it a lion be a king ?
Closely shut vp within this tower of stone.
  Man was made free, and lord o're euery creature :
  To be in bondage then, is gainst his nature.

The husbandman more glad is at the plough,
That browne-bread, crusts, and rustie bacon eates :
Then th'imprisoned king that hath inough,
Of wastell cakes ; and far more lushious meates.
  No bird takes solace by her songs in hold,
  Although her meate be curds, her cage of gold.

Nor vnto mee that lay in prison bound,
In musicke mirth was, or in riches pleasure,
Iingling of fetters had no merie sound,
My griefe too much, for ioyes on earth to measure.
  But now I'm free ; my keeper he remaines
  To taste my sorrowes ; vndergoe my paines.

Nor can I judge, I being misst the morrow,
His griefe's extreame, though foolishnes it be,
For treasure lost, to waile, or make great sorrow :
When, whosoeuer greeues in that degree,
  Counting his losse, and afterward his paine,
  He of one sorrow maketh sorrowes twaine.

of Sir Iohn Oldcastle, knight. 225

But the remembrance of my prisonment,
In little ease fast bound in yron chaines,
Did breede more comfort, joy, and soules content,
When libertie had loosenes of the raines,
  One by another contraries delight,
  Daie is delightsome in respect of night.

And though I am escaped from the Tower,
Feare yet my soule in prison fast doth hold,
Other mishaps pursue me eu'ry hower,
Burnt childe dreadeth fire, the prouerb's old,
  Who dreades no danger, in danger must fall,
  What foole once at large, would make himselfe thrall?

Sir Roger Acton, in the priests displeasure,
Of my escape was thought the chiefe procurement;
Onely when t'was the night, which gaue me leasure,
(Whose shade for freedome is the sole allurement:)
  To thinke of flight, effecting what I thought,
  With both together my escape I wrought.

Night the beginning of this massie round,
The worlds mother, shaddow of the earth,
Greate Demogorgons issue from the ground,
The ancientest of Goddesses by birth,
  Louers delight; loues fittest time to play,
  Venus bright star, and Cupides clearest day.

The ease of care, for ease the sweetest rest,
The peace of minde, the quiet seate of peace,
The soule of sleepe, the sleepe of soules opprest,
Desires best meane, impris'nments release :
    Aboue all nights, nights, dayes, each hower remember,
    To solemnize the twenteth of Nouember.

Mounting her chariot of darke Ebony,
Whilst thorn-backt Cinthia held her Iennets raine,
Adorned in her winters liuery,
Of stars three millions following as her traine,
    She rockt the world with sense-sure-binding sleeps,
    And bade me lanch forth to the Ocean deeps.

Tide for the ship, and ship was for the tide,
Wind for the tide, and tide was for the wind,
For Neptune men, and Neptune them to guide,
Thames wanton-currant stealing on behind,
    Night, Neptune, men, ship, tide, the Thames, and
    For my escape were all in one combind.   [wind,

And whilst I cut this dangerous swelling sourse,
The brest-bare-loue-enticing Naiedes,
Play on before me, and direct my course
To the dew-bedangled Oceanitides,
    For whose sweete sake I'm entertain'd a stranger,
    And harmelesse sau'd frō waves, frō wind, frō danger.

What time the gloomie morning from her bed,
Muffled in mists, and raukie vapours rose,
With watrie lockes about her shoulders spred
Regardlessely; because she did suppose
   Our quiuering flags and streamers did out-braue
   The golden sun, vpon the siluer waue.

I rode on Goodwins mercie-wanting sand,
Or sea-mans swallowing gulfe drunke Hecates,
And like Vlisses to his dearest land,
I scour'd the Scillaes and Simphlegades,
   Ariuing at my wisht-for hauen Douer,
   And thorow Kent to Cowling I came ouer.

Ship, slice the sea, and be thou deifi'd,
Shine brightest on this starre-bestudded vaile,
In heauen more worthy to be stellifi'd,
Than that wherein the Argonautes did saile:
   Let frothie waues die o're thy pitchie blacke,
   And in Elisiums deepe last suffer wracke.

But home, no harbour was for mine estate;
I'm still pursu'd so with mine enemies,
E're thrise the sun did ope his Eastern gate,
I with my houshould were constrain'd to flee:
   Tost long vpon the Bishops Sea, at last
   Neere to saint Albones we our anchor cast.

But by misfortune t'was the Abbots land,
Whereas we lay ; so by his priuie spies,
The fat-backt tumbrell soone did vnderstand,
And vnawares asleepe did vs surprise,
 Three of my men he tooke, my bookes, my wife,
 Onely with one I fled, and sau'd my life.

My men to treate the Abbot now begin,
My Margarites beauty, streaming on his face,
Fairenesse no fauour in his sight would win,
Their wordes no pittie moue, their lookes no grace :
 Then she gan speake, but spake vnto the wind,
 Remorse did neuer lodge in clownish mind.

Dumb stoode my doue, and wrung her hands, whilst often
Low kneeling downe, teares from her eies did shower :
Hard is that hart which beauty cannot soften,
Yet mourning beautie had on him no power :
 Although her teares were like his christall beads,
 Which melted, wash the place whereon he treades.

Stil she intreates, and still the pearles round
Stil through her eies, and wel vpon her face,
Such hony drops on roses I haue found,
When bright Apollo held the morne in chace :
 But both the charmes of teares and sugred words
 For their release no aide at all afordes.

Thus [kneeld], thus prai'd, thus wept my beuteous
    Queene,
T[o see my loving] mens imprisonment :
[Thus wisht shee] rather that they might haue seene
Her dying day, or endlesse banishment :
    And in remembrance I was mist among,
    Her weakned sorrowes therby grew more strong.

But now the limbecke of her blood-shot eies,
Burnt vp with sighs, their springing teares haue staid,
No hope of life in her the Abbot sees ;
So backe to Cowling safe she was conuaid :
    She drowps, she faints, she swownds, she comfort
    I was her comfort, comfortlesse she dieth.   [flieth,

I trauel still, like to the wandering knight
For ladies loue, on strange aduentures bownd,
As counceller, I made the tonglesse night
Of my distresse, which all in silence drown'd,
    Least to the world, day should my griefe discoucr,
    I striue, vntill hart, eies, sighs, teares, ran ouer.

Through many bywaies, many countries fle[d,]
In midst of Cheshire now I am on a riuer,
By more crookt winding which her curr[ent led,]
Then I had gone by-wayes ; her name the W[eev]er :
    On whose prowde banke such entertaine I had,
    As longer, if I might, I would haue staid.

[The passages within brackets are illegible in the book from which this
edition is printed, and they have been supplied from another source.]

Still doe I wander by the banks of Weeuer,
With gorgeous buildings stately ritch adorned :
Buildings the banks, and banks outbraue the Riuer ;
Shee swels o're banks and buildings, them shee scorned,
 Limits there be for euery thing beside,
 No banks can limit in the sea of pride.

Her tumbling streame my guide was to vaile roiall,
Through all the Wyches vnto Ashtons chappell,
Frodsham, Rockesauage, Thus I had a triall,
How she vnloaded all her rolling Channell :
 With neare embracements Weeuer Mersey met,
 And both together th'Irish Seas they gret.

I will but wade neare to this Riuers briuk,
And of her deepnesse make this shallow boast :
Her cooling water those dry countries drink :
So shee makes fruitfull all the western coast ;
 That no lesse famous, no lesse faire a riuer,
 Then the fift Auon, or third Ouzo, is Weeuer.

To Lancashire from hence my journey lies,
Where plentie dwels, where pleasantnesse of Aire
Breathes forth like baulme from rose-strawne Paradies,
At the first blushing of the morning faire :
 Where beutie, vertue, loue, wit, and the Graces,
 Sit all in triumph on the weemens faces.

I doe salute this climate in my way,
On which the heauens such fauours did bestow:
But t'was too hote for me therein to stay,
Except I would myselfe a Papist show:
   So there, through many paines and perils past,
   I'm safe returned back to Wales at last.

Here Cobham liues, oh doe not say he liues,
But dying liues, or liuing howerly dies;
A liuing death exilement alwaies giues,
A banisht man still on his death bed lies.
   Mine high estate is low misfortunes graue,
   My power restrain'd is now a glorious slaue.

What in exilement to my sect befell,
Daigne to vnfould mellifluous Mercurie:
Nay stay, why shouldst thou to the world tell
That with thy tong all eies abhord to see:
   Yet greefe kept in oftimes doth grow more fell,
   For riuers damm'd aboue the bank doe swell.

This Act proclaim'd and disanuld in many,
Twice twentie hundred soules were martyred:
Out of the land to Spaine, and Germanie,
Bohemia, Fraunce, and Scotland, others fled:
   Who would not flie, what patient man can bide,
   In Clergie men ambitious hautie pride?

Sir Roger Acton, Browne, and Beuerley,
Knight, Squire, and Preacher, valorous, vertuous, good:
In Christenmas vpon Saint Thomas day,
Gainst certain Priests vpon a quarrell stood :
   For which so hainous and inhumane wrong,
   They were attacht, and into prison flong.

Now was the month which Ianus hath to name,
Of old new christened by Pompilius;
And wondrous proud that he had got such fame:
Added feeld-purging Februarius :
   Ianus bifronted, one which bids adew
   Vnto the old yeare, entertaines the new.

When Roger Acton, Beuerley, and Browne,
Of Heresie conuicted by the Act :
To Thicket feelds vpon an hurdle drawne,
Were hang'd, and burn'd (O more then monstrous fact:)
   And through the Realme all Artists it would cumber,
   By that sore Act the martyres all to number.

Some two yeares after was a mutinie,
An vproare, tumult, or rebellion,
In Saint Gyles feelds ; the which conspiracie
Acton and I, some doe affirme begone ;
   But the Kings power not able to with-stand,
   We fled, were taken, burned out of hand.

Which time tree-garnisht Cambriaes loftie mountaines
Did ouer-shade me with their beetle browes,
And by Elysiums Nectar-spouting fountaines
Acton did march in Saint-triumphing showes:
    From Wales returne I could not then to fight,
    From Heauen Acton would not if he might.

Twice told, two twelue months now the howers haue
Their morning slumbers on the Sun to tend,   [broke,
And bring his horses to the charriots yoke:
Mark now the period of my dolefull end:
    The Clergies mallice (not ore-blowne) will haue me,
    Though heauen and earth & all had sworn to saue
                                                  [me.

With lordlie gifts and kinglie promises
They fed Lord Powis (gouernour in Wales,)
He came to me pretending holinesse;
To true Religion for a time he falls:
    And last, his Iudas kindnes did bewray me,
    Seeking all meanes how that he might betray me.

Powis his promise faine would haue forsaken,
Before the meanes for my attach he wrought:
I was not one so easie to be taken,
With his owne blood his bribes he dearlie bought:
    But I not able to withstand his strength,
    (Not Hercules gainst two) was tooke at length.

In greatest greefe this one thing made me glad,
(Though hard tis fasten mirth with miserie,)
That in mine absence Arundell was dread,
Which was resolu'd before, my death to see:
　But seld comes better, he, though void of grace,
　Yet was a man, the Deuill came in his place.

Thus ill at worst doth alway gin to mend,
And by example good doth often gaine:
That by degrees so rising in the end,
To perfect goodnesse it returnes againe:
　So since his time they haue so risen still,
　Thriuing in good, as they decaid in ill.

Now goodnesse raised to her highest pitch,
In snow-white robes is sent vs for a gift:
The radiant splendour of this Empire ritch,
Whose shining lustre heauens doth enlight:
　O that I could a spirit in thee breathe,
　Whose life preserues diuinitie from death.

By Chichley Archbishop of Canterburie,
And Bedford Prorex (oh the King was absent:)
Of Treason I'm condemn'd and Heresie;
A double crime, a double punishment:
　My iudgement giuen; of death, the day and hower
　Appointed; I am sent back to the Tower.

Death, the pale daughter of black Erebus,
What fashion to appeare in doth not know:
But councell takes of Nox and Morpheus,
What forme most terrour and amaze will show:
   Hell, Sleepe, Night, Death, are troubled to deuise,
   What new found shape might please these tyrants
                                          [eies.

Two fyrie coursers foming clottred blood,
Whurries; at last, Death bound in iron chaines;
Whil'st goblings (gaping like a whirle-poole) wood,
Doe lash their goarie sides, with steeled yaines:
   Blood and reuenge by in a chariot ride,
   Millions of furies scudding by their side.

Which all at once doe vomit Sulphure flakes,
Throw scorching brands, which wrapt in brimston, choke
The trembling Audience; that affrighted quakes,
To vew the Sun eclipst with steaming smoke:
   To heare deuils, ghosts, and feends howle, roare, &
   Filling the earth, as though they empted hell.   [yell,

To Thickets feeld thus was Oldcastle hurried,
The gallowes built of purpose wondrous hie:
Neare to the top of which (as one lies buried)
In three cold chaines mine aged corps doe lie:
   The faggots fyr'd, with me the gallows burne,
   I call on God, and to the fyre I turne.

The Prelates curse, alowd the people crie,
One would rebell, another him aswageth,
One sighs, to vew anothers blubred eie,
One murmuring railes, another inlie rageth,
 All weep, some howle, some faint, some swound,
 Deafing the heauens, darkening the skie. [some die.

The bundels cracke; with that the mourning Aire
Comes whisking round to coole the raging flame,
When he perceiues his breathes but bellowes are,
Rather to kindle than to coole the same :
 He turnes himselfe to water, and he raines
 To quench the fyre, and ease me of my paines.

The fyre, red-blushing of his fact ashamed,
Clad him in smoke, the smoke to Aire he turned,
That aire to water, water earth receiued,
Earth, like the fyre to melt to water, burned :
 Earth, Water, Aire, Fyre, symboliz'd in one,
 To quench, or coole, Oldcastl's Martyrdome.

But now I gaspe, I fry, I drop, I fall,
My Chaines doe yeeld, Spectators stand agast,
To make the which abhorred more of all,
My Bootes and Spurs must in the fyre be cast.
 O death! strange death! which to describe at large
 Would aske sweet Ouids wit, and Nestors age.

If wits pearle-dropping Opobalsamum,
In Amber-streaming Eloquence were drie ;
Vnto my bleached cindars she might come,
And take a fluent Helicon supplie :
　Mine Ashes bath'd in th'vnguent of her eies,
　A siluer-fethered Phœnix would arise.

Ah no ! my bodies snow-white burned ashes,
(Those harmlesse reliques) cast were in the riuer,
Whose salt-fresh-meeting waues betwixt them washes,
Like Lethe, my remembrance not to liue here :
　My vertues fame is like my bodies death,
　Kindled with a blast, and burnt out with a breath.

And in this idle age who's once forgotten,
Obliuion dims the brightnesse of his glory :
Enuie is ripe before his bones be rotten,
And ouerthrowes the truth of vertues story :
　Despoil's his name, and robs him of his merits :
　For naught but fame man after death inherits.

Nor can my soule within the sable night,
When all (but louers) welcome carelesse rest :
Like to some subtle shade, or wandring spright,
With goarie sides, and deeper lanched brest ;
　Holding in tho'ne hand wildfyre, in the other
　A torch, to stifle th'aire with pitchie smother.

With deep sunke eyes, lanke cheeks, and pallide hew,
Dismembred armes, sharpe visage, doubtfull sight,
Enter some watchfull Poets secret mew,
His heauenly thoughts, and quiet studies fright;
  With hollow voice: commaunding him set forth
  Immortall verse for my entomblesse worth.

Then should the world on brasen pillers view me,
With great Achilles, in the house of Fame;
His Tutor'd pen with Tropheis would renew me,
And still repaire the ruin of my name:
  But I'm inuirond with the Elisian feelds,
  Which for departed soules no passage yeelds.

But Wickleues soule now beares me company,
And Ierome Prages, within the highest heauen,
(These were my comfort in calamitie)
Whose ioyes (Rome sayes) her curses hath bereauen;
  Thus (if they could) they would denie vs t'haue,
  In heauen our soules, as in the earth our graue.

Iewes burie him which railes on Moses lawes,
Turkes him which worships not their Alkaron,
Tartarians him which Cham no reuerence shawes,
The Persians him which worships not the sun;
  More rigorous cruell then this Romish crew
  Then Persian, Turke, Tartarian, or Iew.

Their dead in banquets Scithians deuoure,
Their dead with dogs Hircanians do eate,
Phagi with fish; with foule th'Assirian poure,
The Troglodites to wormes are giuen for meate :
  More heath'nish papists, they deny me t'haue,
  In beast, fish, foule, in man, or worme, my graue.

Becket was wounded in his priests apparrell,
In Romes defence; his death was glorious;
I burnt, vnburied, drown d for Christs owne quarrell,
My death to most was ignominious;
  He prais'd, adornd, and for a martyr sainted,
  Whilst I (Romes scoffe) my rites of buriall wanted.

For Beckets sake erected was a tombe,
Like an Egiptian high Pyramides,
Millions of bare-foote pilgrims yeerely come,
With tapers burning to his holynes,
  Till Henry th'eight, by Cromwells good procurement,
  Cast downe this mocke-ape toy, this vaine alurement.

The glorious beutie of this brightest shrine,
The treasorie of euer-springing gold :
Becket is set; now doth Oldcastle shine :
Him for a Saint within your Kalends hold.
  Thus fooles admire what wisest men despiseth,
  Thus fond affects doe fall, when vertue riseth.

Wit, spend thy vigour, Poets, wits quintessence,
Hermes, make great the worlds eies with teares :
Actors make sighes a burden for each sentence :
That he may sob which reades, he swound which heares.
  Mean time, till life in death you doe renew,
  Wit, Poets, Hermes, Actors, all adew.

FINIS.

www.ingramcontent.com/pod-product-compliance
Lightning Source LLC
Chambersburg PA
CBHW031420230426
43668CB00007B/376